FO...

I was introduced to Darkchylde when I first read Randy Queen's screenplay and the popular comic books he created in 1996. I fell in love with the dark child Ariel and the Lovecraftian mythos that haunts her teenage life. Randy created a true original; a beautiful heroine innocently becomes a portal for ghastly creatures trying to regain their foothold in this world from a dark, foreboding plane beyond ours. It was, and is, absolutely brilliant.

Now you hold DREAMS OF DARKCHYLDE in your hands, and I envy the discoveries you'll make reading this volume. You're going to learn more about Ariel's past, her internal terrain, her conflicted nature, the darkness that literally inhabits her. DREAMS includes Randy's favorite short, 'NO POSSIBLE HARM'. I think it's mine too.

I'm honored to introduce Randy Queen's latest vision of Ariel and her world. Now turn the page, the best is yet to come.

John Carpenter

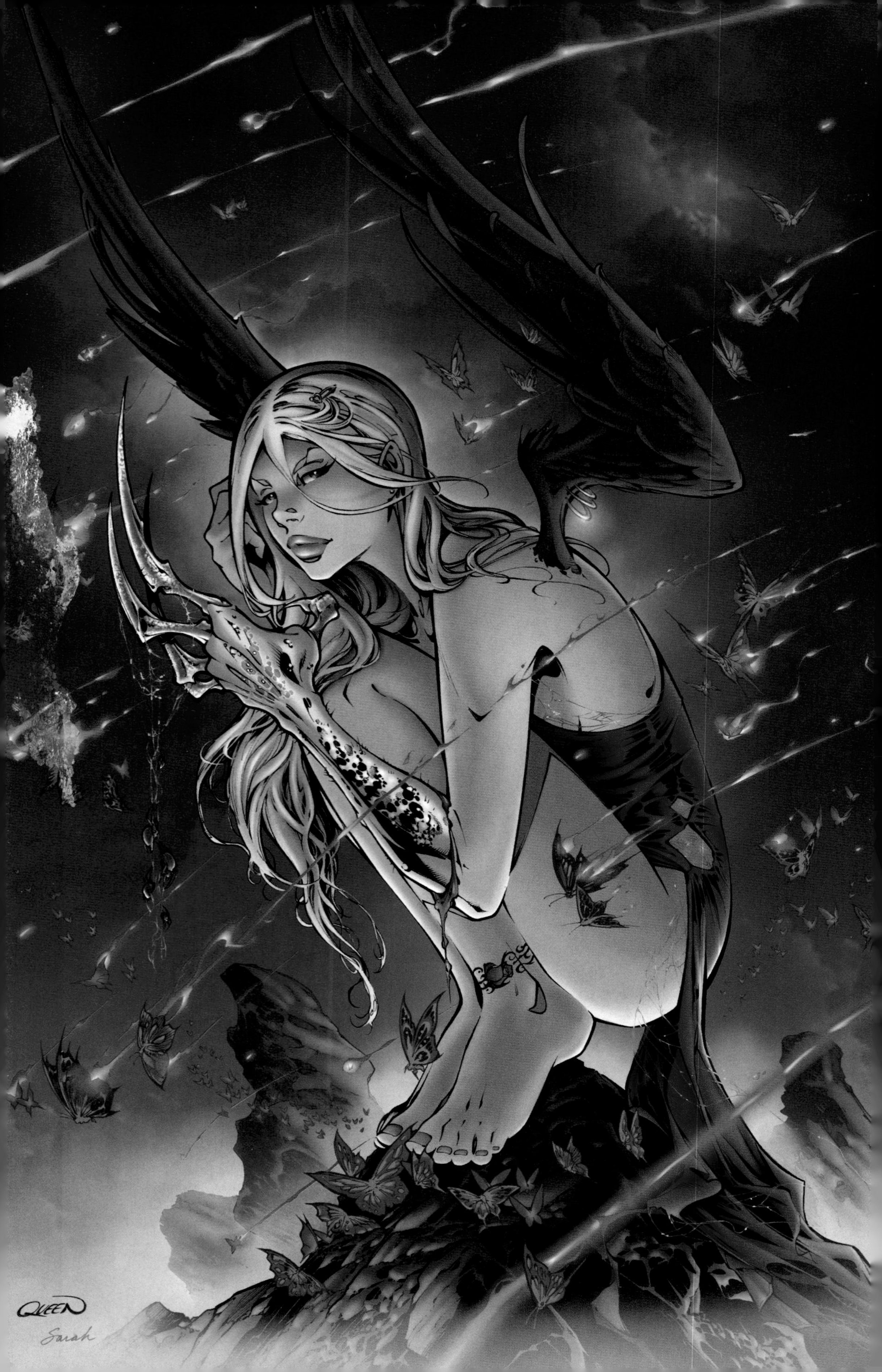
QUEEN
Sarah

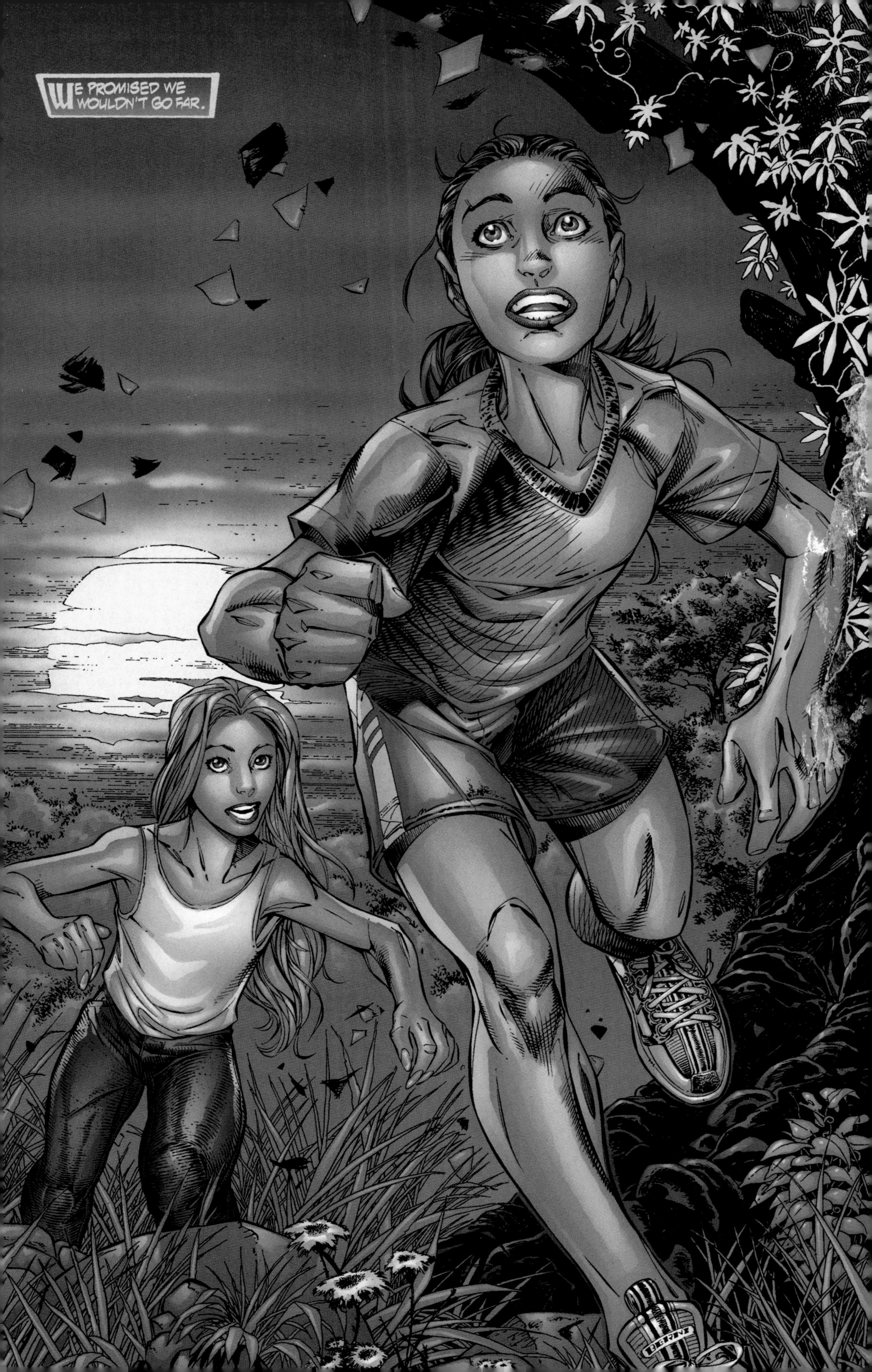
WE PROMISED WE WOULDN'T GO FAR.

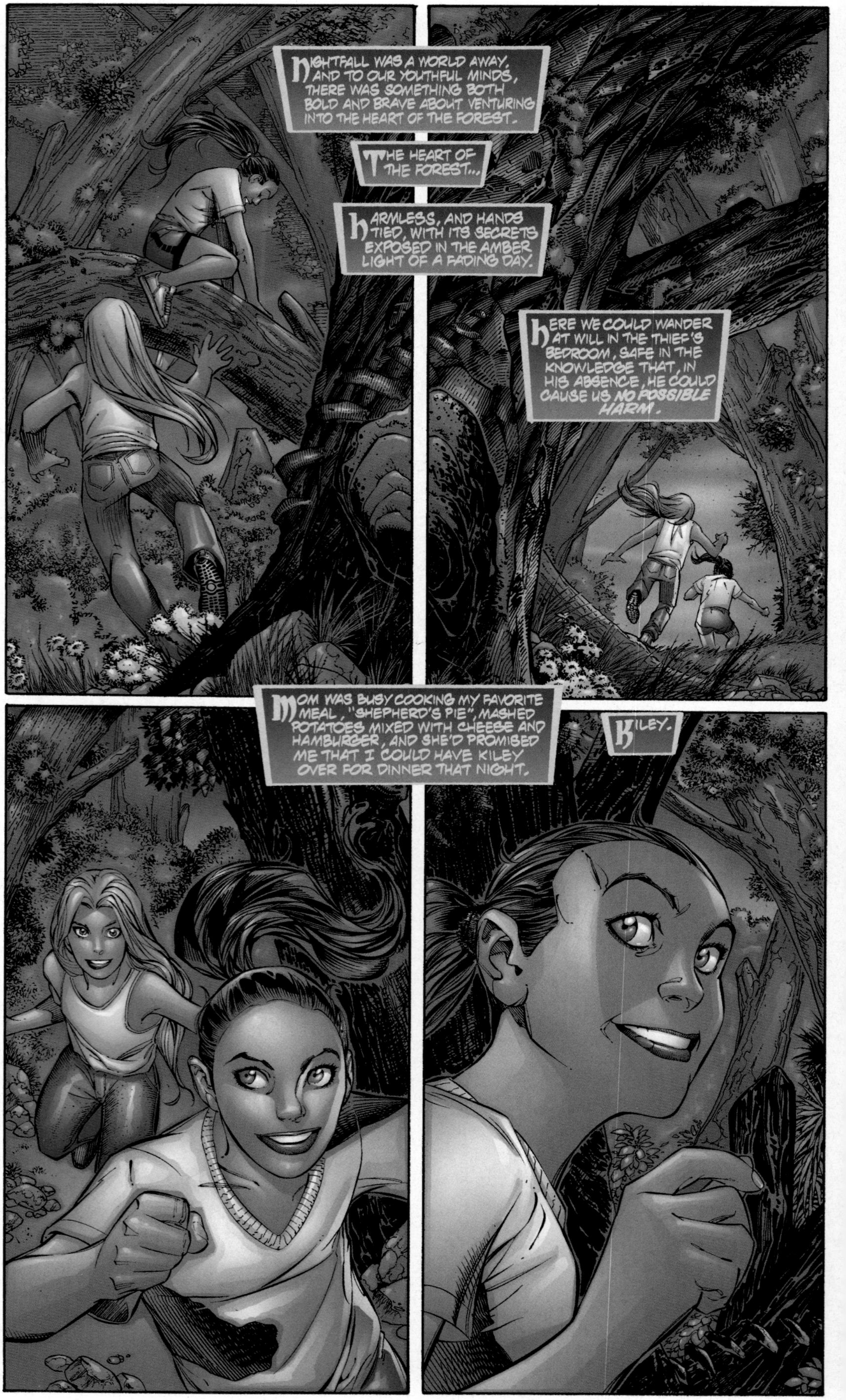
NIGHTFALL WAS A WORLD AWAY, AND TO OUR YOUTHFUL MINDS, THERE WAS SOMETHING BOTH BOLD AND BRAVE ABOUT VENTURING INTO THE HEART OF THE FOREST.
THE HEART OF THE FOREST...
HARMLESS, AND HANDS TIED, WITH ITS SECRETS EXPOSED IN THE AMBER LIGHT OF A FADING DAY.
HERE WE COULD WANDER AT WILL IN THE THIEF'S BEDROOM, SAFE IN THE KNOWLEDGE THAT, IN HIS ABSENCE, HE COULD CAUSE US NO POSSIBLE HARM.
MOM WAS BUSY COOKING MY FAVORITE MEAL, "SHEPHERD'S PIE", MASHED POTATOES MIXED WITH CHEESE AND HAMBURGER, AND SHE'D PROMISED ME THAT I COULD HAVE KILEY OVER FOR DINNER THAT NIGHT.
KILEY.

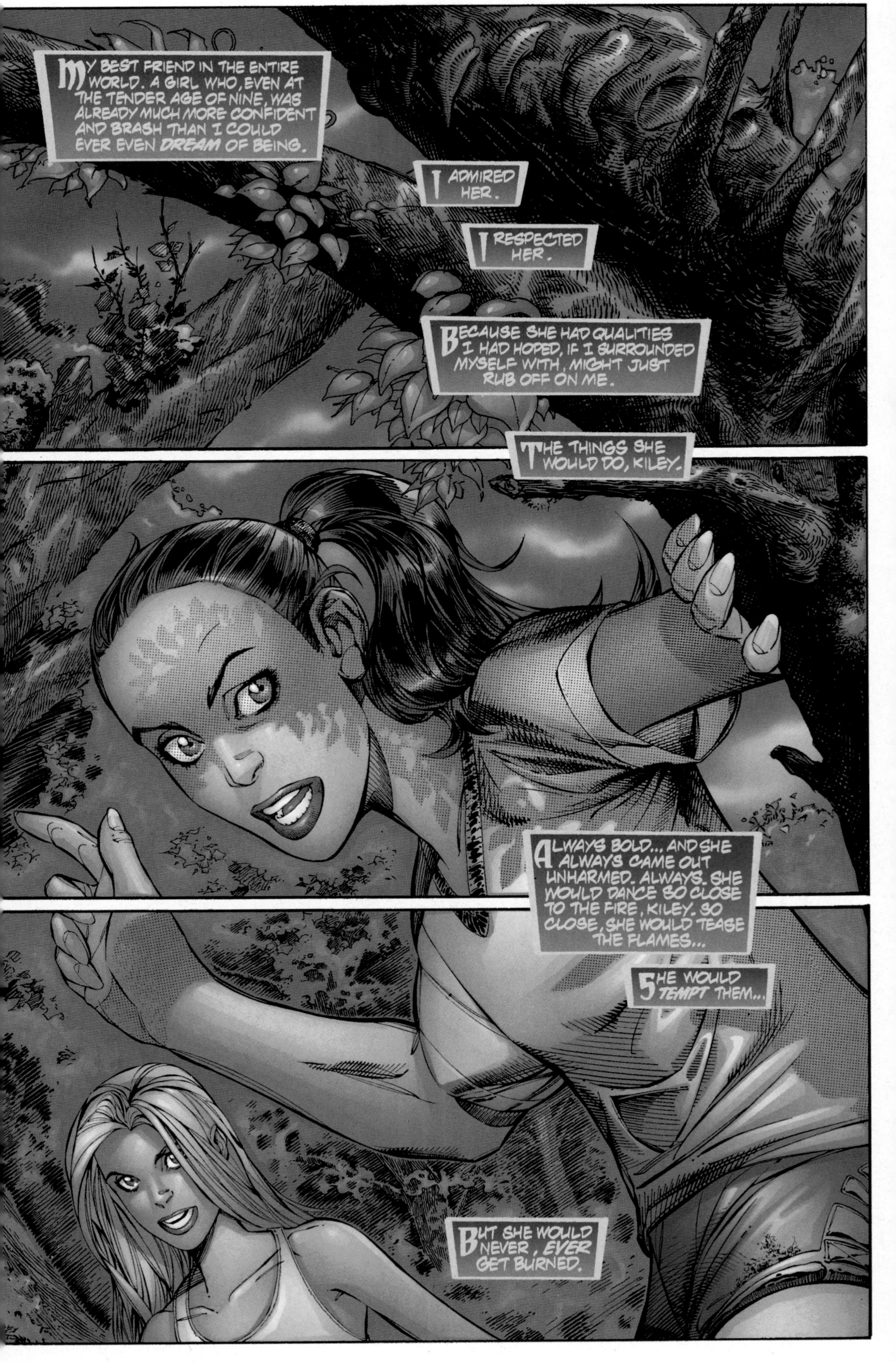

MY BEST FRIEND IN THE ENTIRE WORLD. A GIRL WHO, EVEN AT THE TENDER AGE OF NINE, WAS ALREADY MUCH MORE CONFIDENT AND BRASH THAN I COULD EVER EVEN *DREAM* OF BEING.
I ADMIRED HER.
I RESPECTED HER.
BECAUSE SHE HAD QUALITIES I HAD HOPED, IF I SURROUNDED MYSELF WITH, MIGHT JUST RUB OFF ON ME.
THE THINGS SHE WOULD DO, KILEY.
ALWAYS BOLD... AND SHE ALWAYS CAME OUT UNHARMED. ALWAYS. SHE WOULD DANCE SO CLOSE TO THE FIRE, KILEY. SO CLOSE, SHE WOULD TEASE THE FLAMES...
SHE WOULD *TEMPT* THEM...
BUT SHE WOULD NEVER, *EVER* GET BURNED.

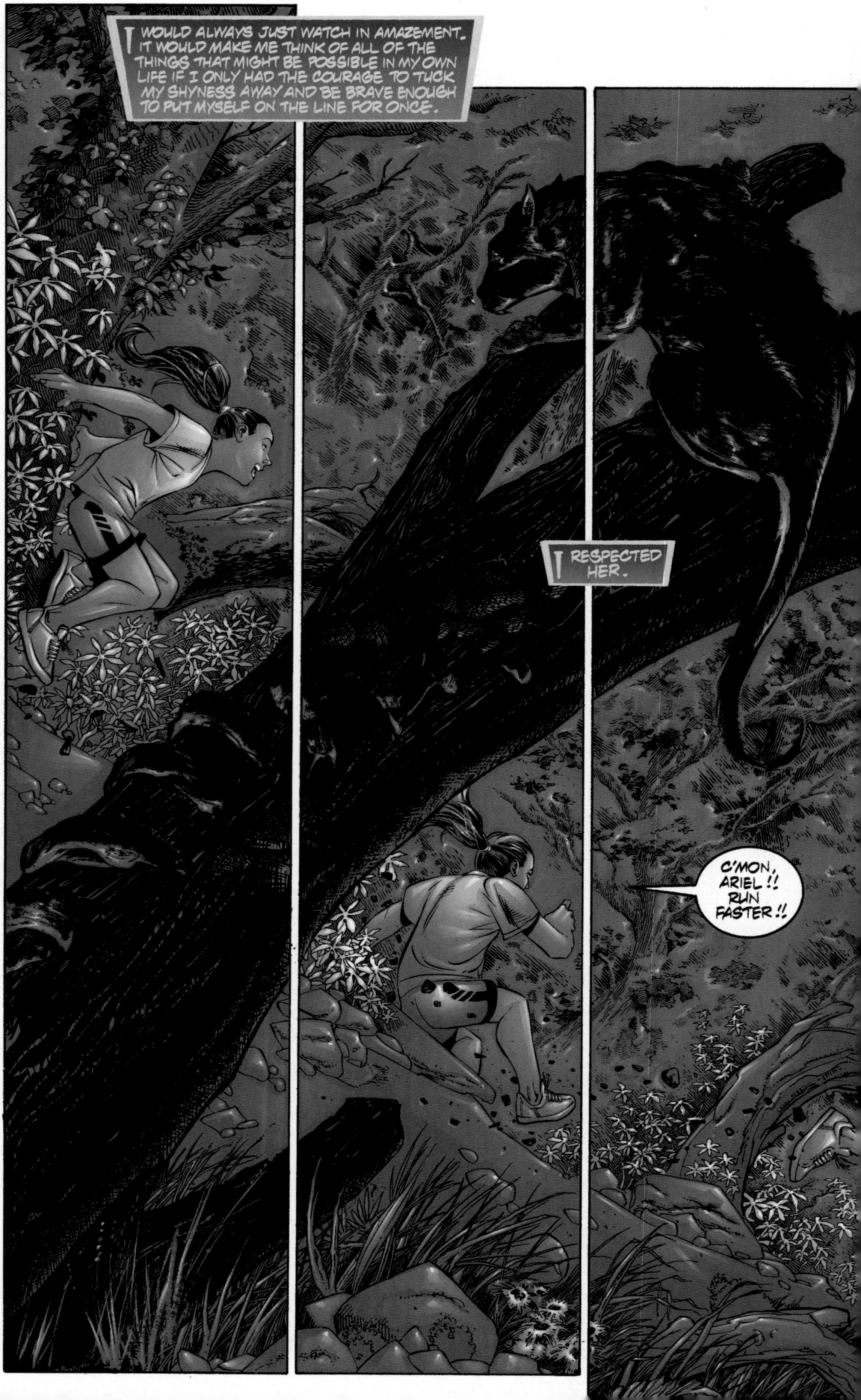
I WOULD ALWAYS JUST WATCH IN AMAZEMENT. IT WOULD MAKE ME THINK OF ALL OF THE THINGS THAT MIGHT BE POSSIBLE IN MY OWN LIFE IF I ONLY HAD THE COURAGE TO TUCK MY SHYNESS AWAY AND BE BRAVE ENOUGH TO PUT MYSELF ON THE LINE FOR ONCE.
I RESPECTED HER.
C'MON, ARIEL!! RUN FASTER!!

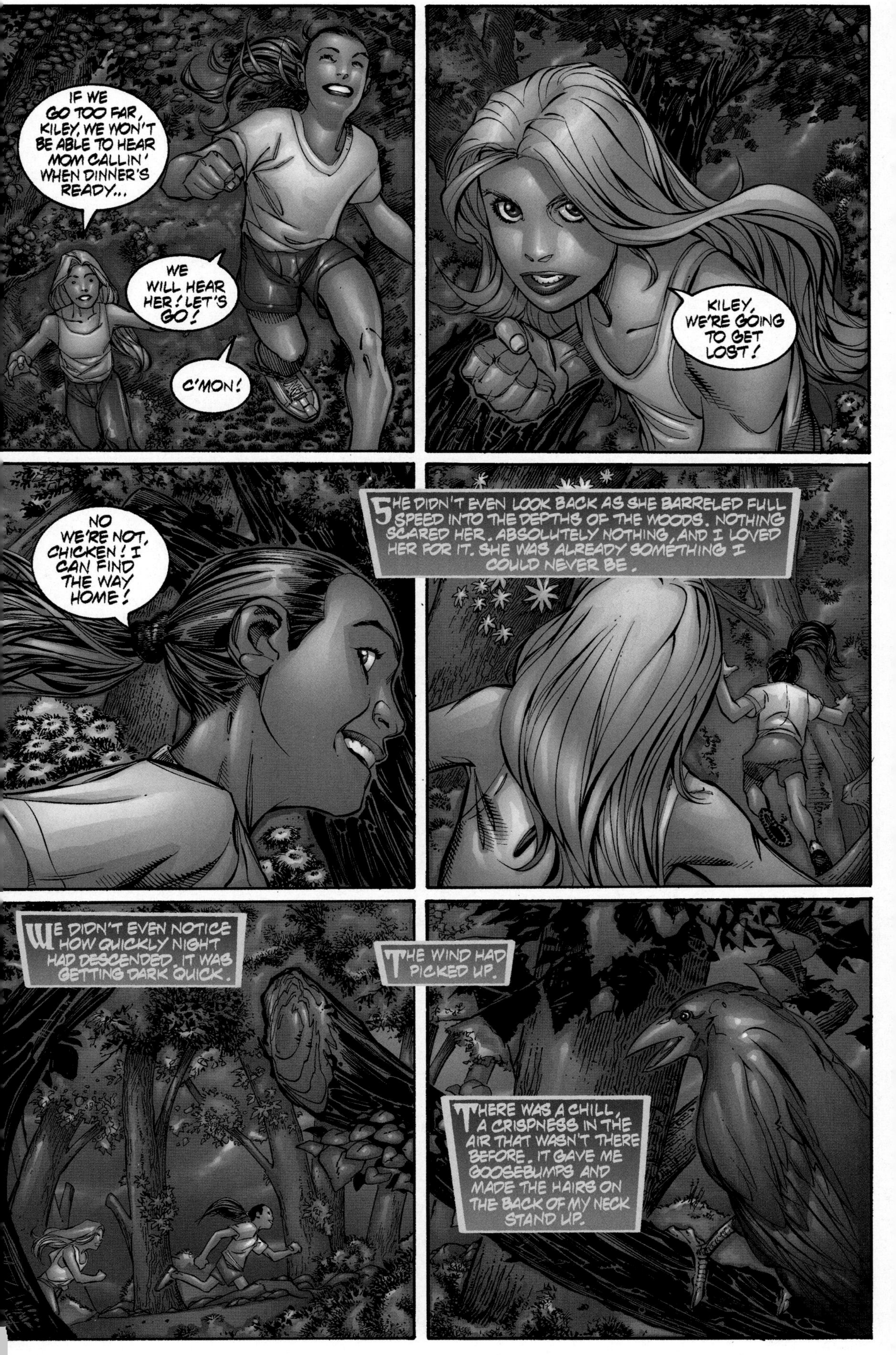
IF WE GO TOO FAR, KILEY, WE WON'T BE ABLE TO HEAR MOM CALLIN' WHEN DINNER'S READY...
WE WILL HEAR HER! LET'S GO!
C'MON!
KILEY, WE'RE GOING TO GET LOST!
NO WE'RE NOT, CHICKEN! I CAN FIND THE WAY HOME!
SHE DIDN'T EVEN LOOK BACK AS SHE BARRELED FULL SPEED INTO THE DEPTHS OF THE WOODS. NOTHING SCARED HER. ABSOLUTELY NOTHING, AND I LOVED HER FOR IT. SHE WAS ALREADY SOMETHING I COULD NEVER BE.
WE DIDN'T EVEN NOTICE HOW QUICKLY NIGHT HAD DESCENDED. IT WAS GETTING DARK QUICK.
THE WIND HAD PICKED UP.
THERE WAS A CHILL, A CRISPNESS IN THE AIR THAT WASN'T THERE BEFORE. IT GAVE ME GOOSEBUMPS AND MADE THE HAIRS ON THE BACK OF MY NECK STAND UP.

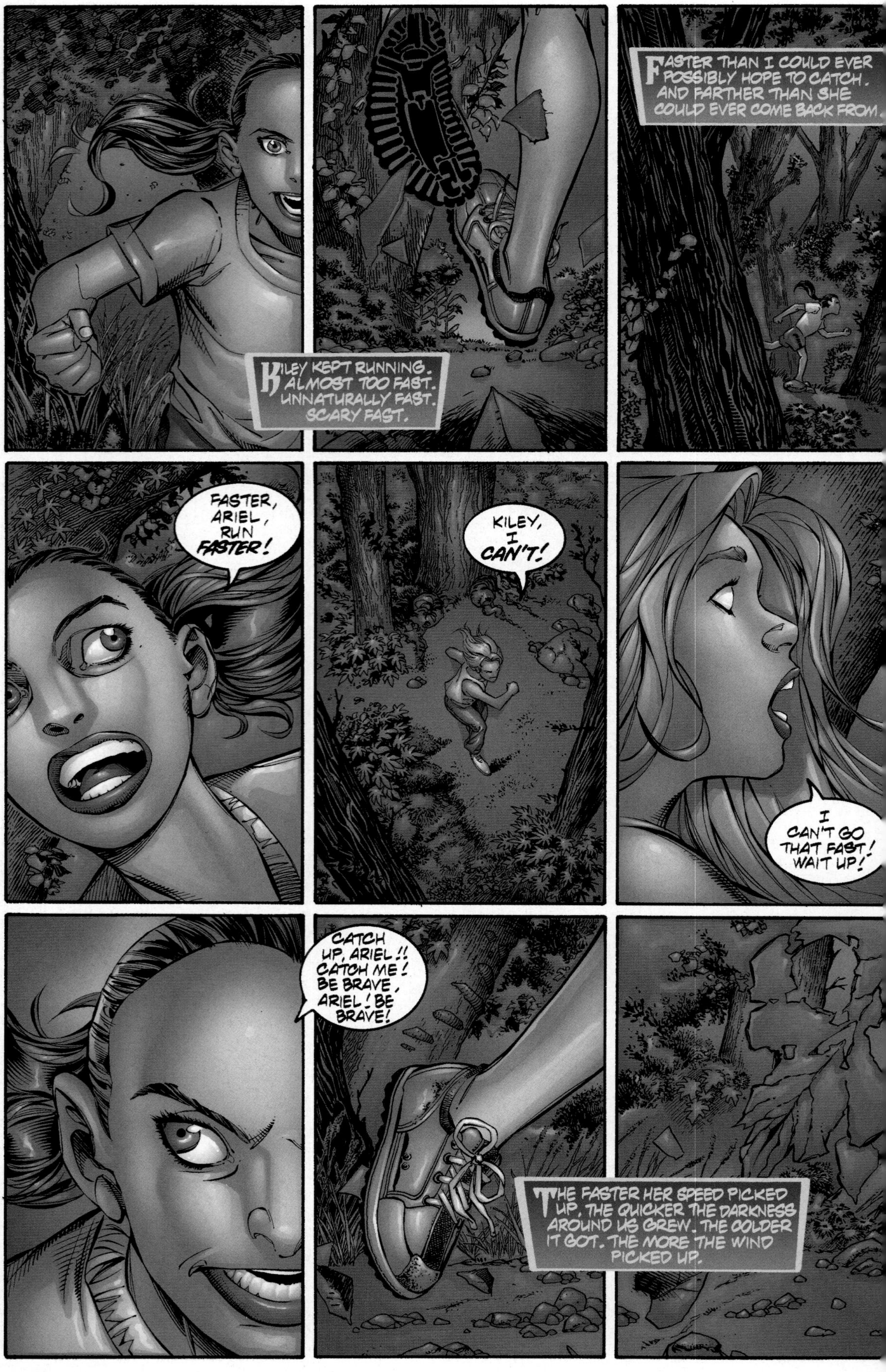
KILEY KEPT RUNNING. ALMOST TOO FAST. UNNATURALLY FAST. SCARY FAST.
FASTER THAN I COULD EVER POSSIBLY HOPE TO CATCH. AND FARTHER THAN SHE COULD EVER COME BACK FROM.
FASTER, ARIEL, RUN FASTER!
KILEY, I CAN'T!
I CAN'T GO THAT FAST! WAIT UP!
CATCH UP, ARIEL!! CATCH ME! BE BRAVE, ARIEL! BE BRAVE!
THE FASTER HER SPEED PICKED UP, THE QUICKER THE DARKNESS AROUND US GREW. THE COLDER IT GOT. THE MORE THE WIND PICKED UP.

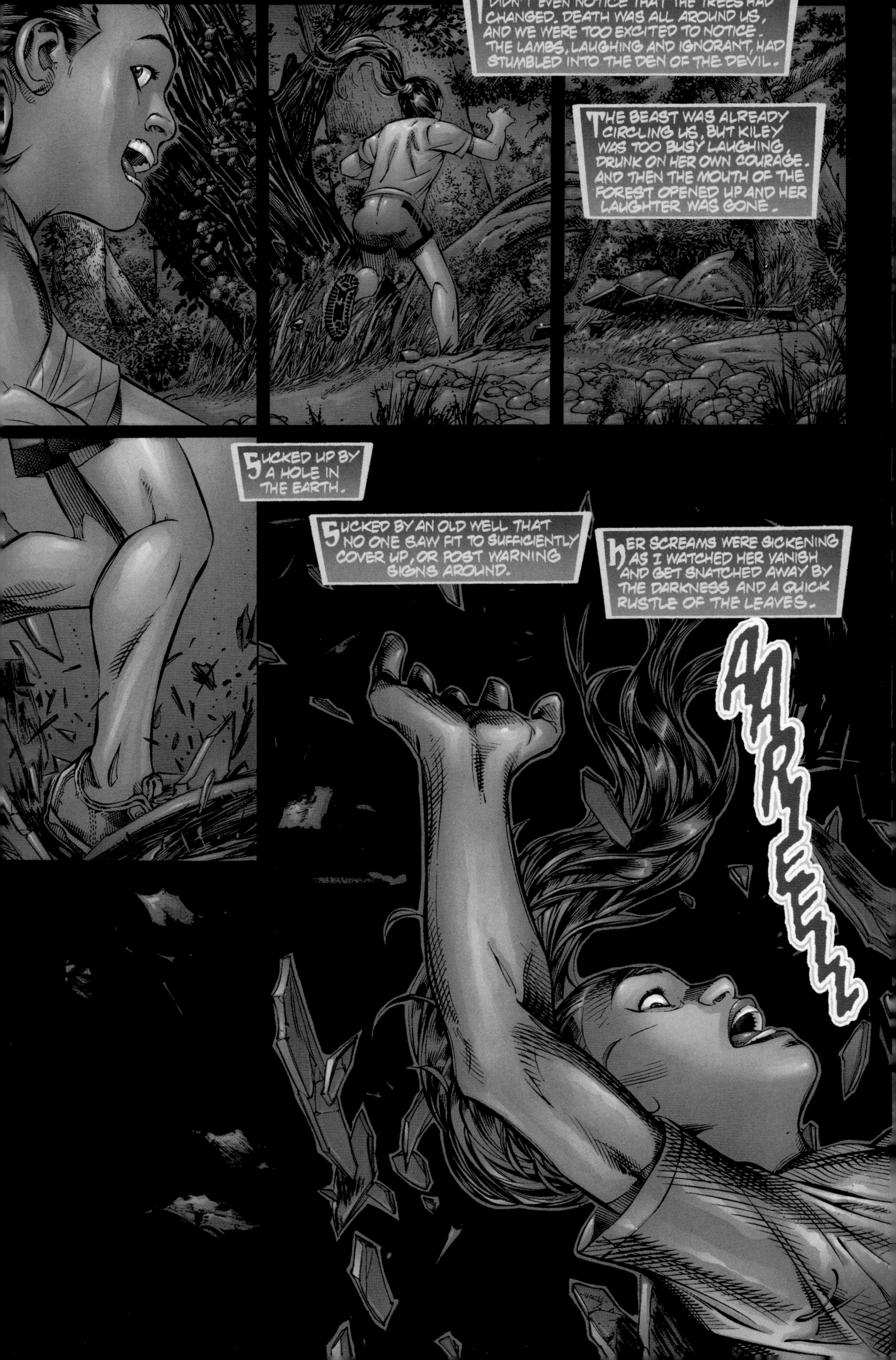
I DIDN'T EVEN NOTICE THAT THE TREES HAD CHANGED. DEATH WAS ALL AROUND US, AND WE WERE TOO EXCITED TO NOTICE. THE LAMBS, LAUGHING AND IGNORANT, HAD STUMBLED INTO THE DEN OF THE DEVIL.
THE BEAST WAS ALREADY CIRCLING US, BUT KILEY WAS TOO BUSY LAUGHING, DRUNK ON HER OWN COURAGE. AND THEN THE MOUTH OF THE FOREST OPENED UP AND HER LAUGHTER WAS GONE.
SUCKED UP BY A HOLE IN THE EARTH.
SUCKED BY AN OLD WELL THAT NO ONE SAW FIT TO SUFFICIENTLY COVER UP, OR POST WARNING SIGNS AROUND.
HER SCREAMS WERE SICKENING AS I WATCHED HER VANISH AND GET SNATCHED AWAY BY THE DARKNESS AND A QUICK RUSTLE OF THE LEAVES.
AARRIEEEW

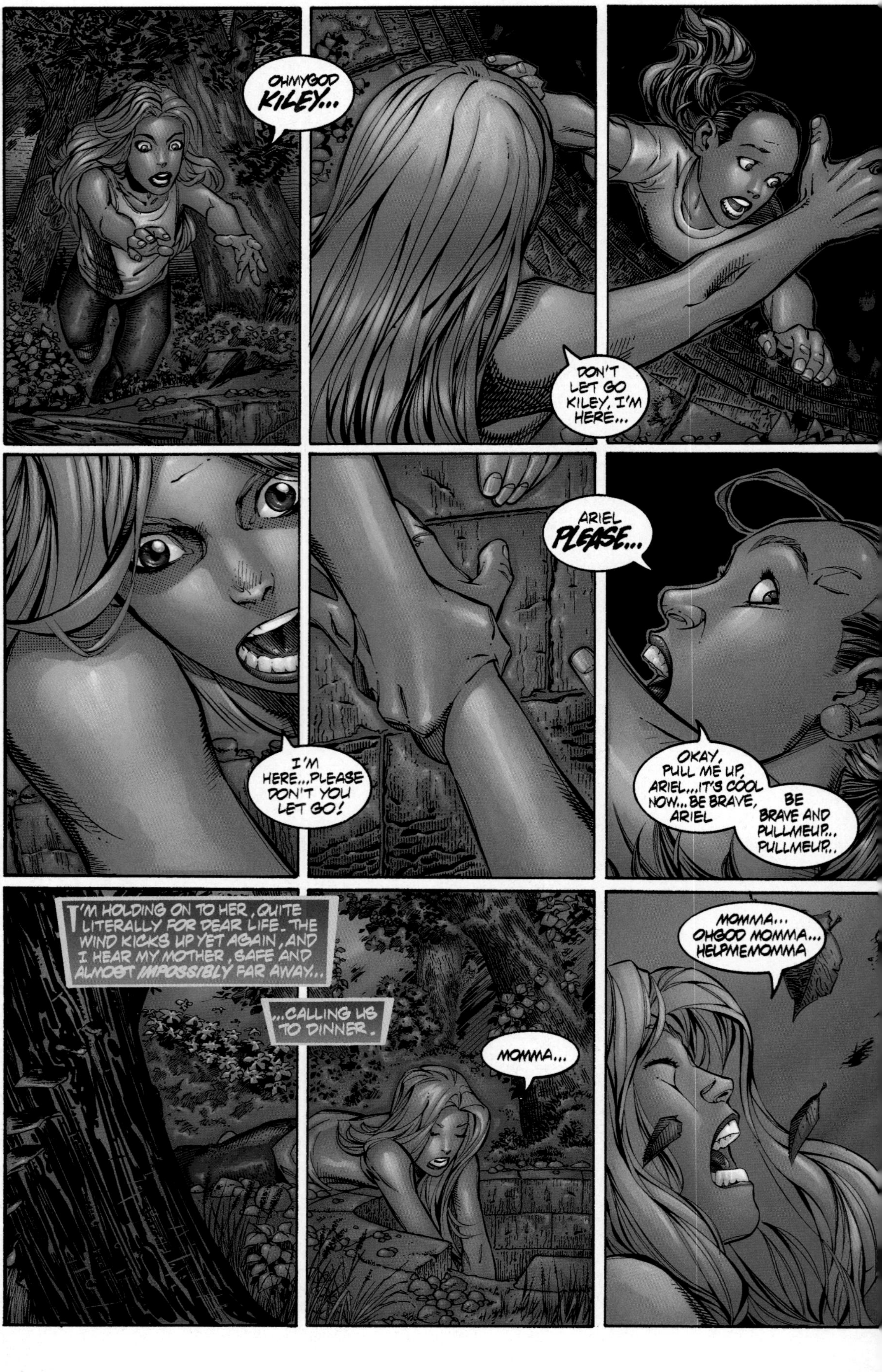
OHMYGOD KILEY...
DON'T LET GO KILEY, I'M HERE...
I'M HERE...PLEASE DON'T YOU LET GO!
ARIEL PLEASE...
OKAY, PULL ME UP, ARIEL...IT'S COOL NOW...BE BRAVE, ARIEL
BE BRAVE AND PULLMEUP... PULLMEUP...
I'M HOLDING ON TO HER, QUITE LITERALLY FOR DEAR LIFE. THE WIND KICKS UP YET AGAIN, AND I HEAR MY MOTHER, SAFE AND ALMOST IMPOSSIBLY FAR AWAY...
...CALLING US TO DINNER.
MOMMA...
MOMMA... OHGOD MOMMA... HELPMEMOMMA

THE TREES START TO MOVE... UNNATURALLY...IN WAYS THAT COULDN'T POSSIBLY JUST BE THE WIND.

AND I HEARD LAUGHTER...

...SOFT, EVIL, UNNATURAL LAUGHTER...COMING FROM THE BOTTOM OF THAT DARK HOLE... LAUGHTER THAT WOULD LOVE FOR NOTHING MORE THAN FOR ME TO JUST LET KILEY FALL.

SHE'S SLIPPING AND SHE GETS A LOOK IN HER EYES THAT'S VERY FAR AWAY... A LOOK THAT SAYS SHE KNOWS SHE'LL NEVER BE ON THE OTHER SIDE OF THIS WELL AGAIN.

MOMMA... PLEASE GOD HELP ME... PLEASE MOMMA DON'T LET HER...

SHE'S SLIPPING.

MOMMA PLEASE HELP...

PLEASE DON'T LET HERDIE

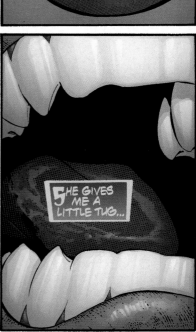

SHE GIVES ME A LITTLE TUG...

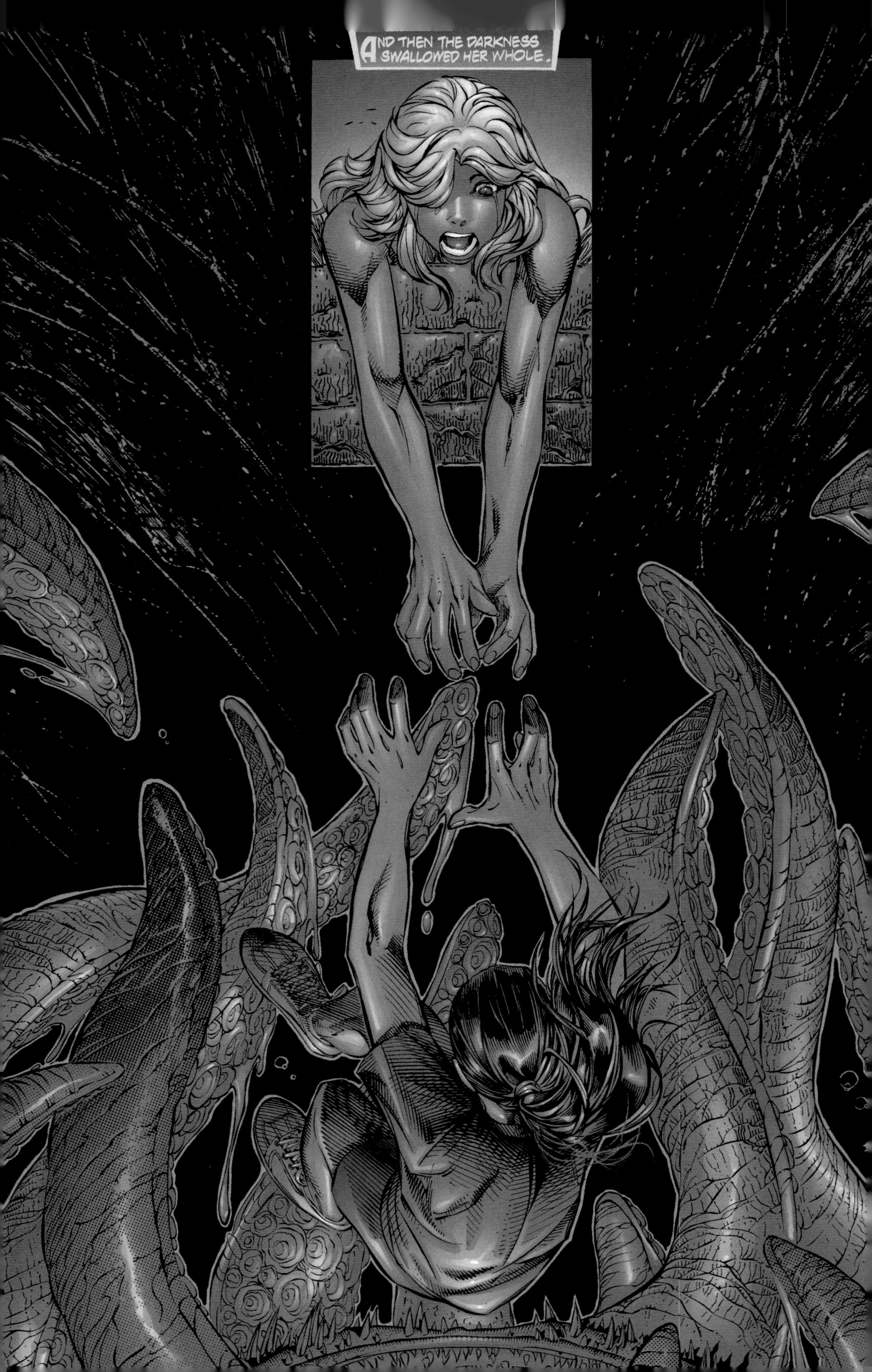
AND THEN THE DARKNESS SWALLOWED HER WHOLE.

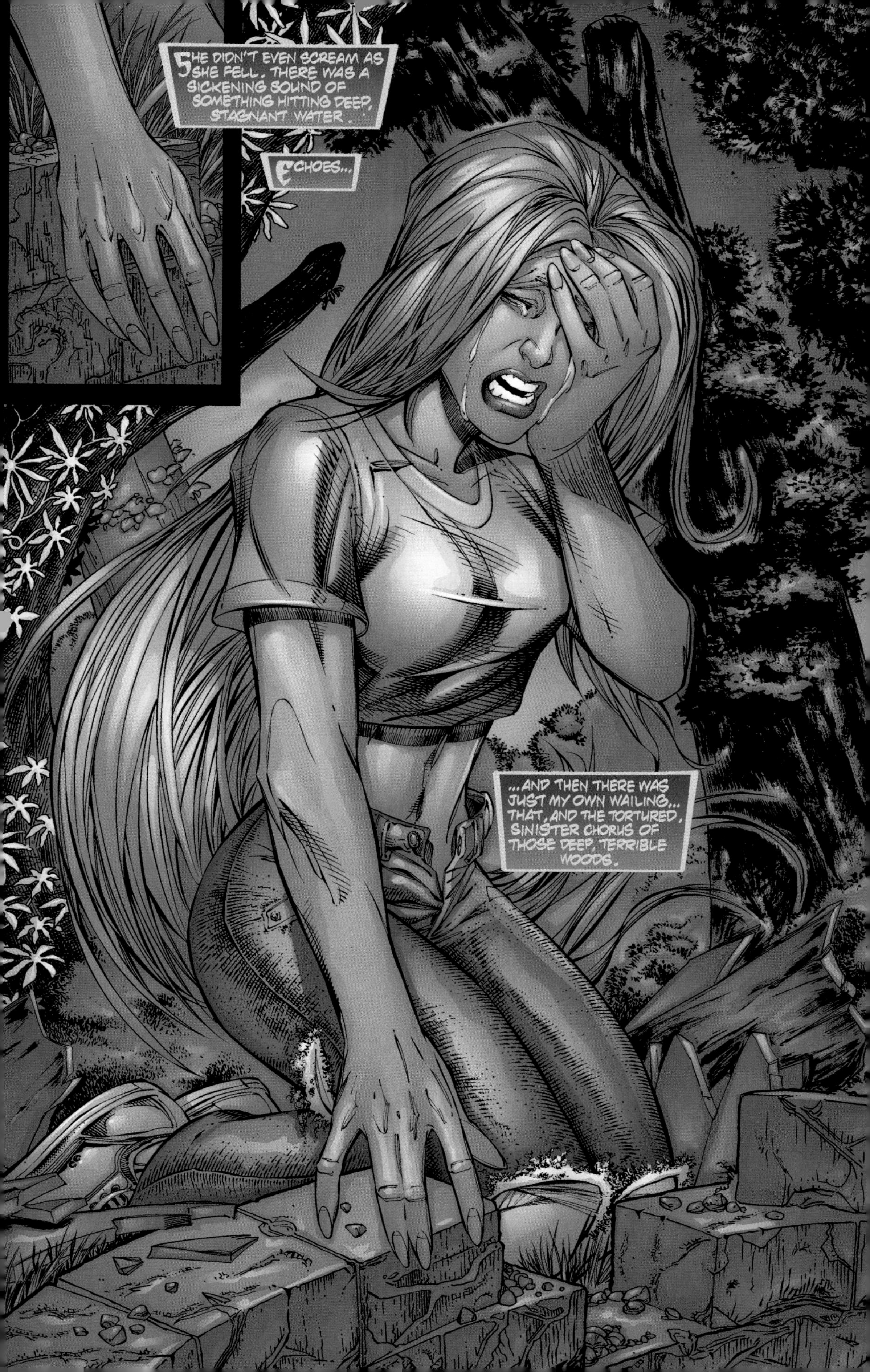
SHE DIDN'T EVEN SCREAM AS SHE FELL. THERE WAS A SICKENING SOUND OF SOMETHING HITTING DEEP, STAGNANT WATER.
ECHOES...
...AND THEN THERE WAS JUST MY OWN WAILING... THAT, AND THE TORTURED, SINISTER CHORUS OF THOSE DEEP, TERRIBLE WOODS.

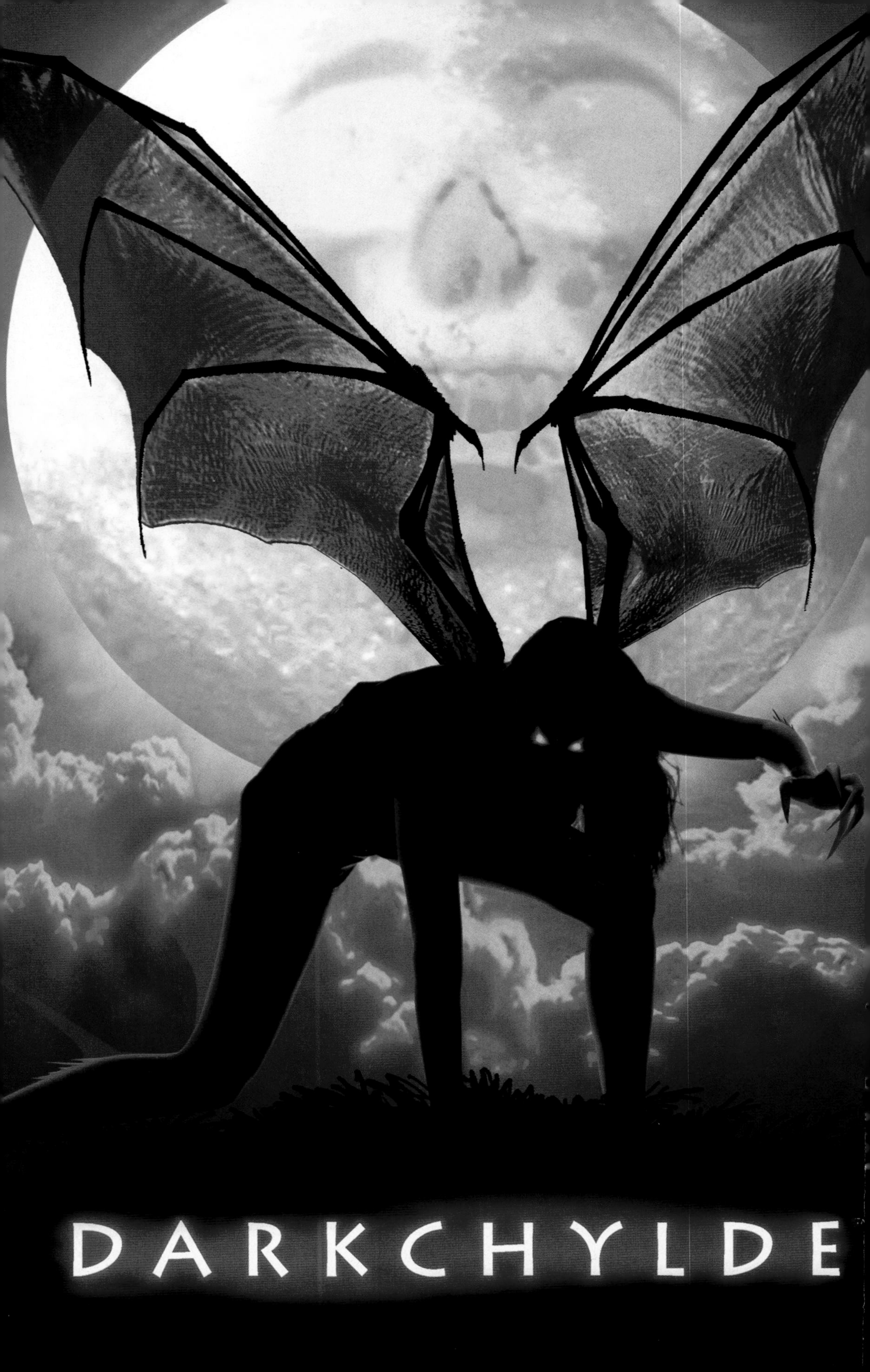
DARKCHYLDE

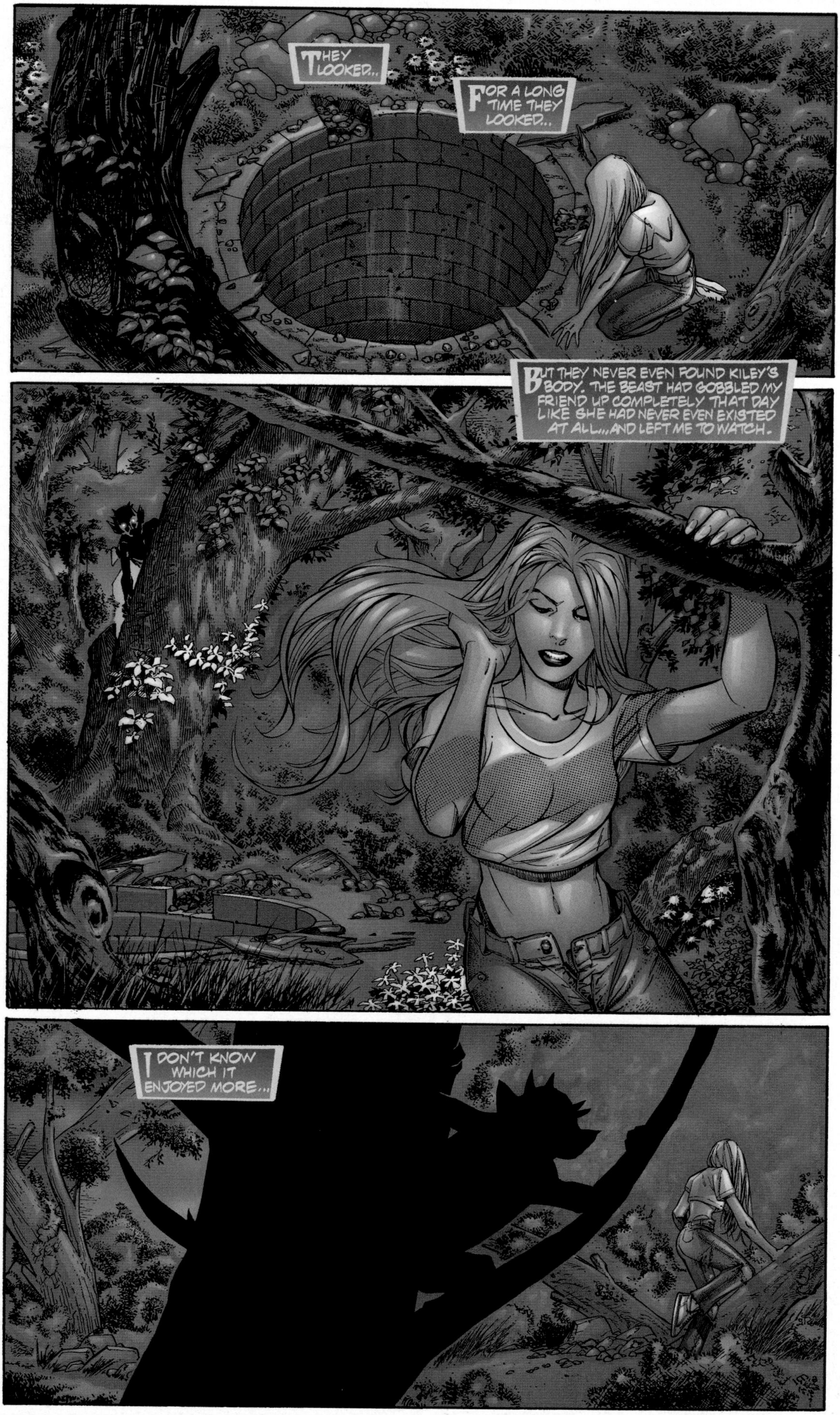
THEY LOOKED...
FOR A LONG TIME THEY LOOKED...
BUT THEY NEVER EVEN FOUND KILEY'S BODY. THE BEAST HAD GOBBLED MY FRIEND UP COMPLETELY THAT DAY LIKE SHE HAD NEVER EVEN EXISTED AT ALL...AND LEFT ME TO WATCH.
I DON'T KNOW WHICH IT ENJOYED MORE...

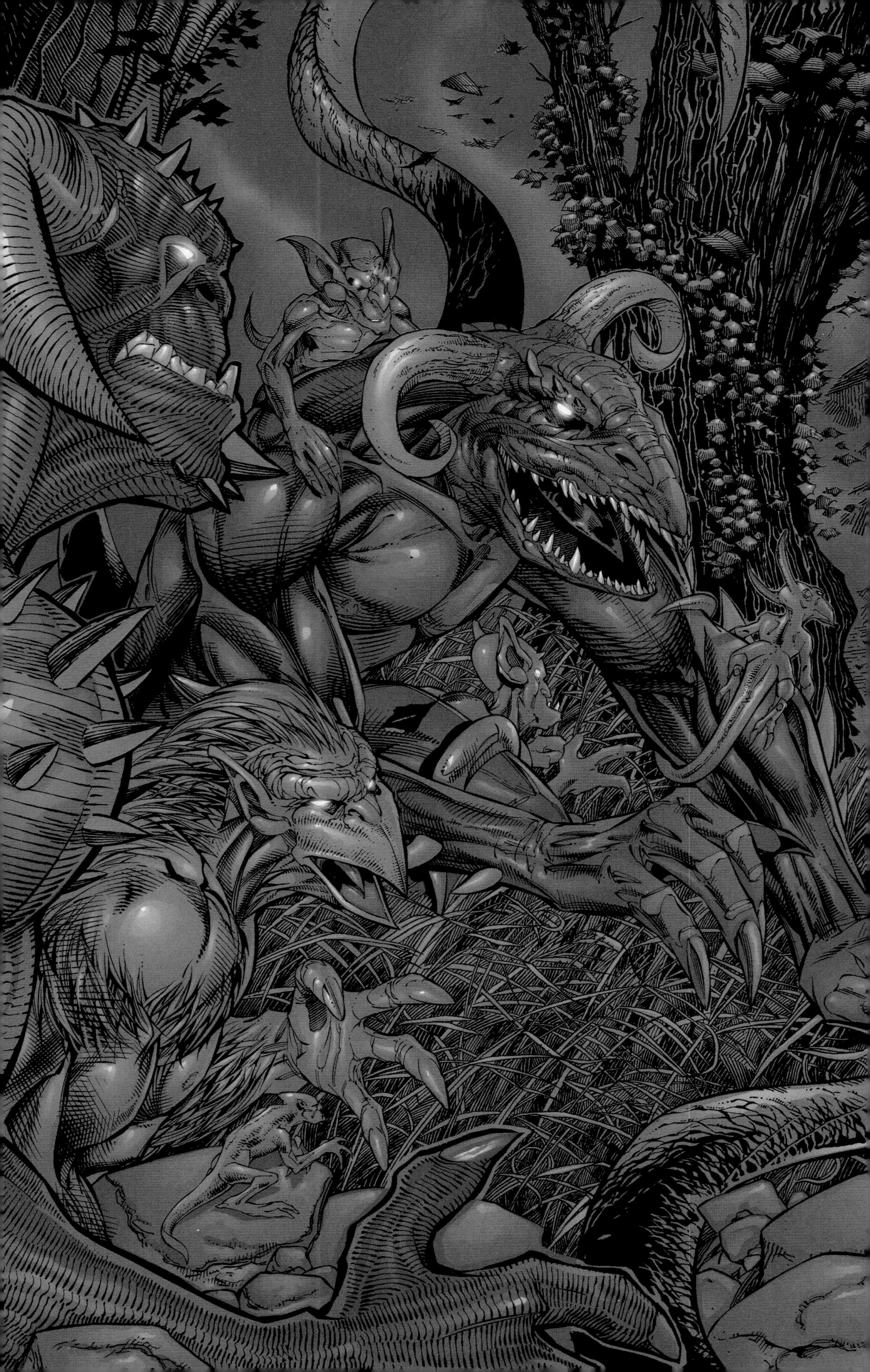

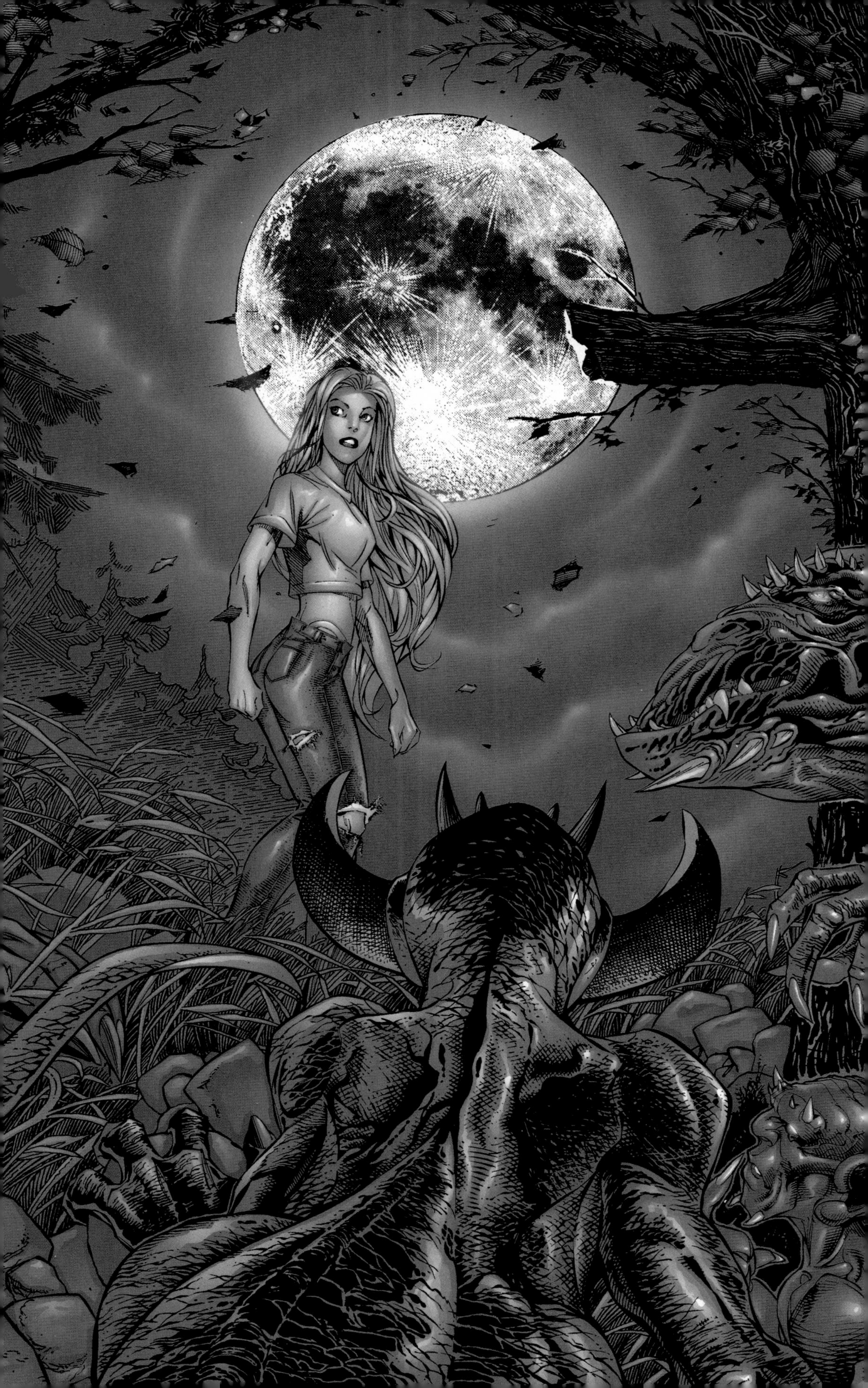

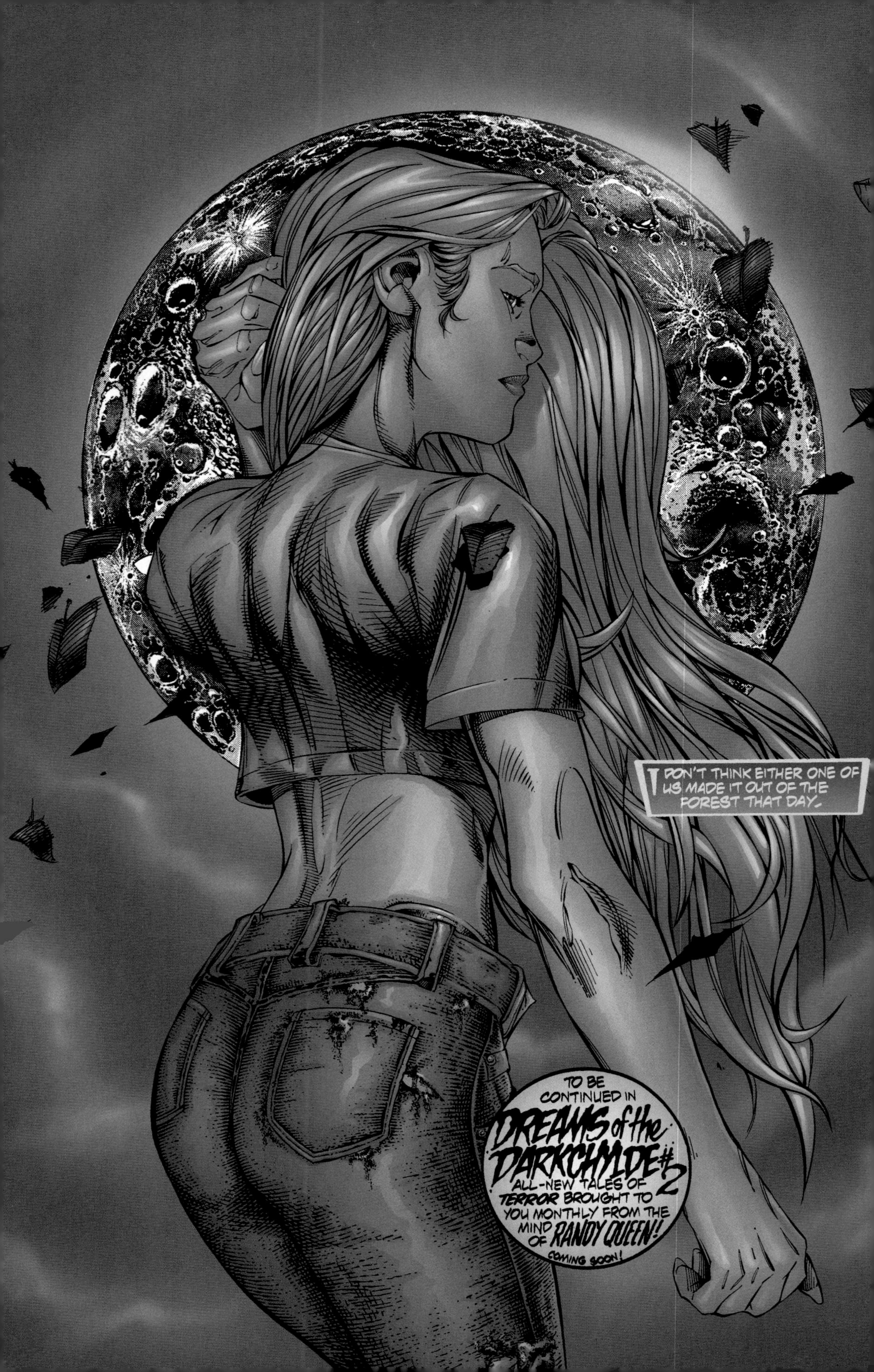
I DON'T THINK EITHER ONE OF US MADE IT OUT OF THE FOREST THAT DAY.
TO BE CONTINUED IN DREAMS of the DARKCHYLDE #2
ALL-NEW TALES OF TERROR BROUGHT TO YOU MONTHLY FROM THE MIND OF RANDY QUEEN!
COMING SOON!

"Night is calling again
an open tapestry is my mind
awake in wide wonder
and trembling at what I'll find..."

A Treasury of Sorrows

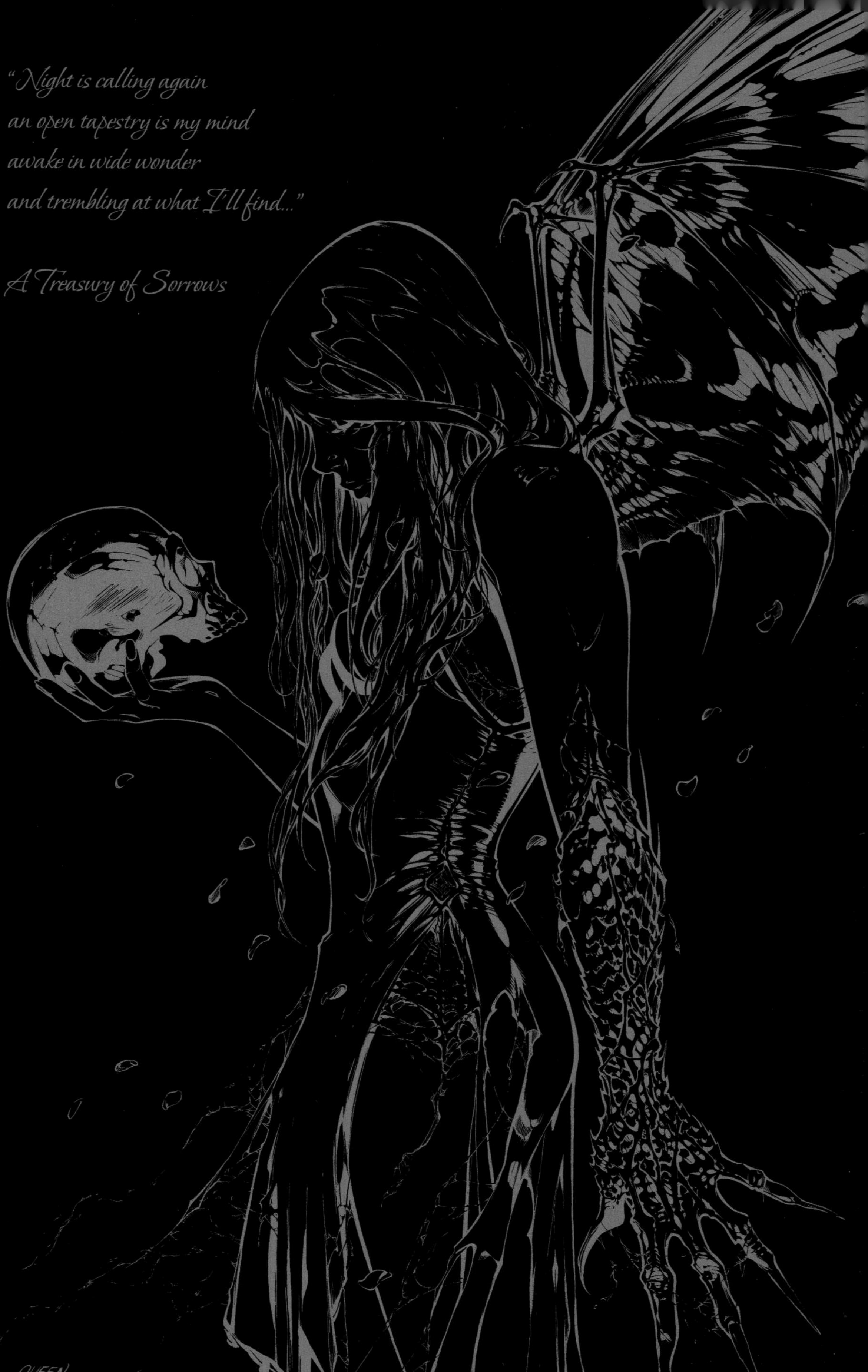
QUEEN

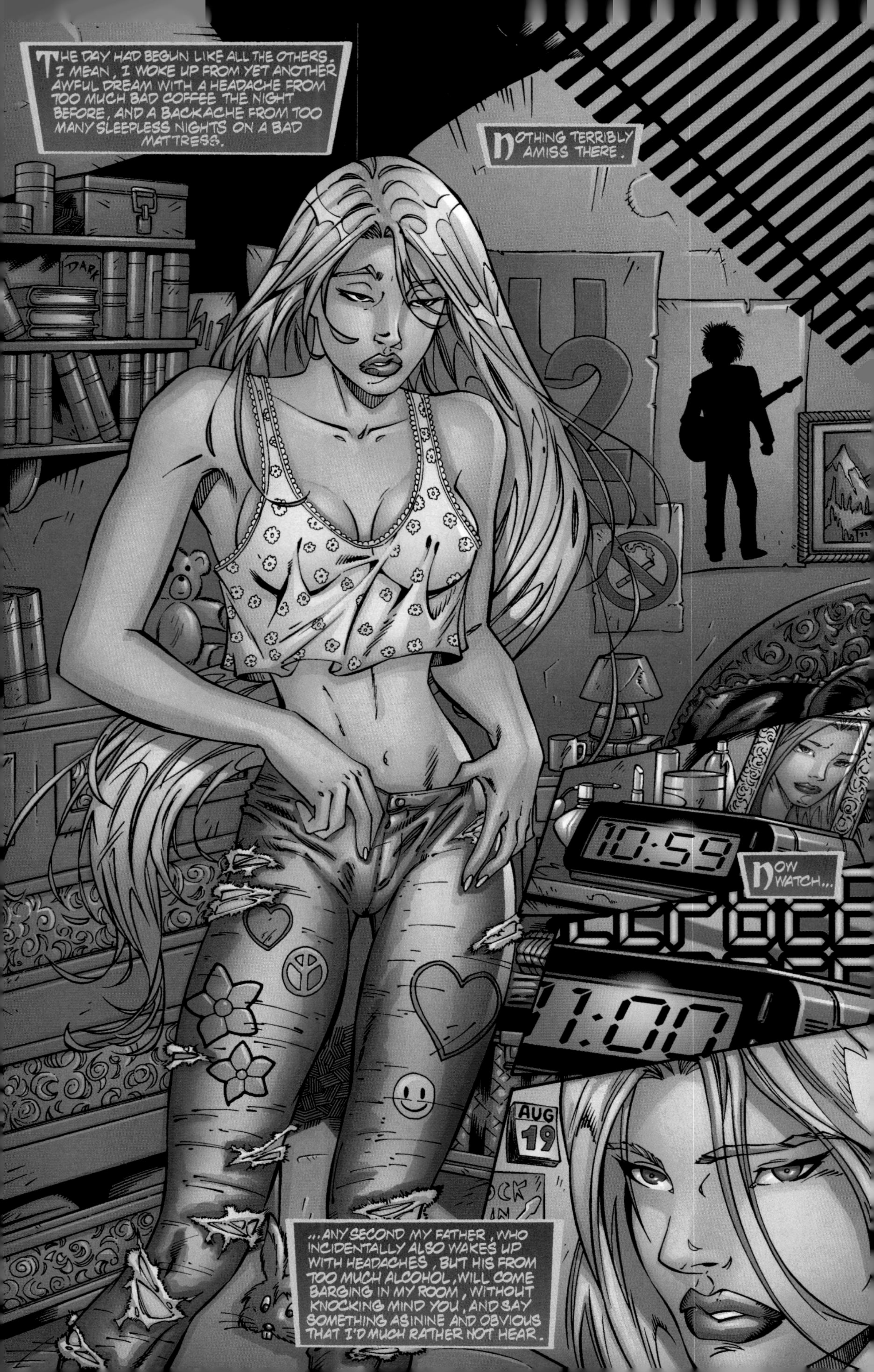
THE DAY HAD BEGUN LIKE ALL THE OTHERS. I MEAN, I WOKE UP FROM YET ANOTHER AWFUL DREAM WITH A HEADACHE FROM TOO MUCH BAD COFFEE THE NIGHT BEFORE, AND A BACKACHE FROM TOO MANY SLEEPLESS NIGHTS ON A BAD MATTRESS.
NOTHING TERRIBLY AMISS THERE.
DARK
10:59
NOW WATCH...
11:00
AUG 19
...ANY SECOND MY FATHER, WHO INCIDENTALLY ALSO WAKES UP WITH HEADACHES, BUT HIS FROM TOO MUCH ALCOHOL, WILL COME BARGING IN MY ROOM, WITHOUT KNOCKING MIND YOU, AND SAY SOMETHING ASININE AND OBVIOUS THAT I'D MUCH RATHER NOT HEAR.

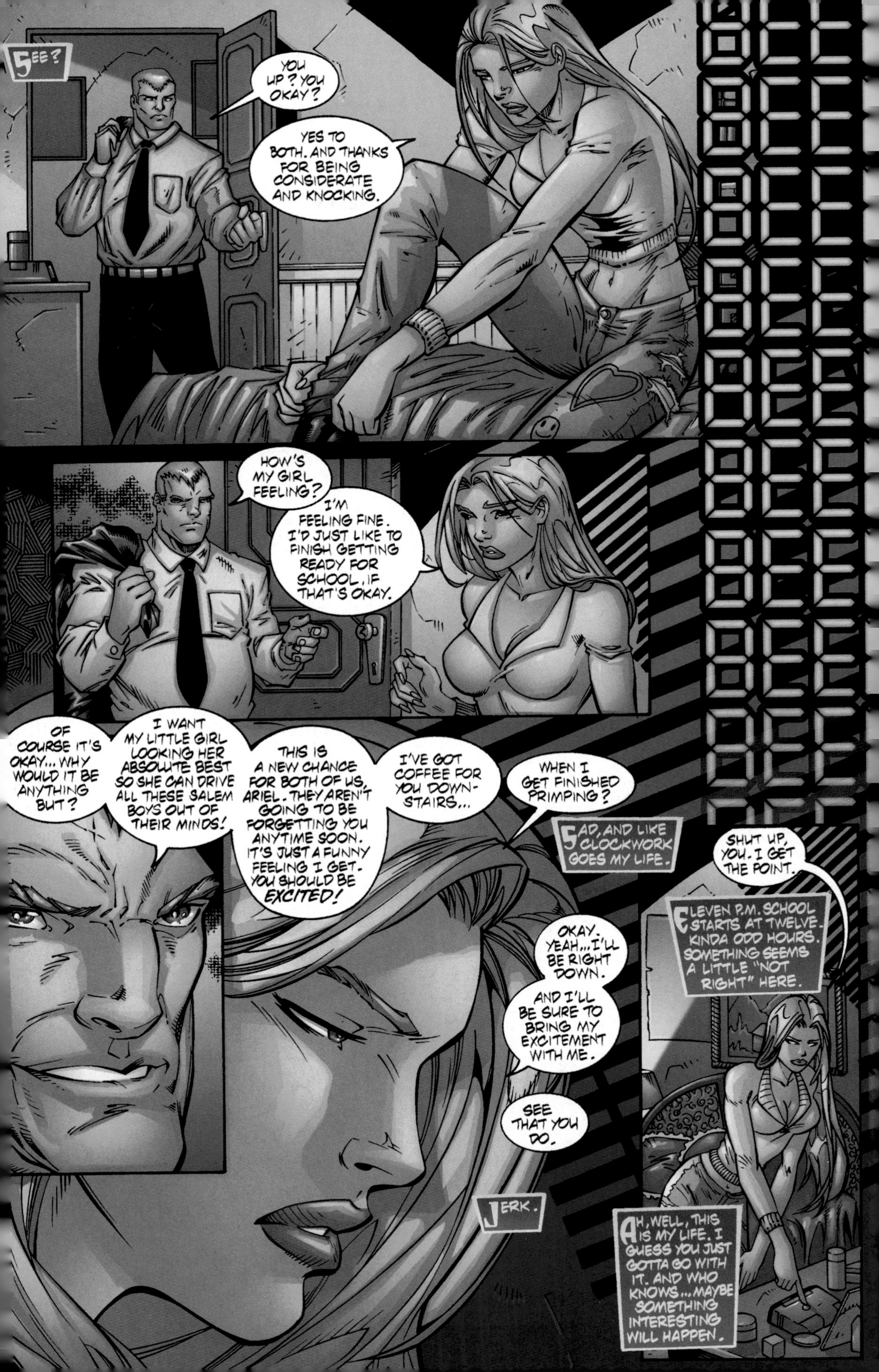
SEE?
YOU UP? YOU OKAY?
YES TO BOTH. AND THANKS FOR BEING CONSIDERATE AND KNOCKING.
HOW'S MY GIRL FEELING?
I'M FEELING FINE. I'D JUST LIKE TO FINISH GETTING READY FOR SCHOOL, IF THAT'S OKAY.
OF COURSE IT'S OKAY... WHY WOULD IT BE ANYTHING BUT?
I WANT MY LITTLE GIRL LOOKING HER ABSOLUTE BEST SO SHE CAN DRIVE ALL THESE SALEM BOYS OUT OF THEIR MINDS!
THIS IS A NEW CHANCE FOR BOTH OF US, ARIEL. THEY AREN'T GOING TO BE FORGETTING YOU ANYTIME SOON. IT'S JUST A FUNNY FEELING I GET. YOU SHOULD BE EXCITED!
I'VE GOT COFFEE FOR YOU DOWN-STAIRS...
WHEN I GET FINISHED PRIMPING?
SAD, AND LIKE CLOCKWORK GOES MY LIFE.
OKAY. YEAH... I'LL BE RIGHT DOWN.
AND I'LL BE SURE TO BRING MY EXCITEMENT WITH ME.
SEE THAT YOU DO.
JERK.
SHUT UP, YOU. I GET THE POINT.
ELEVEN P.M. SCHOOL STARTS AT TWELVE. KINDA ODD HOURS. SOMETHING SEEMS A LITTLE "NOT RIGHT" HERE.
AH, WELL, THIS IS MY LIFE. I GUESS YOU JUST GOTTA GO WITH IT. AND WHO KNOWS... MAYBE SOMETHING INTERESTING WILL HAPPEN.

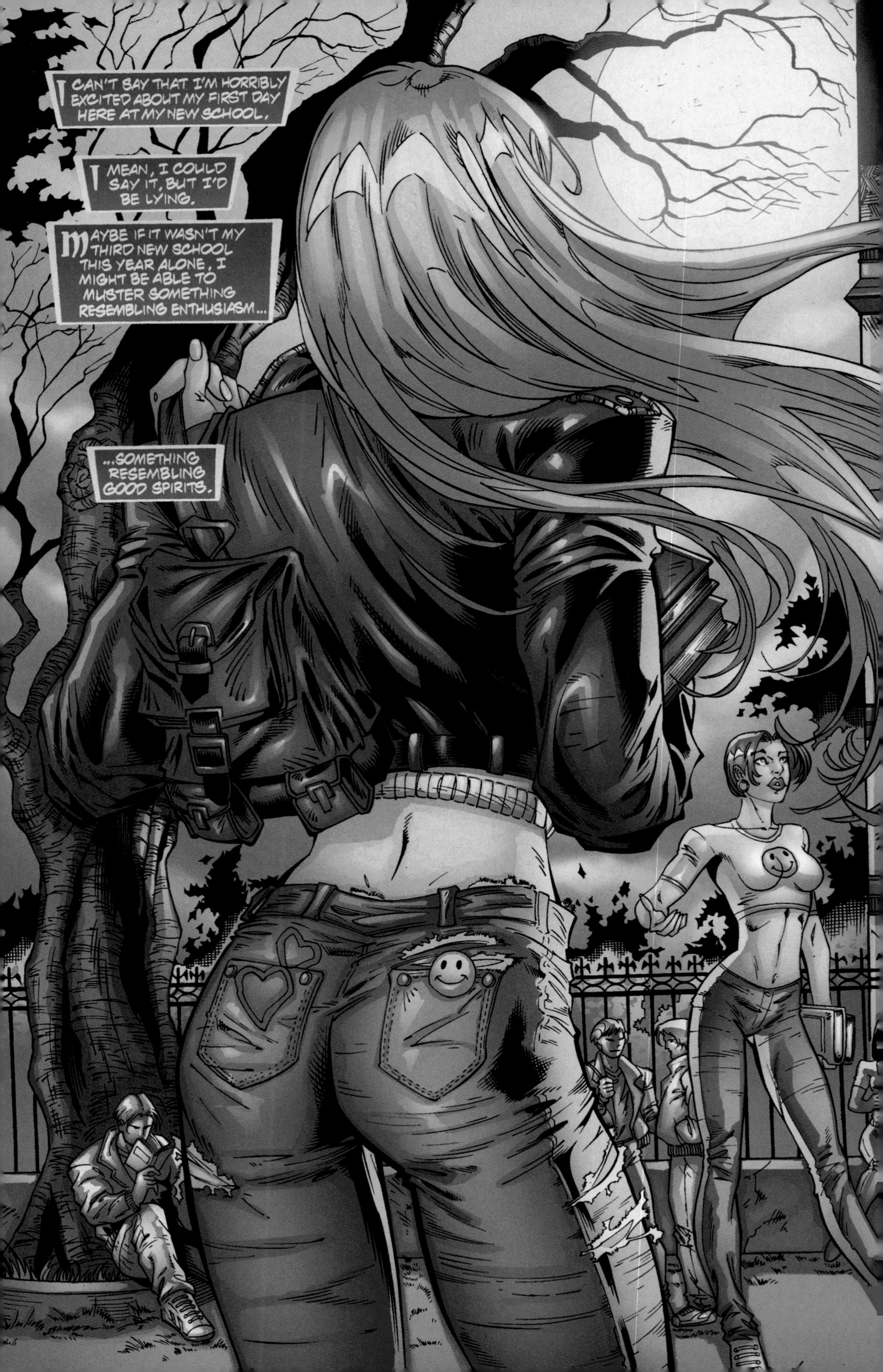
I CAN'T SAY THAT I'M HORRIBLY EXCITED ABOUT MY FIRST DAY HERE AT MY NEW SCHOOL.
I MEAN, I COULD SAY IT, BUT I'D BE LYING.
MAYBE IF IT WASN'T MY THIRD NEW SCHOOL THIS YEAR ALONE, I MIGHT BE ABLE TO MUSTER SOMETHING RESEMBLING ENTHUSIASM...
...SOMETHING RESEMBLING GOOD SPIRITS.

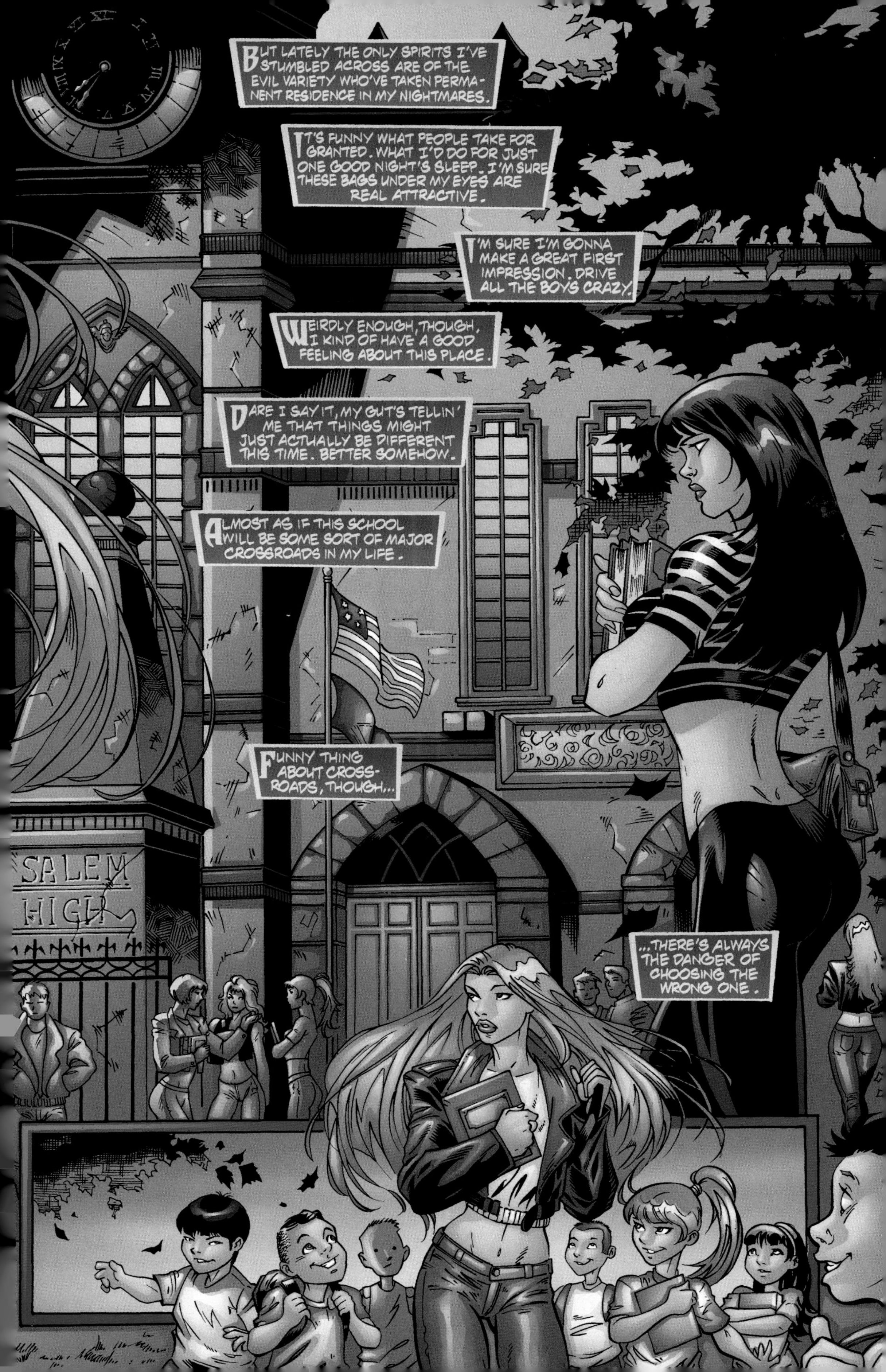
BUT LATELY THE ONLY SPIRITS I'VE STUMBLED ACROSS ARE OF THE EVIL VARIETY WHO'VE TAKEN PERMANENT RESIDENCE IN MY NIGHTMARES.
IT'S FUNNY WHAT PEOPLE TAKE FOR GRANTED. WHAT I'D DO FOR JUST ONE GOOD NIGHT'S SLEEP. I'M SURE THESE BAGS UNDER MY EYES ARE REAL ATTRACTIVE.
I'M SURE I'M GONNA MAKE A GREAT FIRST IMPRESSION. DRIVE ALL THE BOYS CRAZY.
WEIRDLY ENOUGH, THOUGH, I KIND OF HAVE A GOOD FEELING ABOUT THIS PLACE.
DARE I SAY IT, MY GUT'S TELLIN' ME THAT THINGS MIGHT JUST ACTUALLY BE DIFFERENT THIS TIME. BETTER SOMEHOW.
ALMOST AS IF THIS SCHOOL WILL BE SOME SORT OF MAJOR CROSSROADS IN MY LIFE.
FUNNY THING ABOUT CROSS-ROADS, THOUGH...
SALEM HIGH
...THERE'S ALWAYS THE DANGER OF CHOOSING THE WRONG ONE.

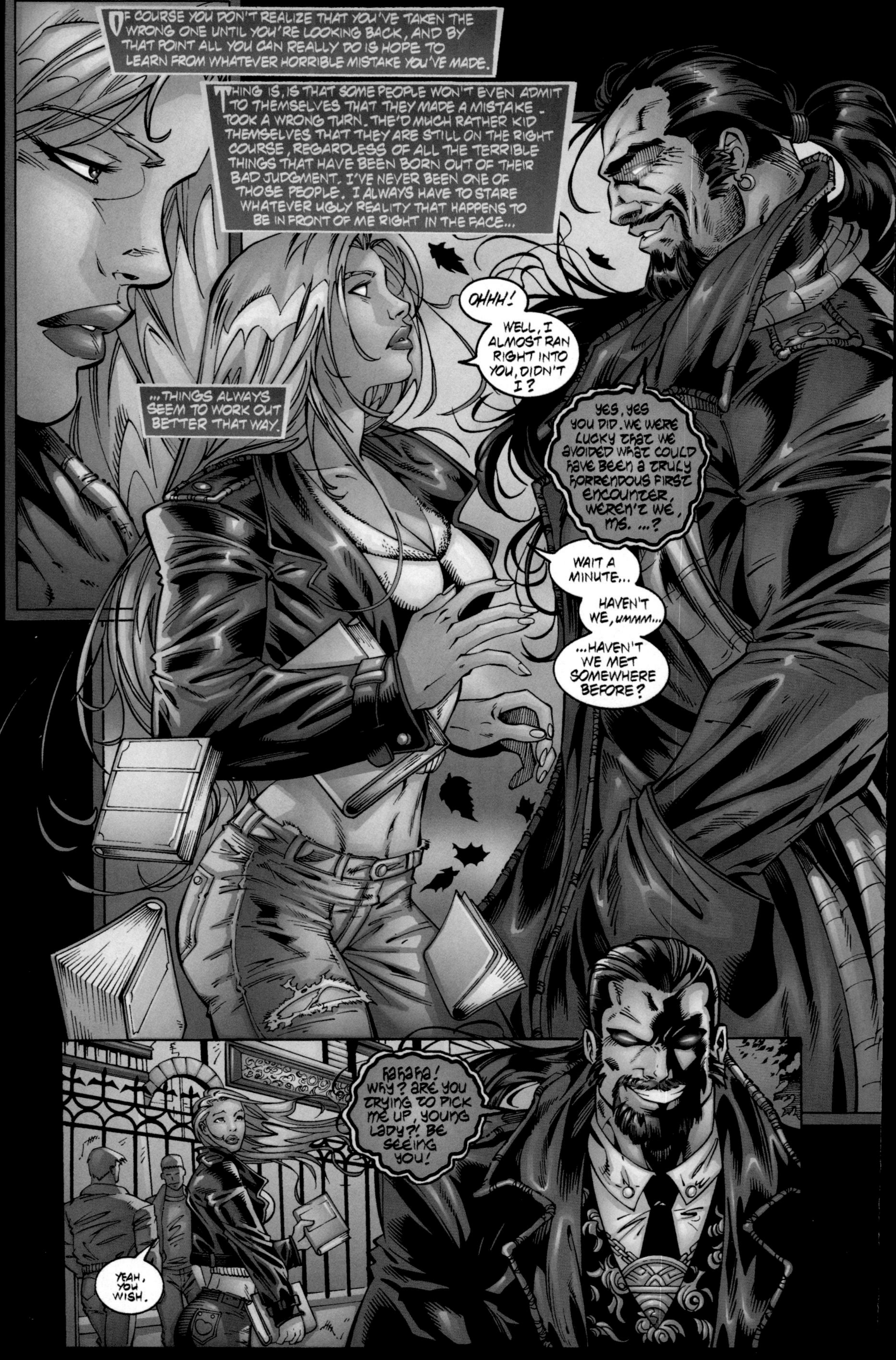

OF COURSE YOU DON'T REALIZE THAT YOU'VE TAKEN THE WRONG ONE UNTIL YOU'RE LOOKING BACK, AND BY THAT POINT ALL YOU CAN REALLY DO IS HOPE TO LEARN FROM WHATEVER HORRIBLE MISTAKE YOU'VE MADE.
THING IS, IS THAT SOME PEOPLE WON'T EVEN ADMIT TO THEMSELVES THAT THEY MADE A MISTAKE - TOOK A WRONG TURN. THE'D MUCH RATHER KID THEMSELVES THAT THEY ARE STILL ON THE RIGHT COURSE, REGARDLESS OF ALL THE TERRIBLE THINGS THAT HAVE BEEN BORN OUT OF THEIR BAD JUDGMENT. I'VE NEVER BEEN ONE OF THOSE PEOPLE. I ALWAYS HAVE TO STARE WHATEVER UGLY REALITY THAT HAPPENS TO BE IN FRONT OF ME RIGHT IN THE FACE...
...THINGS ALWAYS SEEM TO WORK OUT BETTER THAT WAY.
OHHH!
WELL, I ALMOST RAN RIGHT INTO YOU, DIDN'T I?
YES, YES YOU DID. WE WERE LUCKY THAT WE AVOIDED WHAT COULD HAVE BEEN A TRULY HORRENDOUS FIRST ENCOUNTER, WEREN'T WE, MS. ...?
WAIT A MINUTE...
HAVEN'T WE, UMMM...
...HAVEN'T WE MET SOMEWHERE BEFORE?
HAHAHA! WHY? ARE YOU TRYING TO PICK ME UP, YOUNG LADY?! BE SEEING YOU!
YEAH, YOU WISH.

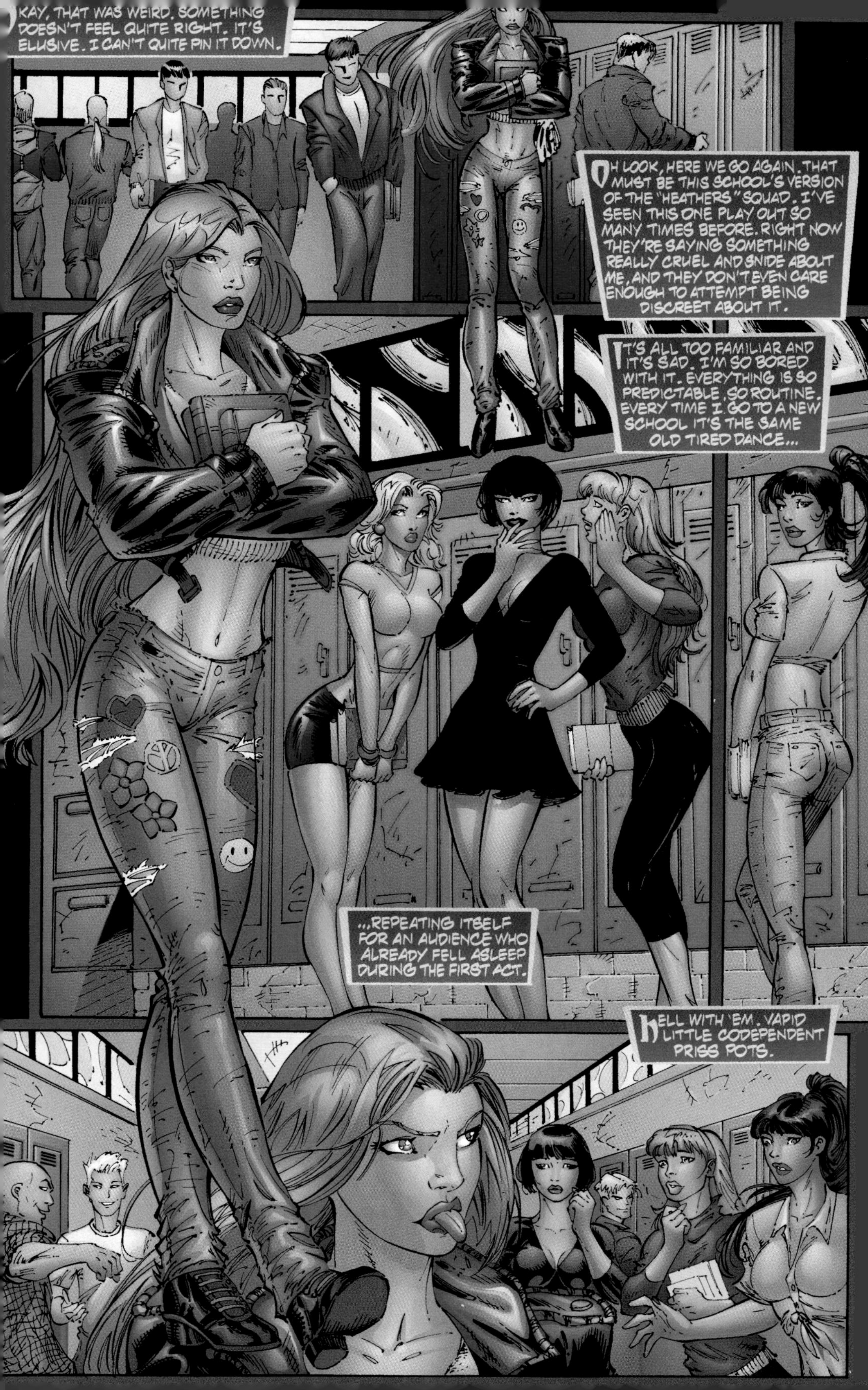
OKAY, THAT WAS WEIRD. SOMETHING DOESN'T FEEL QUITE RIGHT. IT'S ELUSIVE. I CAN'T QUITE PIN IT DOWN.
OH LOOK, HERE WE GO AGAIN. THAT MUST BE THIS SCHOOL'S VERSION OF THE "HEATHERS" SQUAD. I'VE SEEN THIS ONE PLAY OUT SO MANY TIMES BEFORE. RIGHT NOW THEY'RE SAYING SOMETHING REALLY CRUEL AND SNIDE ABOUT ME, AND THEY DON'T EVEN CARE ENOUGH TO ATTEMPT BEING DISCREET ABOUT IT.
IT'S ALL TOO FAMILIAR AND IT'S SAD. I'M SO BORED WITH IT. EVERYTHING IS SO PREDICTABLE, SO ROUTINE. EVERY TIME I GO TO A NEW SCHOOL IT'S THE SAME OLD TIRED DANCE...
...REPEATING ITSELF FOR AN AUDIENCE WHO ALREADY FELL ASLEEP DURING THE FIRST ACT.
HELL WITH 'EM. VAPID LITTLE CODEPENDENT PRISS POTS.

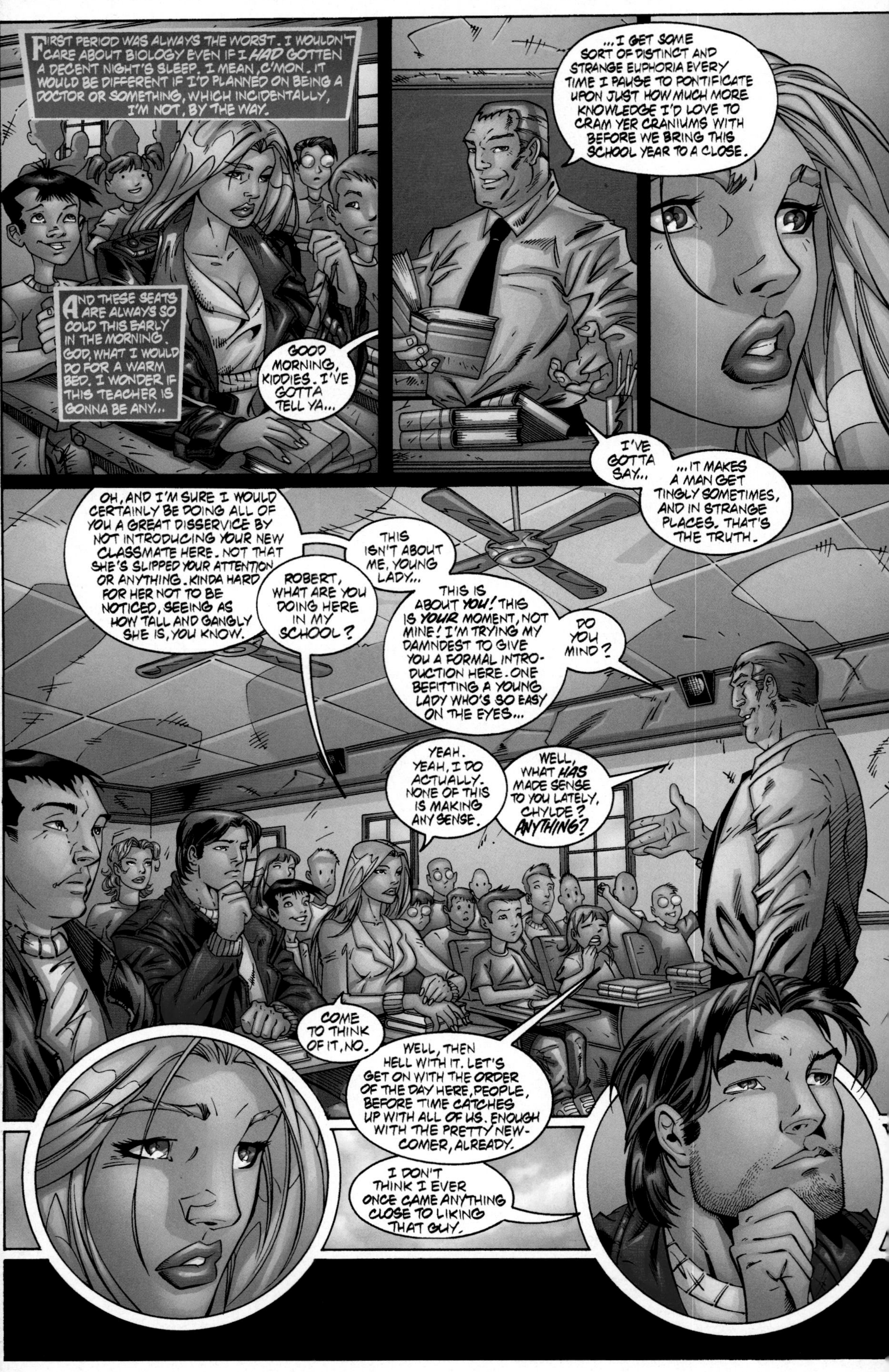
FIRST PERIOD WAS ALWAYS THE WORST. I WOULDN'T CARE ABOUT BIOLOGY EVEN IF I HAD GOTTEN A DECENT NIGHT'S SLEEP. I MEAN, C'MON. IT WOULD BE DIFFERENT IF I'D PLANNED ON BEING A DOCTOR OR SOMETHING, WHICH INCIDENTALLY, I'M NOT, BY THE WAY.
AND THESE SEATS ARE ALWAYS SO COLD THIS EARLY IN THE MORNING. GOD, WHAT I WOULD DO FOR A WARM BED. I WONDER IF THIS TEACHER IS GONNA BE ANY...
GOOD MORNING, KIDDIES. I'VE GOTTA TELL YA...
...I GET SOME SORT OF DISTINCT AND STRANGE EUPHORIA EVERY TIME I PAUSE TO PONTIFICATE UPON JUST HOW MUCH MORE KNOWLEDGE I'D LOVE TO CRAM YER CRANIUMS WITH BEFORE WE BRING THIS SCHOOL YEAR TO A CLOSE.
I'VE GOTTA SAY...
...IT MAKES A MAN GET TINGLY SOMETIMES, AND IN STRANGE PLACES. THAT'S THE TRUTH.
OH, AND I'M SURE I WOULD CERTAINLY BE DOING ALL OF YOU A GREAT DISSERVICE BY NOT INTRODUCING YOUR NEW CLASSMATE HERE. NOT THAT SHE'S SLIPPED YOUR ATTENTION OR ANYTHING. KINDA HARD FOR HER NOT TO BE NOTICED, SEEING AS HOW TALL AND GANGLY SHE IS, YOU KNOW.
ROBERT, WHAT ARE YOU DOING HERE IN MY SCHOOL?
THIS ISN'T ABOUT ME, YOUNG LADY...
THIS IS ABOUT YOU! THIS IS YOUR MOMENT, NOT MINE! I'M TRYING MY DAMNDEST TO GIVE YOU A FORMAL INTRO-DUCTION HERE. ONE BEFITTING A YOUNG LADY WHO'S SO EASY ON THE EYES...
DO YOU MIND?
YEAH. YEAH, I DO ACTUALLY. NONE OF THIS IS MAKING ANY SENSE.
WELL, WHAT HAS MADE SENSE TO YOU LATELY, CHYLDE? ANYTHING?
COME TO THINK OF IT, NO.
WELL, THEN HELL WITH IT. LET'S GET ON WITH THE ORDER OF THE DAY HERE, PEOPLE, BEFORE TIME CATCHES UP WITH ALL OF US. ENOUGH WITH THE PRETTY NEW-COMER, ALREADY.
I DON'T THINK I EVER ONCE CAME ANYTHING CLOSE TO LIKING THAT GUY.

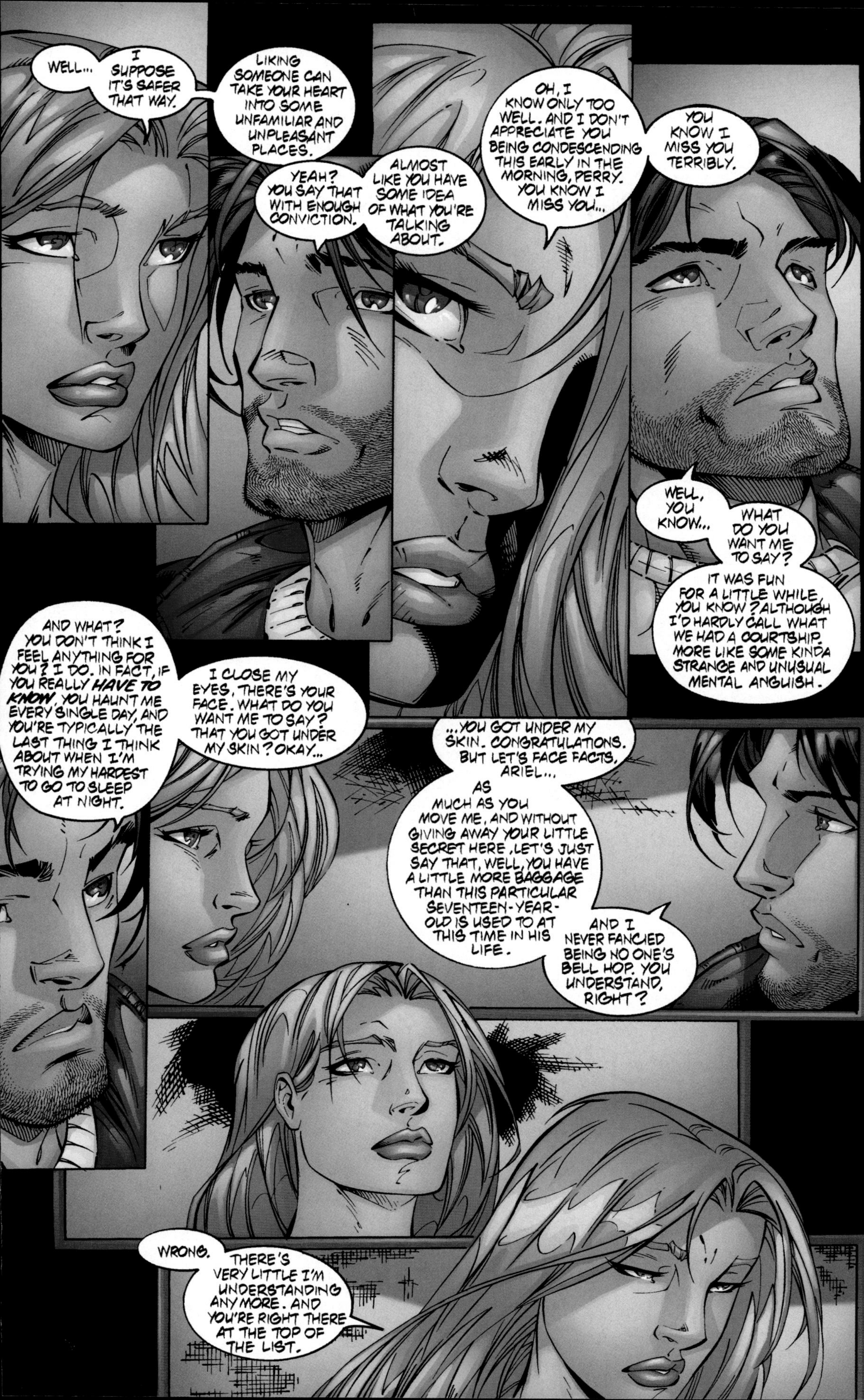
WELL...
I SUPPOSE IT'S SAFER THAT WAY.
LIKING SOMEONE CAN TAKE YOUR HEART INTO SOME UNFAMILIAR AND UNPLEASANT PLACES.
YEAH? YOU SAY THAT WITH ENOUGH CONVICTION.
ALMOST LIKE YOU HAVE SOME IDEA OF WHAT YOU'RE TALKING ABOUT.
OH, I KNOW ONLY TOO WELL. AND I DON'T APPRECIATE YOU BEING CONDESCENDING THIS EARLY IN THE MORNING, PERRY. YOU KNOW I MISS YOU...
YOU KNOW I MISS YOU TERRIBLY.
WELL, YOU KNOW...
WHAT DO YOU WANT ME TO SAY?
IT WAS FUN FOR A LITTLE WHILE, YOU KNOW? ALTHOUGH I'D HARDLY CALL WHAT WE HAD A COURTSHIP. MORE LIKE SOME KINDA STRANGE AND UNUSUAL MENTAL ANGUISH.
AND WHAT? YOU DON'T THINK I FEEL ANYTHING FOR YOU? I DO. IN FACT, IF YOU REALLY **HAVE TO KNOW**, YOU HAUNT ME EVERY SINGLE DAY, AND YOU'RE TYPICALLY THE LAST THING I THINK ABOUT WHEN I'M TRYING MY HARDEST TO GO TO SLEEP AT NIGHT.
I CLOSE MY EYES, THERE'S YOUR FACE. WHAT DO YOU WANT ME TO SAY? THAT YOU GOT UNDER MY SKIN? OKAY...
...YOU GOT UNDER MY SKIN. CONGRATULATIONS. BUT LET'S FACE FACTS, ARIEL...
AS MUCH AS YOU MOVE ME, AND WITHOUT GIVING AWAY YOUR LITTLE SECRET HERE, LET'S JUST SAY THAT, WELL, YOU HAVE A LITTLE MORE BAGGAGE THAN THIS PARTICULAR SEVENTEEN-YEAR-OLD IS USED TO AT THIS TIME IN HIS LIFE.
AND I NEVER FANCIED BEING NO ONE'S BELL HOP. YOU UNDERSTAND, RIGHT?
WRONG.
THERE'S VERY LITTLE I'M UNDERSTANDING ANYMORE. AND YOU'RE RIGHT THERE AT THE TOP OF THE LIST.

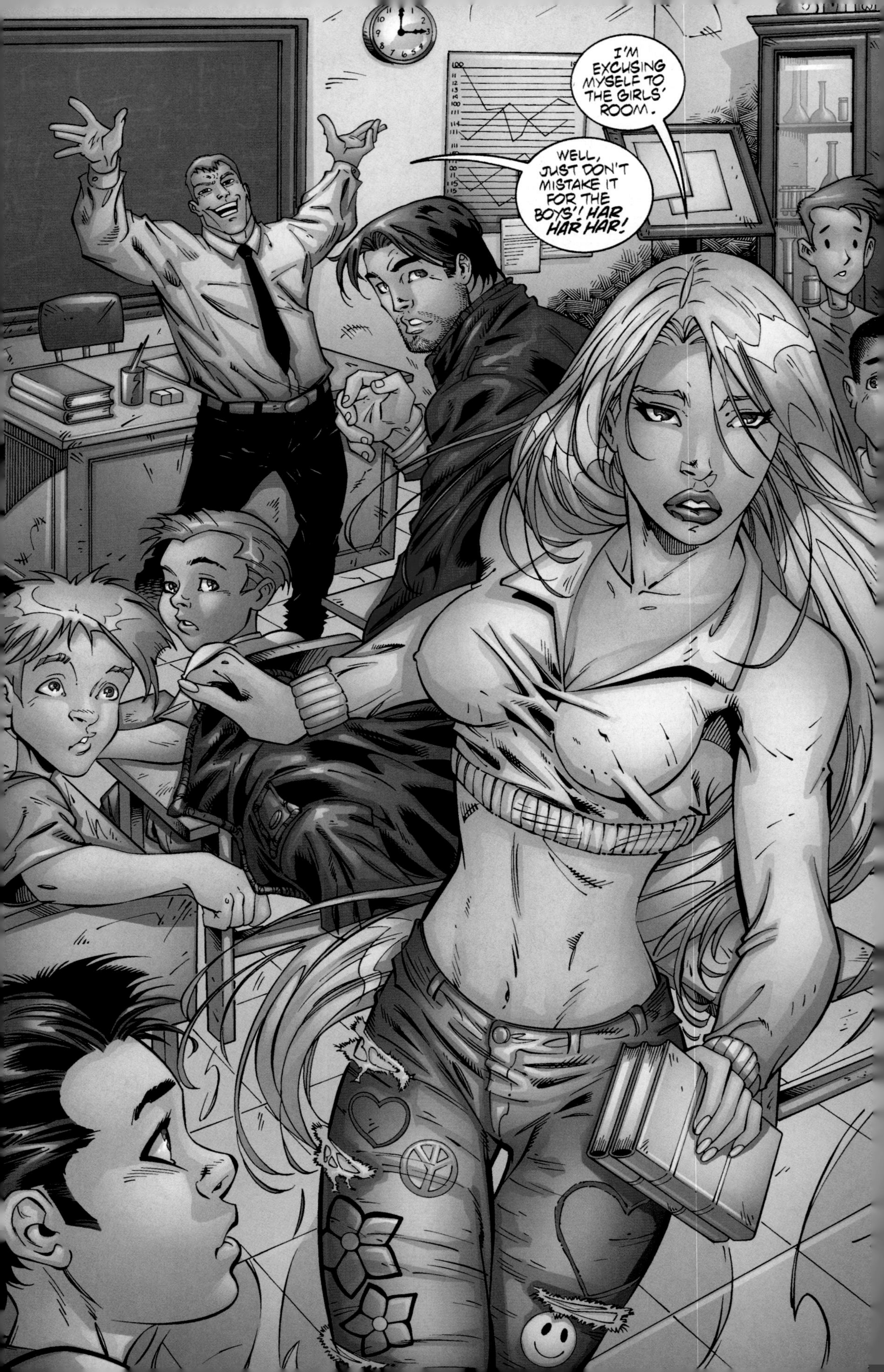
I'M EXCUSING MYSELF TO THE GIRLS' ROOM.
WELL, JUST DON'T MISTAKE IT FOR THE BOYS'! HAR HAR HAR!

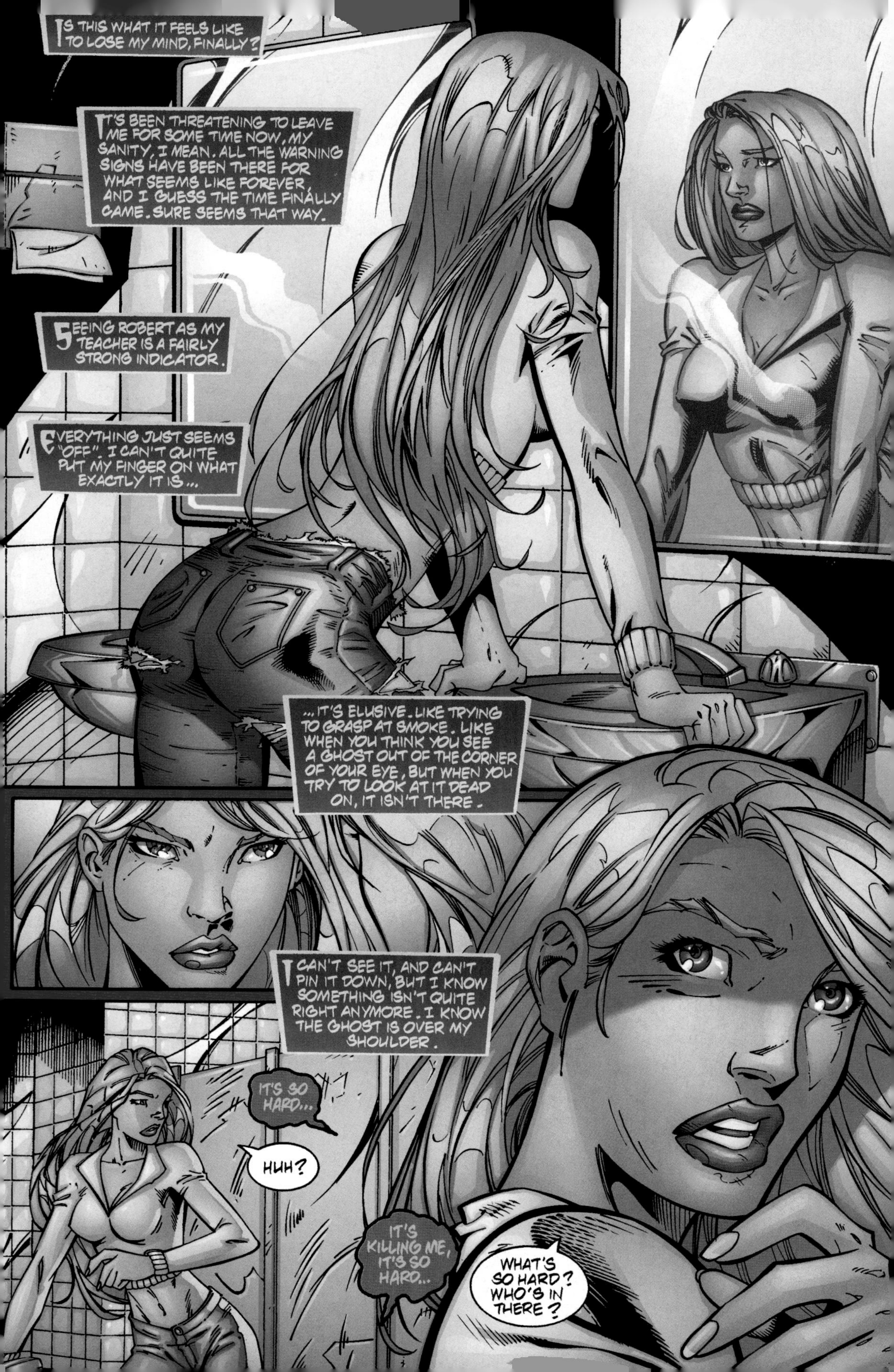

IS THIS WHAT IT FEELS LIKE TO LOSE MY MIND, FINALLY?
IT'S BEEN THREATENING TO LEAVE ME FOR SOME TIME NOW, MY SANITY, I MEAN. ALL THE WARNING SIGNS HAVE BEEN THERE FOR WHAT SEEMS LIKE FOREVER, AND I GUESS THE TIME FINALLY CAME. SURE SEEMS THAT WAY.
SEEING ROBERT AS MY TEACHER IS A FAIRLY STRONG INDICATOR.
EVERYTHING JUST SEEMS "OFF". I CAN'T QUITE PUT MY FINGER ON WHAT EXACTLY IT IS...
...IT'S ELUSIVE. LIKE TRYING TO GRASP AT SMOKE. LIKE WHEN YOU THINK YOU SEE A GHOST OUT OF THE CORNER OF YOUR EYE, BUT WHEN YOU TRY TO LOOK AT IT DEAD ON, IT ISN'T THERE.
I CAN'T SEE IT, AND CAN'T PIN IT DOWN, BUT I KNOW SOMETHING ISN'T QUITE RIGHT ANYMORE. I KNOW THE GHOST IS OVER MY SHOULDER.
IT'S SO HARD...
HUH?
IT'S KILLING ME, IT'S SO HARD...
WHAT'S SO HARD? WHO'S IN THERE?

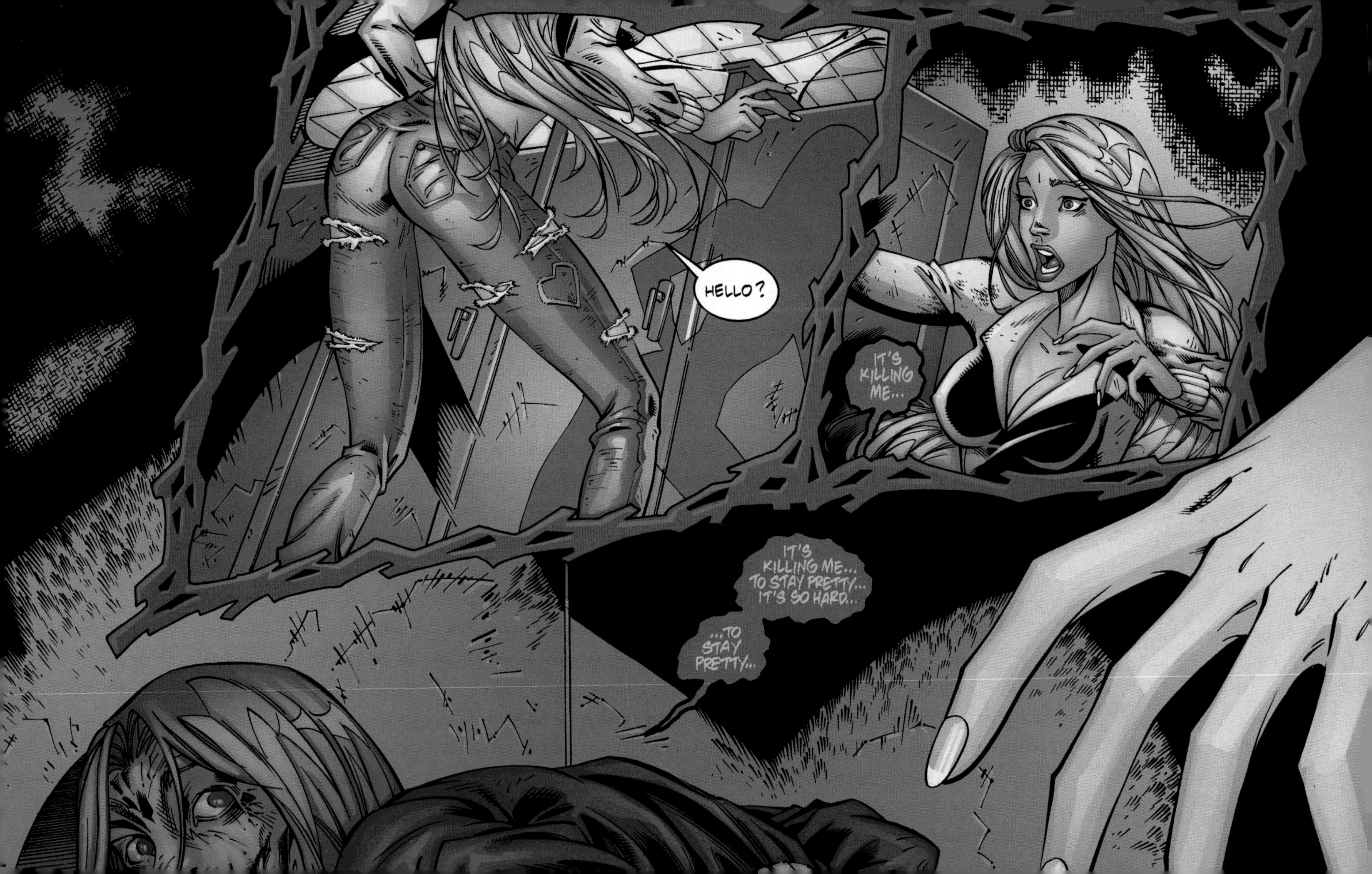
HELLO?
IT'S KILLING ME...
IT'S KILLING ME... TO STAY PRETTY... IT'S SO HARD...
...TO STAY PRETTY...

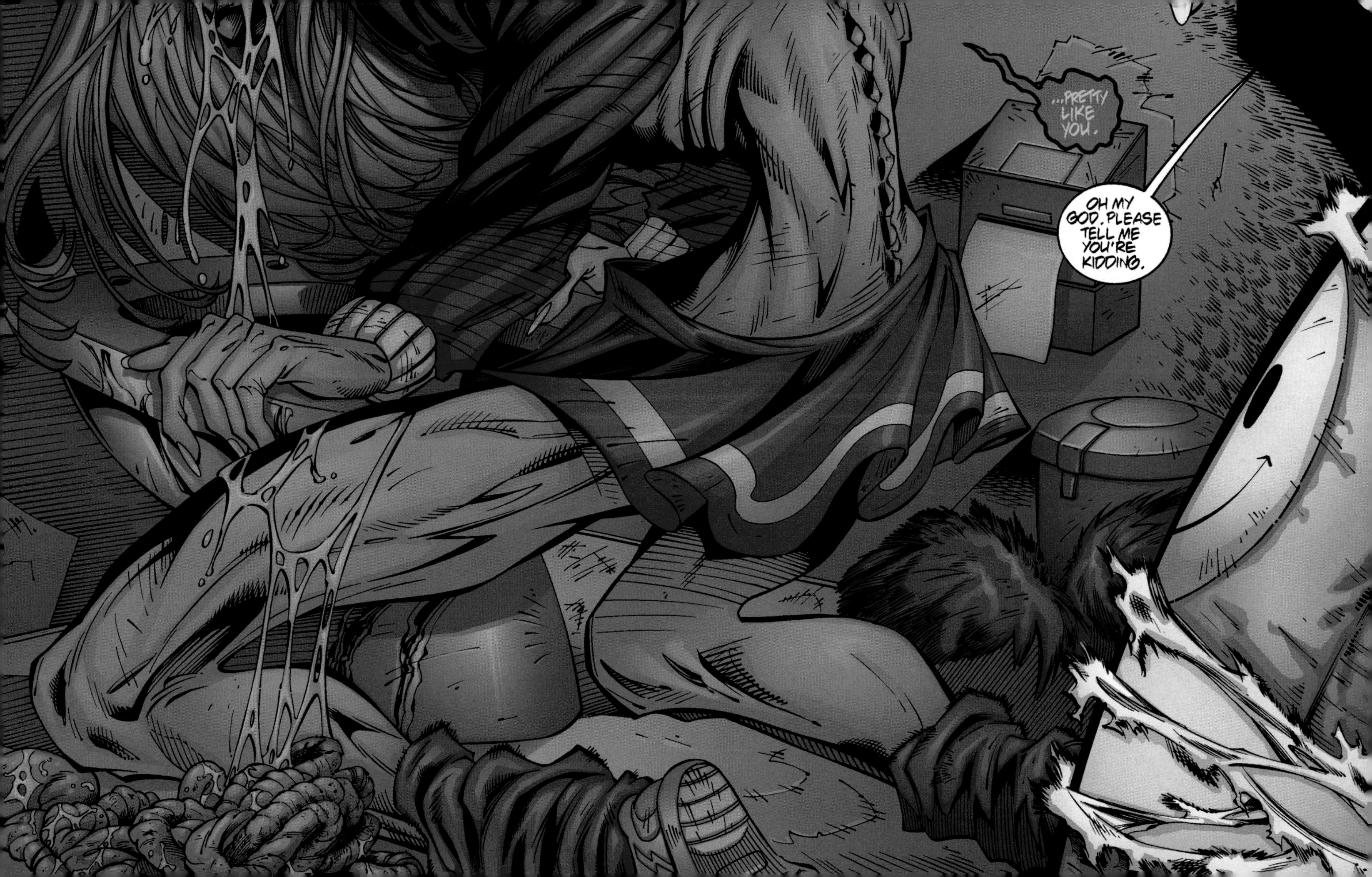
...PRETTY LIKE YOU.
OH MY GOD, PLEASE TELL ME YOU'RE KIDDING.

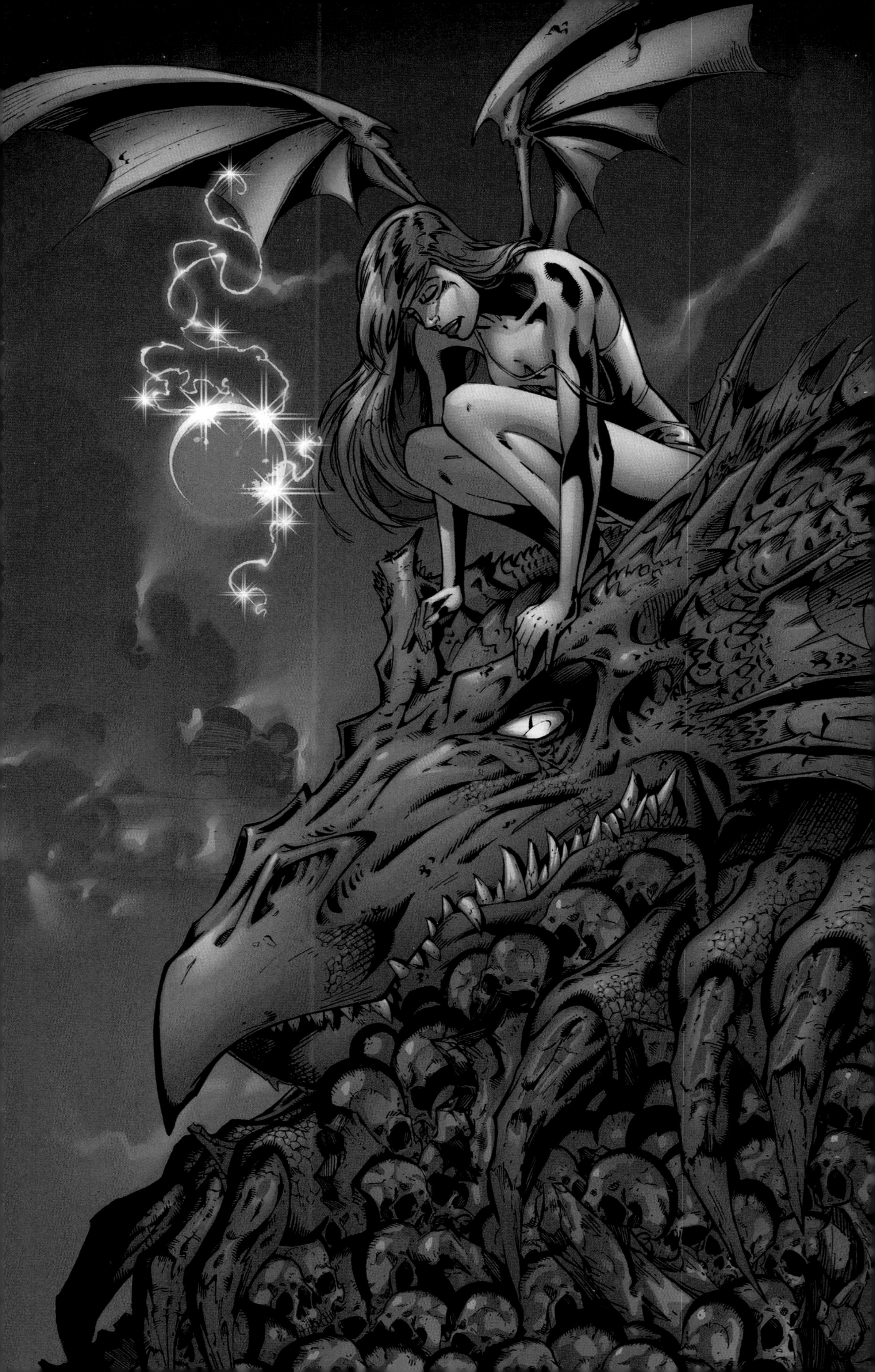

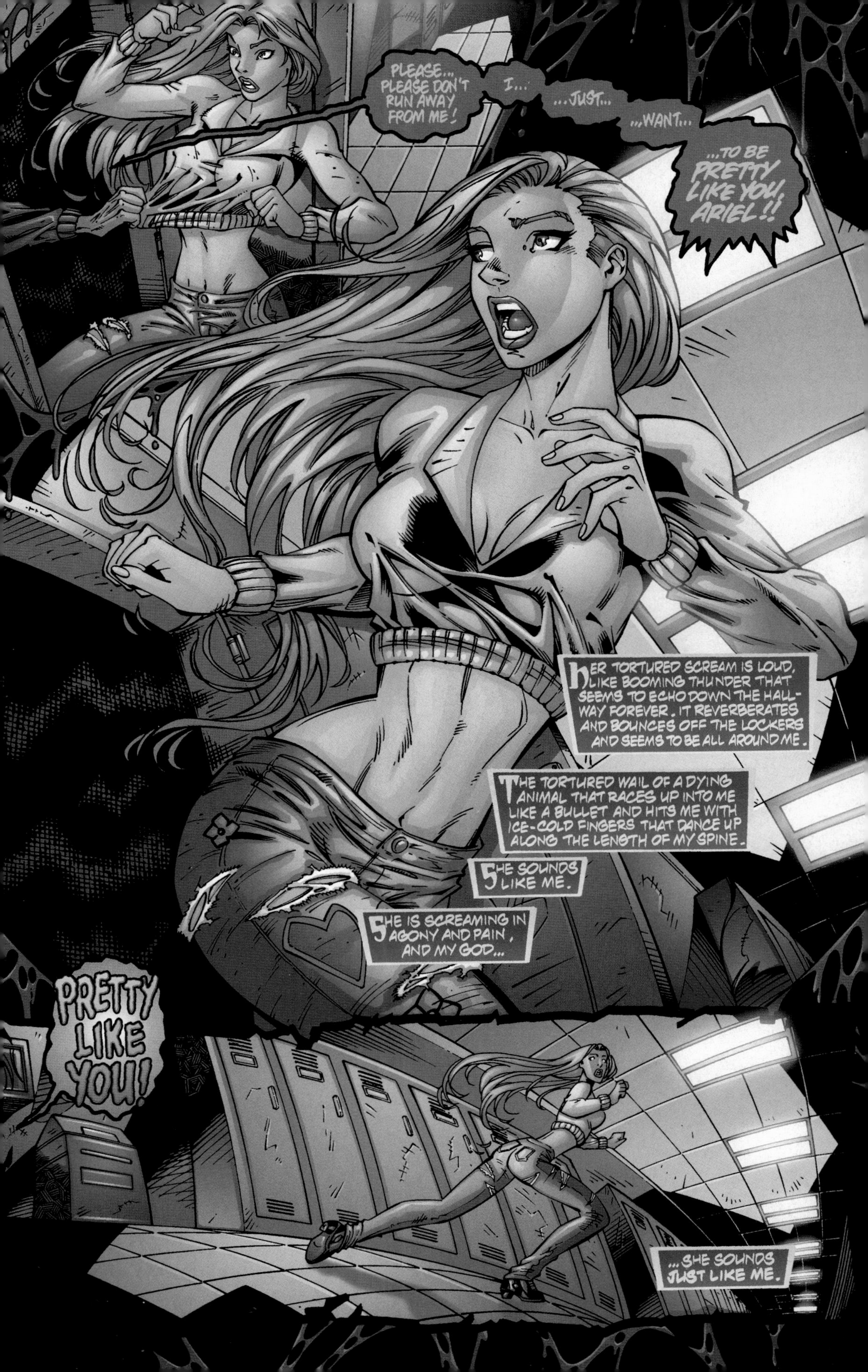
PLEASE... PLEASE DON'T RUN AWAY FROM ME!
I...
...JUST...
...WANT...
...TO BE PRETTY LIKE YOU, ARIEL!!
HER TORTURED SCREAM IS LOUD, LIKE BOOMING THUNDER THAT SEEMS TO ECHO DOWN THE HALLWAY FOREVER. IT REVERBERATES AND BOUNCES OFF THE LOCKERS AND SEEMS TO BE ALL AROUND ME.
THE TORTURED WAIL OF A DYING ANIMAL THAT RACES UP INTO ME LIKE A BULLET AND HITS ME WITH ICE-COLD FINGERS THAT DANCE UP ALONG THE LENGTH OF MY SPINE.
SHE SOUNDS LIKE ME.
SHE IS SCREAMING IN AGONY AND PAIN, AND MY GOD...
PRETTY LIKE YOU!
...SHE SOUNDS JUST LIKE ME.

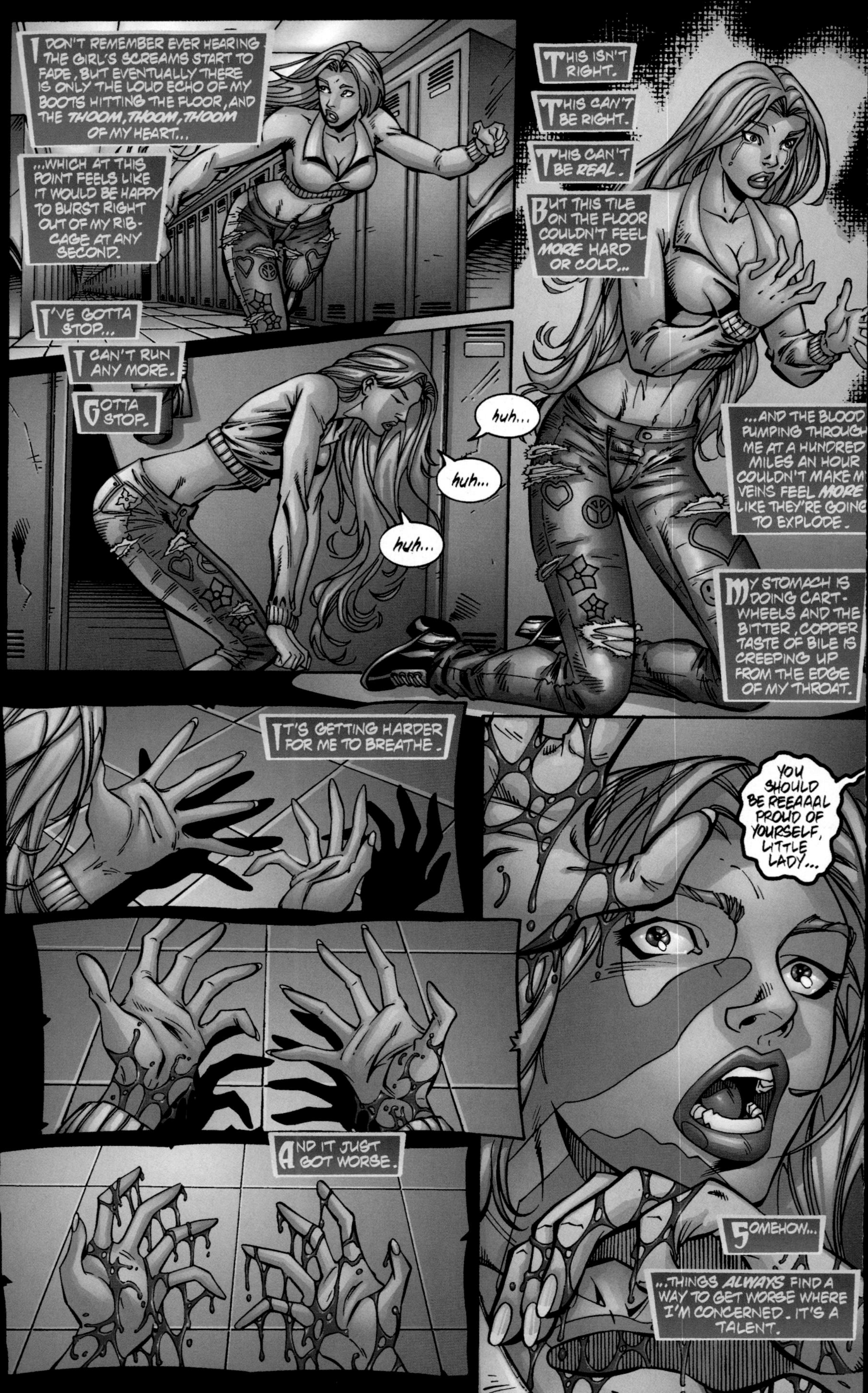
I DON'T REMEMBER EVER HEARING THE GIRL'S SCREAMS START TO FADE, BUT EVENTUALLY THERE IS ONLY THE LOUD ECHO OF MY BOOTS HITTING THE FLOOR, AND THE *THOOM, THOOM, THOOM* OF MY HEART...
...WHICH AT THIS POINT FEELS LIKE IT WOULD BE HAPPY TO BURST RIGHT OUT OF MY RIB-CAGE AT ANY SECOND.
I'VE GOTTA STOP...
I CAN'T RUN ANY MORE.
GOTTA STOP.
huh...
huh...
huh...
THIS ISN'T RIGHT.
THIS CAN'T BE RIGHT.
THIS CAN'T BE *REAL*.
BUT THIS TILE ON THE FLOOR COULDN'T FEEL *MORE* HARD OR COLD...
...AND THE BLOOD PUMPING THROUGH ME AT A HUNDRED MILES AN HOUR COULDN'T MAKE MY VEINS FEEL *MORE* LIKE THEY'RE GOING TO EXPLODE.
MY STOMACH IS DOING CART-WHEELS AND THE BITTER, COPPER TASTE OF BILE IS CREEPING UP FROM THE EDGE OF MY THROAT.
IT'S GETTING HARDER FOR ME TO BREATHE.
AND IT JUST GOT WORSE.
YOU SHOULD BE REEAAAL PROUD OF YOURSELF, LITTLE LADY...
SOMEHOW...
...THINGS *ALWAYS* FIND A WAY TO GET WORSE WHERE I'M CONCERNED. IT'S A TALENT.

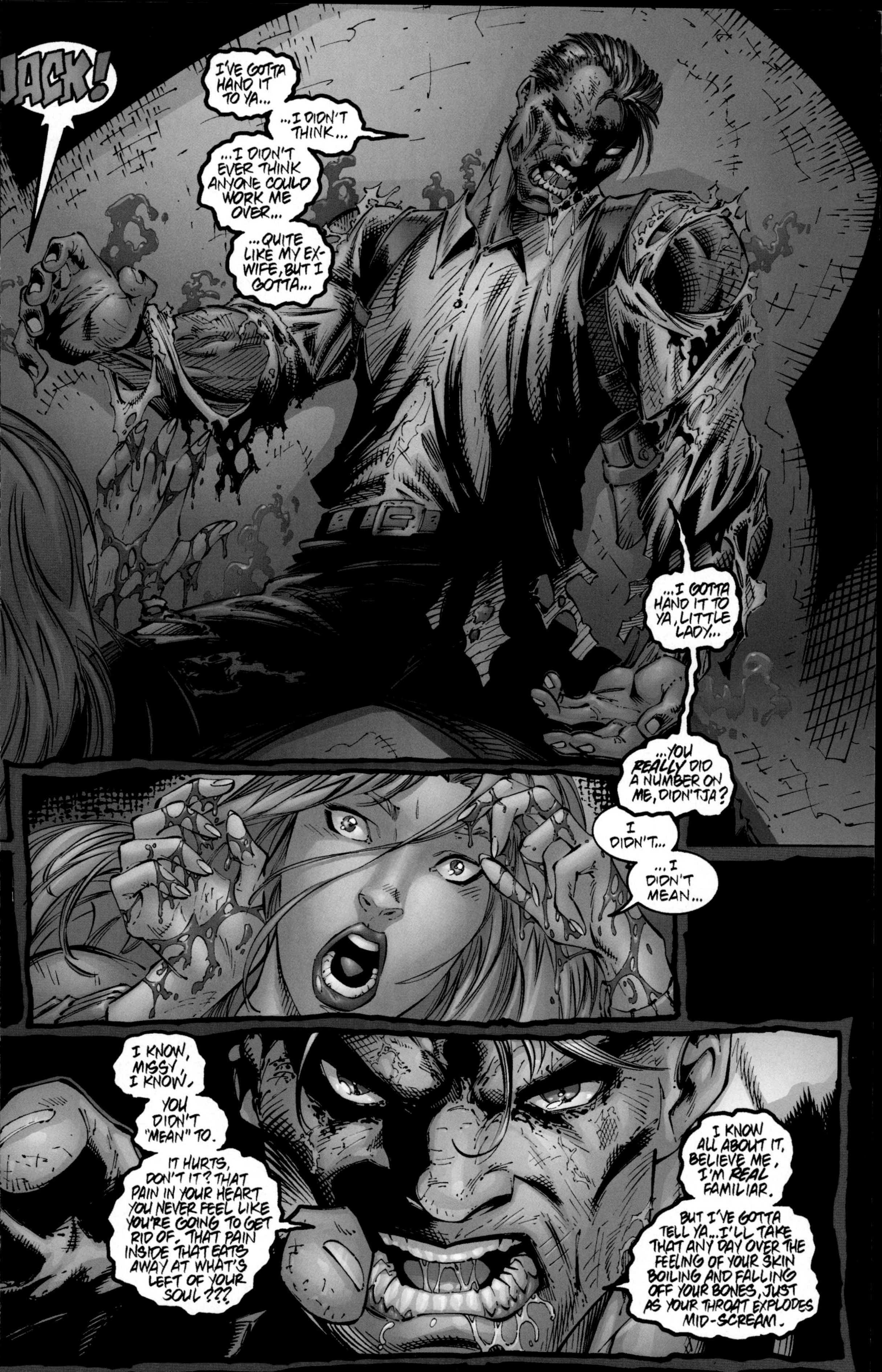

JACK!
I'VE GOTTA HAND IT TO YA...
...I DIDN'T THINK...
...I DIDN'T EVER THINK ANYONE COULD WORK ME OVER...
...QUITE LIKE MY EX-WIFE, BUT I GOTTA...
...I GOTTA HAND IT TO YA, LITTLE LADY...
...YOU REALLY DID A NUMBER ON ME, DIDN'TJA?
I DIDN'T...
...I DIDN'T MEAN...
I KNOW, MISSY, I KNOW.
YOU DIDN'T "MEAN" TO.
IT HURTS, DON'T IT? THAT PAIN IN YOUR HEART YOU NEVER FEEL LIKE YOU'RE GOING TO GET RID OF, THAT PAIN INSIDE THAT EATS AWAY AT WHAT'S LEFT OF YOUR SOUL???
I KNOW ALL ABOUT IT, BELIEVE ME, I'M REAL FAMILIAR.
BUT I'VE GOTTA TELL YA...I'LL TAKE THAT ANY DAY OVER THE FEELING OF YOUR SKIN BOILING AND FALLING OFF YOUR BONES, JUST AS YOUR THROAT EXPLODES MID-SCREAM.

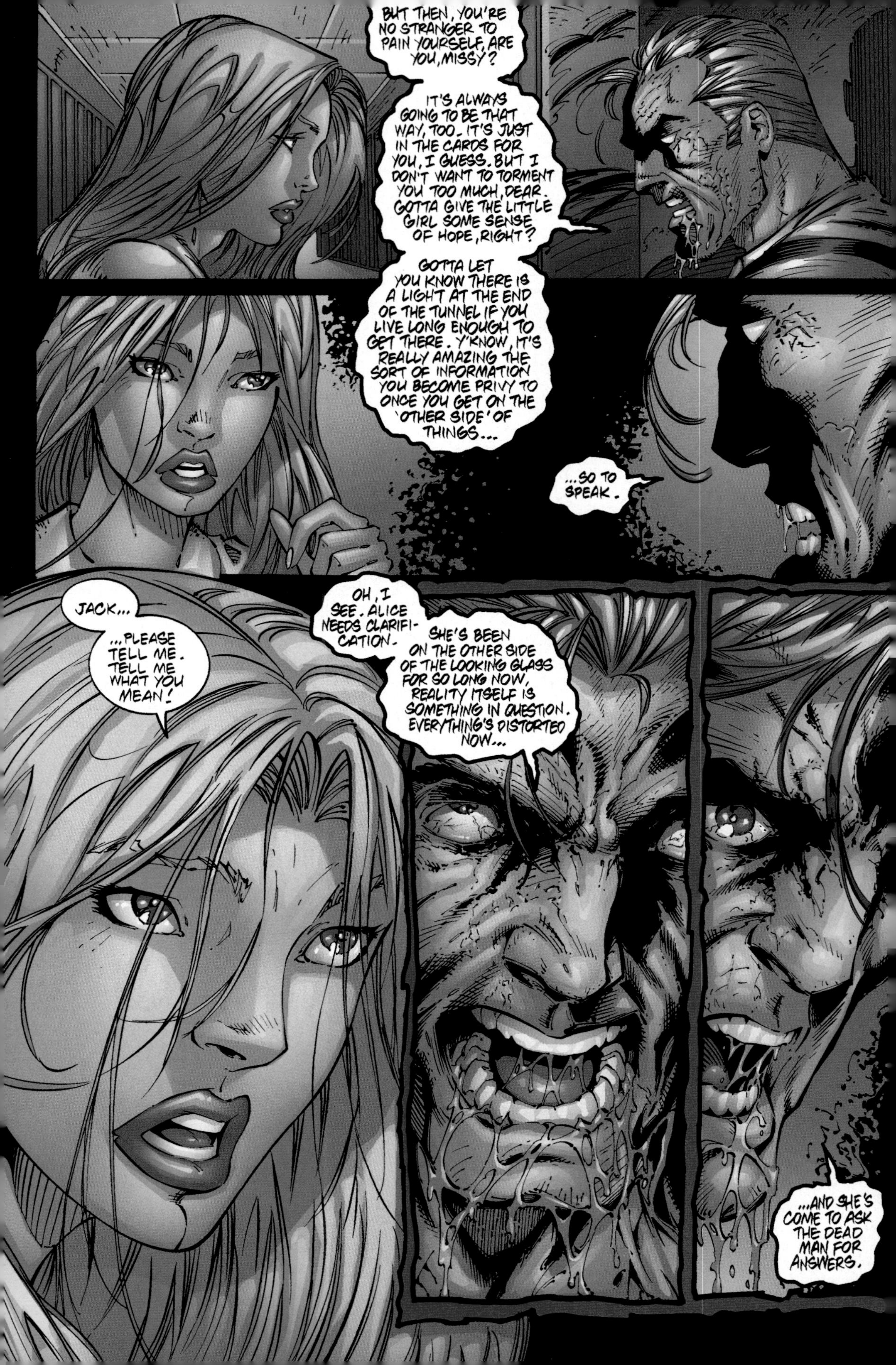
BUT THEN, YOU'RE NO STRANGER TO PAIN YOURSELF, ARE YOU, MISSY?
IT'S ALWAYS GOING TO BE THAT WAY, TOO. IT'S JUST IN THE CARDS FOR YOU, I GUESS. BUT I DON'T WANT TO TORMENT YOU TOO MUCH, DEAR. GOTTA GIVE THE LITTLE GIRL SOME SENSE OF HOPE, RIGHT?
GOTTA LET YOU KNOW THERE IS A LIGHT AT THE END OF THE TUNNEL IF YOU LIVE LONG ENOUGH TO GET THERE. Y'KNOW, IT'S REALLY AMAZING THE SORT OF INFORMATION YOU BECOME PRIVY TO ONCE YOU GET ON THE 'OTHER SIDE' OF THINGS...
...SO TO SPEAK.
JACK...
...PLEASE TELL ME. TELL ME WHAT YOU MEAN!
OH, I SEE. ALICE NEEDS CLARIFI-CATION.
SHE'S BEEN ON THE OTHER SIDE OF THE LOOKING GLASS FOR SO LONG NOW, REALITY ITSELF IS SOMETHING IN QUESTION. EVERYTHING'S DISTORTED NOW...
...AND SHE'S COME TO ASK THE DEAD MAN FOR ANSWERS.

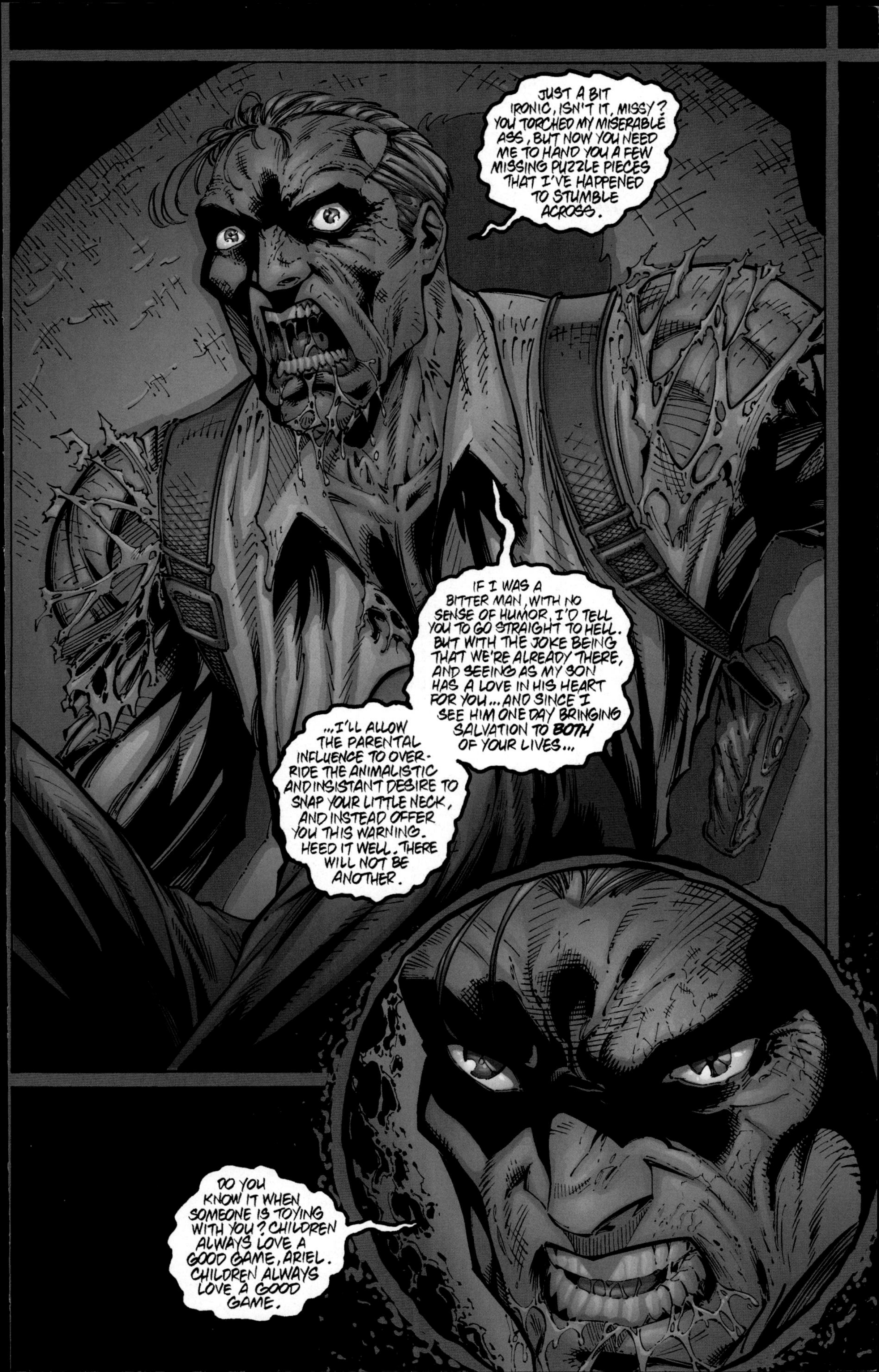
JUST A BIT IRONIC, ISN'T IT, MISSY? YOU TORCHED MY MISERABLE ASS, BUT NOW YOU NEED ME TO HAND YOU A FEW MISSING PUZZLE PIECES THAT I'VE HAPPENED TO STUMBLE ACROSS.
IF I WAS A BITTER MAN, WITH NO SENSE OF HUMOR, I'D TELL YOU TO GO STRAIGHT TO HELL. BUT WITH THE JOKE BEING THAT WE'RE ALREADY THERE, AND SEEING AS MY SON HAS A LOVE IN HIS HEART FOR YOU... AND SINCE I SEE HIM ONE DAY BRINGING SALVATION TO BOTH OF YOUR LIVES...
...I'LL ALLOW THE PARENTAL INFLUENCE TO OVER-RIDE THE ANIMALISTIC AND INSISTANT DESIRE TO SNAP YOUR LITTLE NECK, AND INSTEAD OFFER YOU THIS WARNING. HEED IT WELL. THERE WILL NOT BE ANOTHER.
DO YOU KNOW IT WHEN SOMEONE IS TOYING WITH YOU? CHILDREN ALWAYS LOVE A GOOD GAME, ARIEL. CHILDREN ALWAYS LOVE A GOOD GAME.

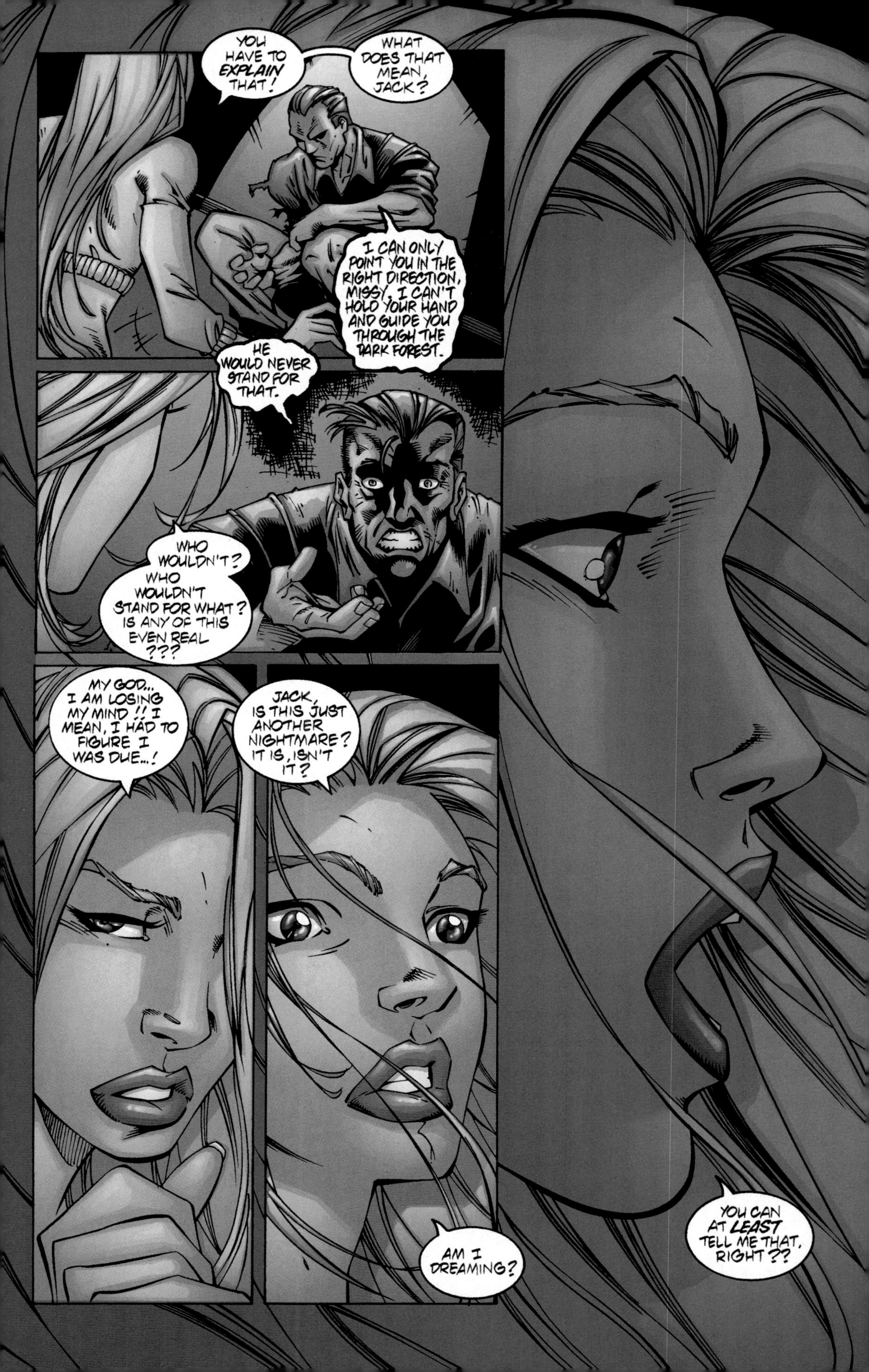
YOU HAVE TO EXPLAIN THAT!
WHAT DOES THAT MEAN, JACK?
I CAN ONLY POINT YOU IN THE RIGHT DIRECTION, MISSY. I CAN'T HOLD YOUR HAND AND GUIDE YOU THROUGH THE DARK FOREST.
HE WOULD NEVER STAND FOR THAT.
WHO WOULDN'T? WHO WOULDN'T STAND FOR WHAT? IS ANY OF THIS EVEN REAL ???
MY GOD... I AM LOSING MY MIND!! I MEAN, I HAD TO FIGURE I WAS DUE...!
JACK, IS THIS JUST ANOTHER NIGHTMARE? IT IS, ISN'T IT?
AM I DREAMING?
YOU CAN AT LEAST TELL ME THAT, RIGHT??

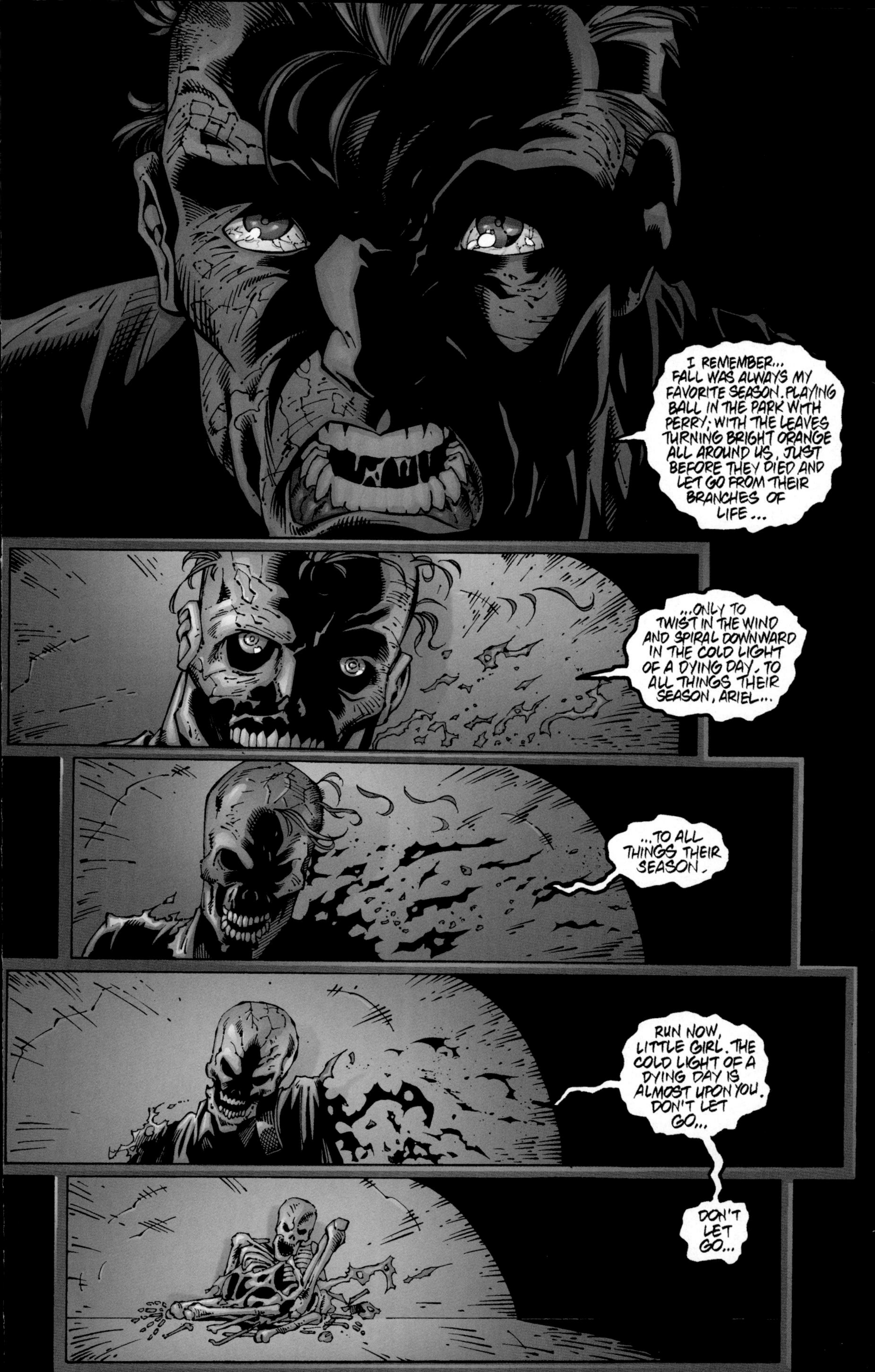
I REMEMBER... FALL WAS ALWAYS MY FAVORITE SEASON. PLAYING BALL IN THE PARK WITH PERRY; WITH THE LEAVES TURNING BRIGHT ORANGE ALL AROUND US, JUST BEFORE THEY DIED AND LET GO FROM THEIR BRANCHES OF LIFE...
...ONLY TO TWIST IN THE WIND AND SPIRAL DOWNWARD IN THE COLD LIGHT OF A DYING DAY. TO ALL THINGS THEIR SEASON, ARIEL...
...TO ALL THINGS THEIR SEASON.
RUN NOW, LITTLE GIRL. THE COLD LIGHT OF A DYING DAY IS ALMOST UPON YOU. DON'T LET GO...
DON'T LET GO...

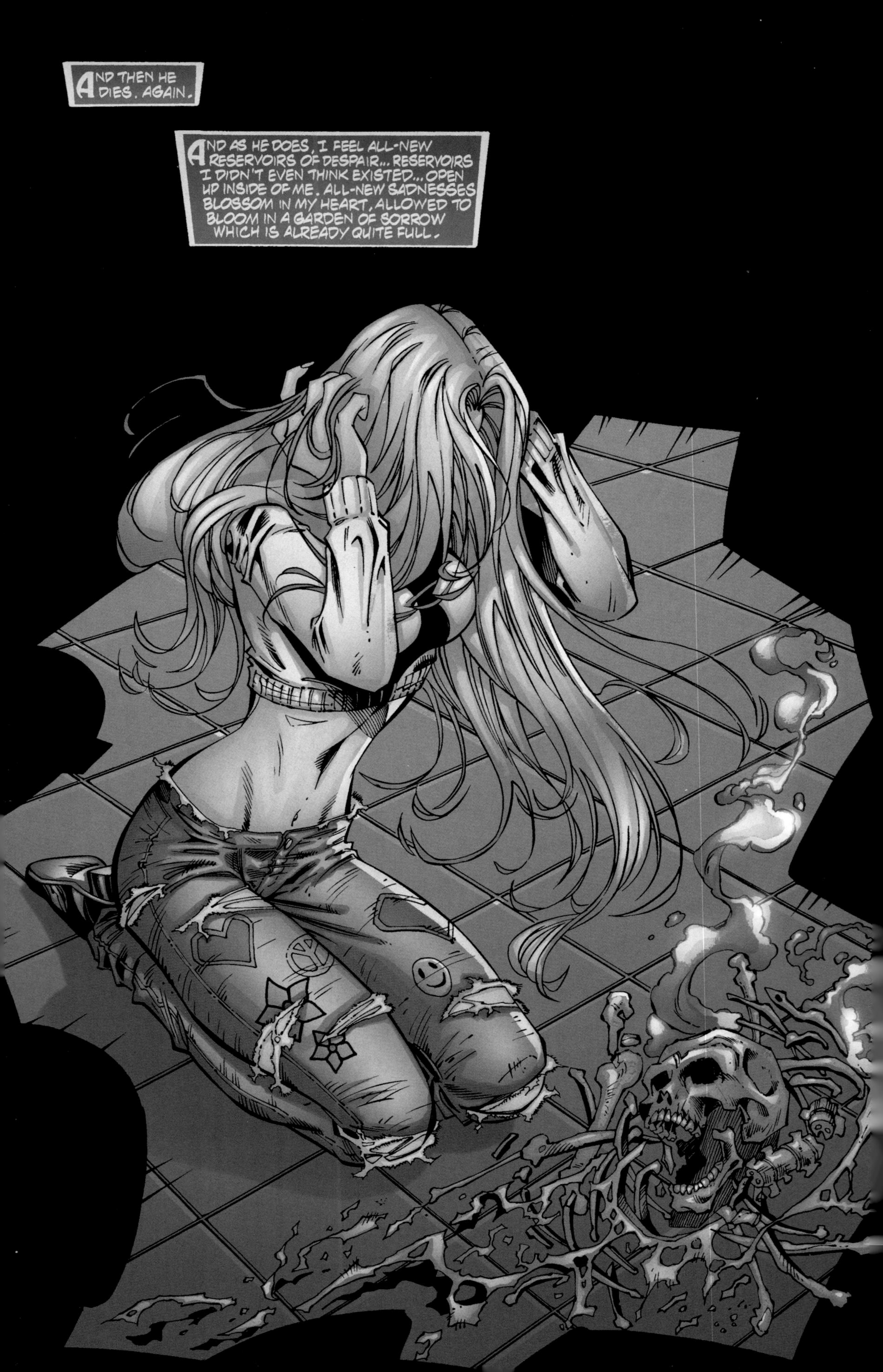
AND THEN HE DIES. AGAIN.
AND AS HE DOES, I FEEL ALL-NEW RESERVOIRS OF DESPAIR... RESERVOIRS I DIDN'T EVEN THINK EXISTED... OPEN UP INSIDE OF ME. ALL-NEW SADNESSES BLOSSOM IN MY HEART, ALLOWED TO BLOOM IN A GARDEN OF SORROW WHICH IS ALREADY QUITE FULL.

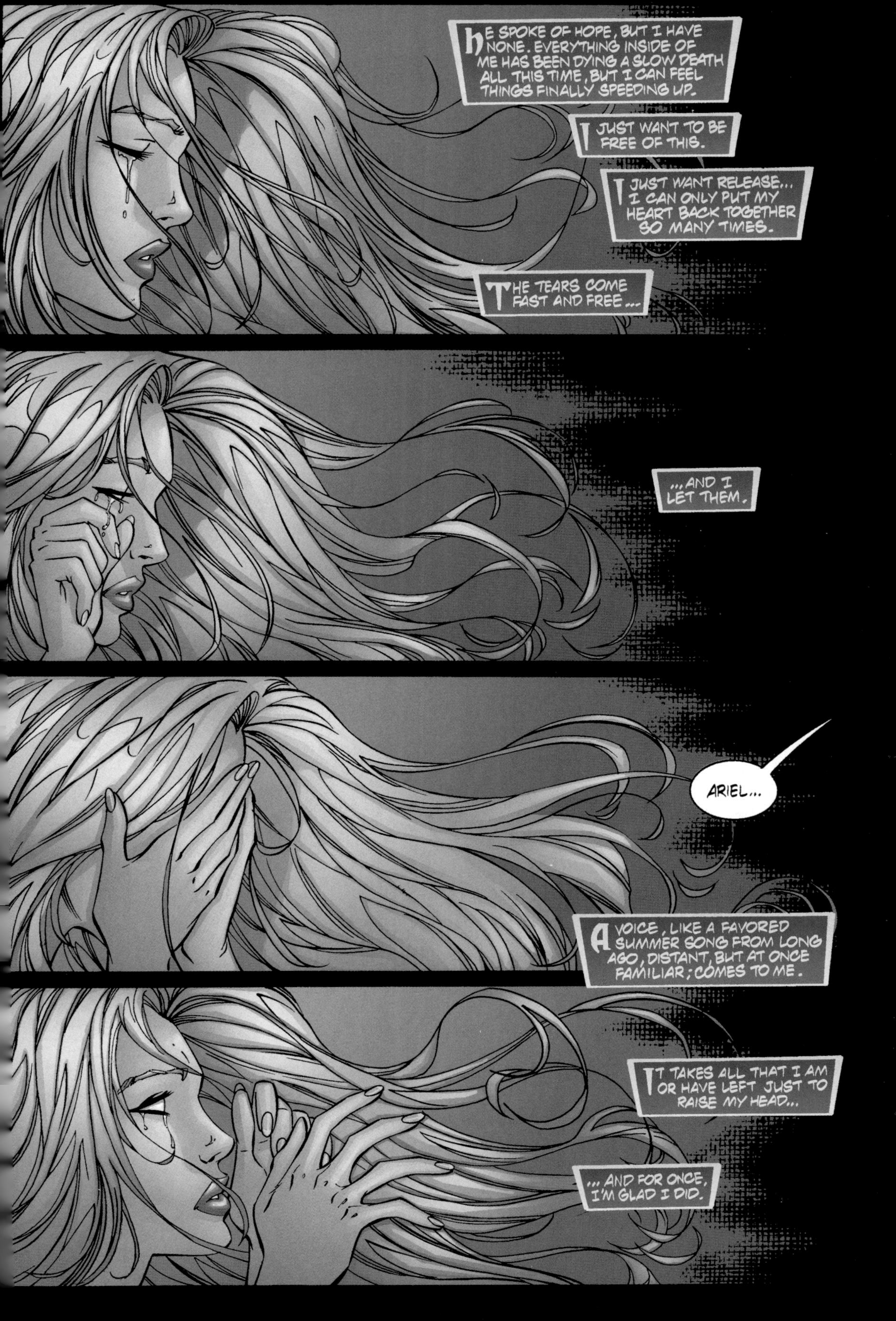
HE SPOKE OF HOPE, BUT I HAVE NONE. EVERYTHING INSIDE OF ME HAS BEEN DYING A SLOW DEATH ALL THIS TIME, BUT I CAN FEEL THINGS FINALLY SPEEDING UP.
I JUST WANT TO BE FREE OF THIS.
I JUST WANT RELEASE... I CAN ONLY PUT MY HEART BACK TOGETHER SO MANY TIMES.
THE TEARS COME FAST AND FREE...
...AND I LET THEM.
ARIEL...
A VOICE, LIKE A FAVORED SUMMER SONG FROM LONG AGO, DISTANT, BUT AT ONCE FAMILIAR; COMES TO ME.
IT TAKES ALL THAT I AM OR HAVE LEFT JUST TO RAISE MY HEAD...
...AND FOR ONCE, I'M GLAD I DID.

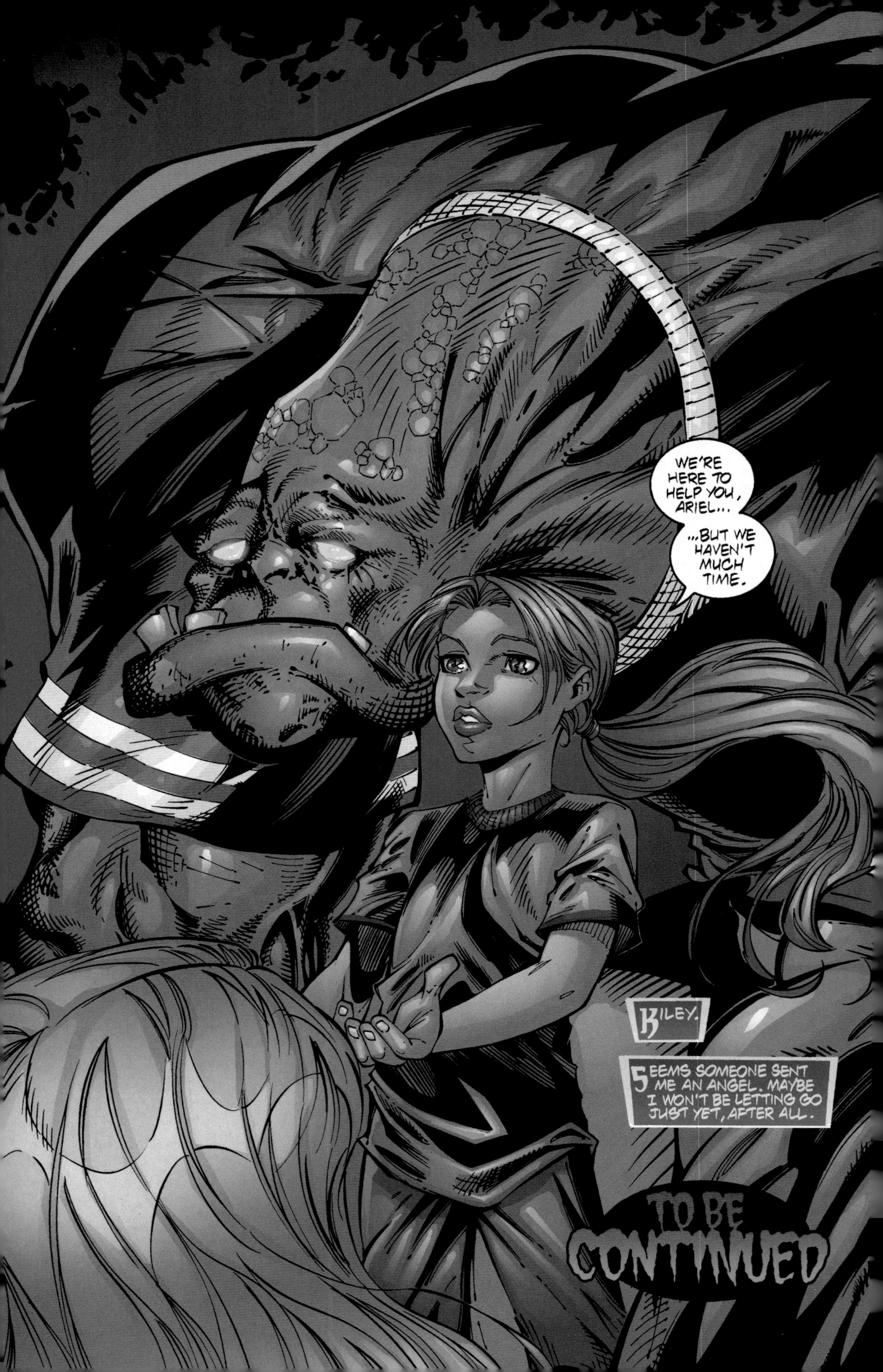
WE'RE HERE TO HELP YOU, ARIEL...
...BUT WE HAVEN'T MUCH TIME.
RILEY.
SEEMS SOMEONE SENT ME AN ANGEL. MAYBE I WON'T BE LETTING GO JUST YET, AFTER ALL.
TO BE CONTINUED

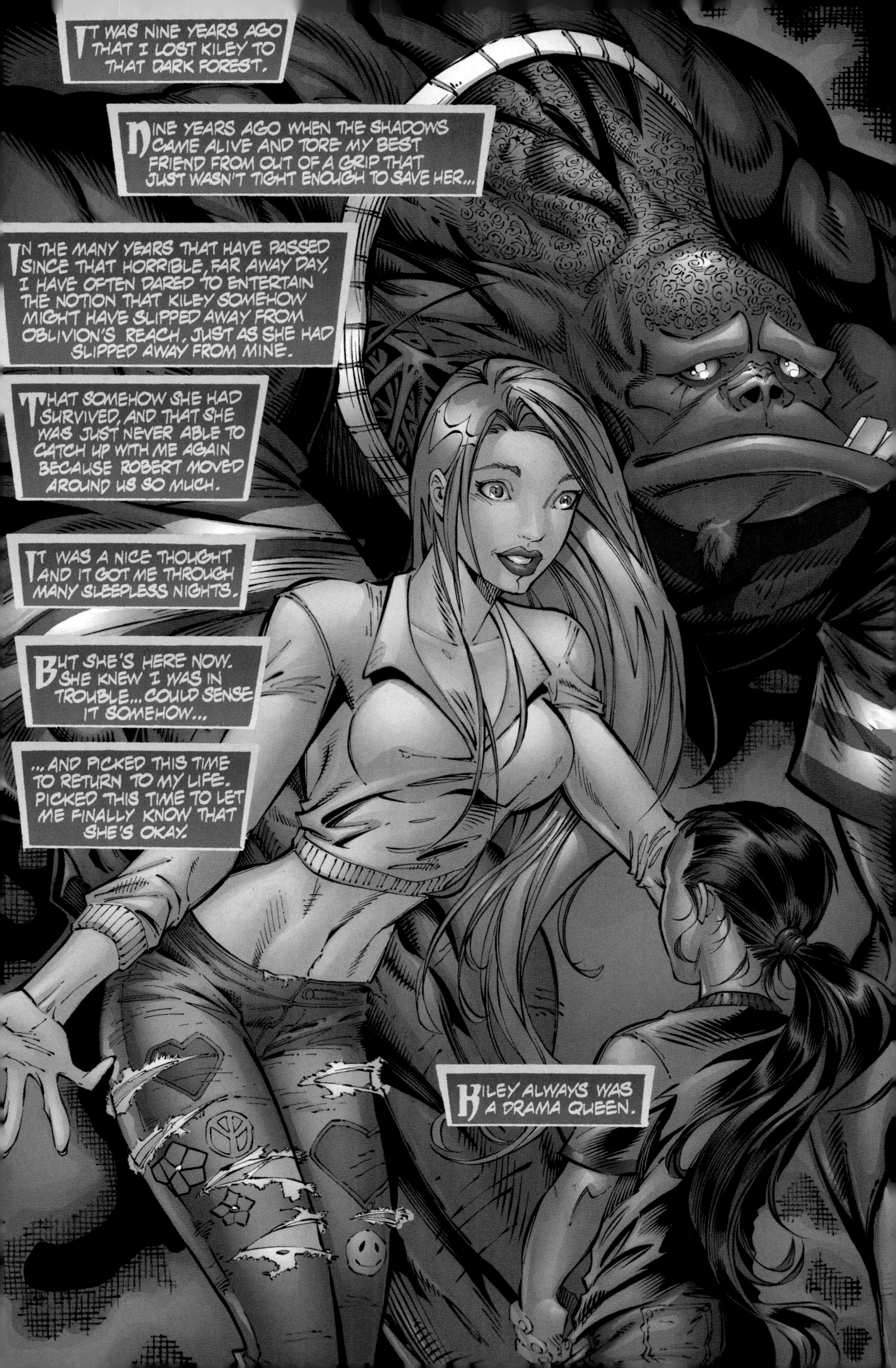
IT WAS NINE YEARS AGO THAT I LOST KILEY TO THAT DARK FOREST.
NINE YEARS AGO WHEN THE SHADOWS CAME ALIVE AND TORE MY BEST FRIEND FROM OUT OF A GRIP THAT JUST WASN'T TIGHT ENOUGH TO SAVE HER...
IN THE MANY YEARS THAT HAVE PASSED SINCE THAT HORRIBLE, FAR AWAY DAY, I HAVE OFTEN DARED TO ENTERTAIN THE NOTION THAT KILEY SOMEHOW MIGHT HAVE SLIPPED AWAY FROM OBLIVION'S REACH, JUST AS SHE HAD SLIPPED AWAY FROM MINE.
THAT SOMEHOW SHE HAD SURVIVED, AND THAT SHE WAS JUST NEVER ABLE TO CATCH UP WITH ME AGAIN BECAUSE ROBERT MOVED AROUND US SO MUCH.
IT WAS A NICE THOUGHT AND IT GOT ME THROUGH MANY SLEEPLESS NIGHTS.
BUT SHE'S HERE NOW. SHE KNEW I WAS IN TROUBLE...COULD SENSE IT SOMEHOW...
...AND PICKED THIS TIME TO RETURN TO MY LIFE. PICKED THIS TIME TO LET ME FINALLY KNOW THAT SHE'S OKAY.
KILEY ALWAYS WAS A DRAMA QUEEN.

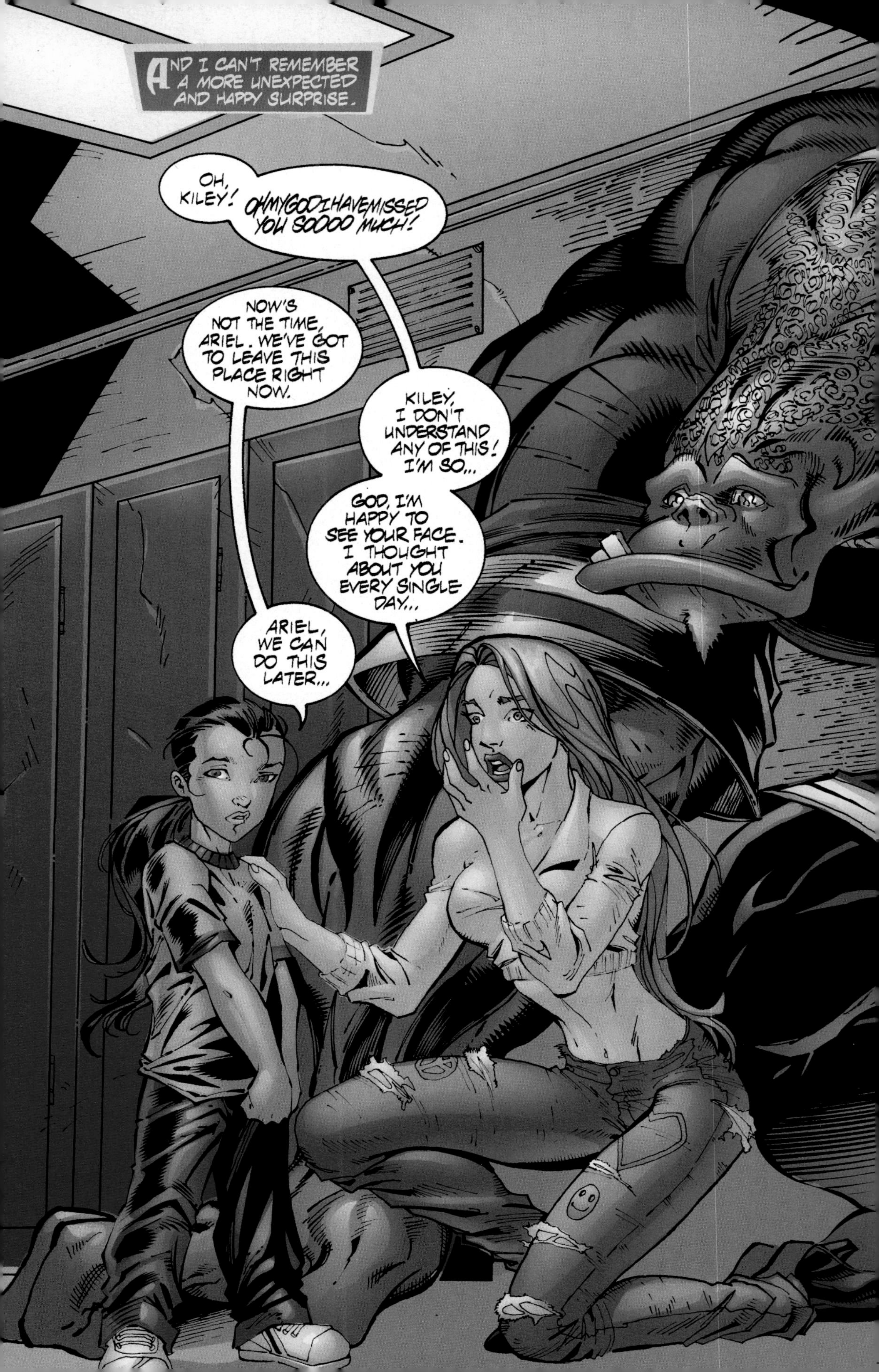
AND I CAN'T REMEMBER A MORE UNEXPECTED AND HAPPY SURPRISE.
OH, KILEY!
OHMYGODIHAVEMISSED YOU SOOOO MUCH!
NOW'S NOT THE TIME, ARIEL. WE'VE GOT TO LEAVE THIS PLACE RIGHT NOW.
KILEY, I DON'T UNDERSTAND ANY OF THIS! I'M SO...
GOD, I'M HAPPY TO SEE YOUR FACE. I THOUGHT ABOUT YOU EVERY SINGLE DAY...
ARIEL, WE CAN DO THIS LATER...

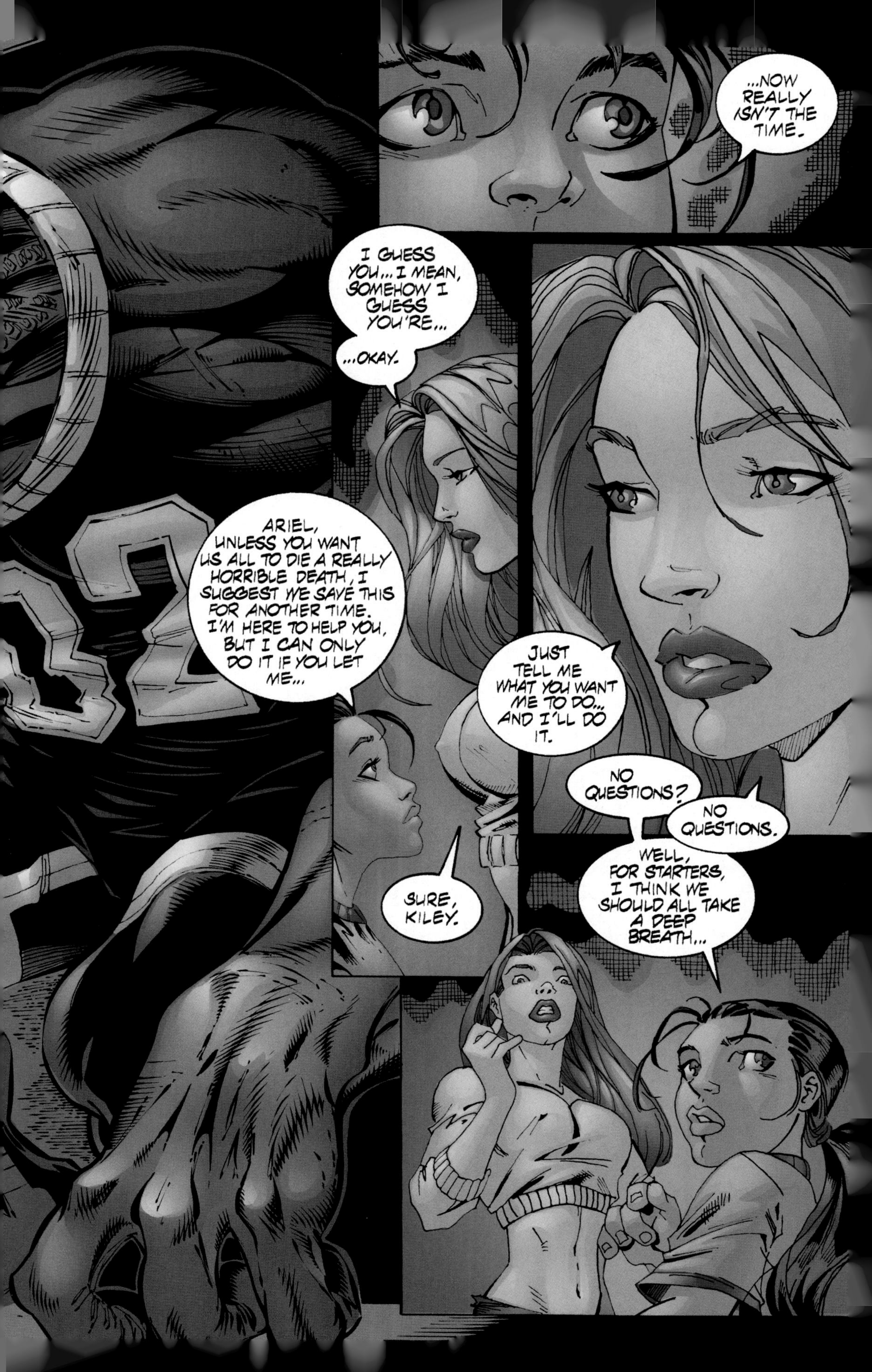
...NOW REALLY ISN'T THE TIME.
I GUESS YOU... I MEAN, SOMEHOW I GUESS YOU'RE...
...OKAY.
ARIEL, UNLESS YOU WANT US ALL TO DIE A REALLY HORRIBLE DEATH, I SUGGEST WE SAVE THIS FOR ANOTHER TIME. I'M HERE TO HELP YOU, BUT I CAN ONLY DO IT IF YOU LET ME...
JUST TELL ME WHAT YOU WANT ME TO DO... AND I'LL DO IT.
SURE, KILEY.
NO QUESTIONS?
NO QUESTIONS.
WELL, FOR STARTERS, I THINK WE SHOULD ALL TAKE A DEEP BREATH...

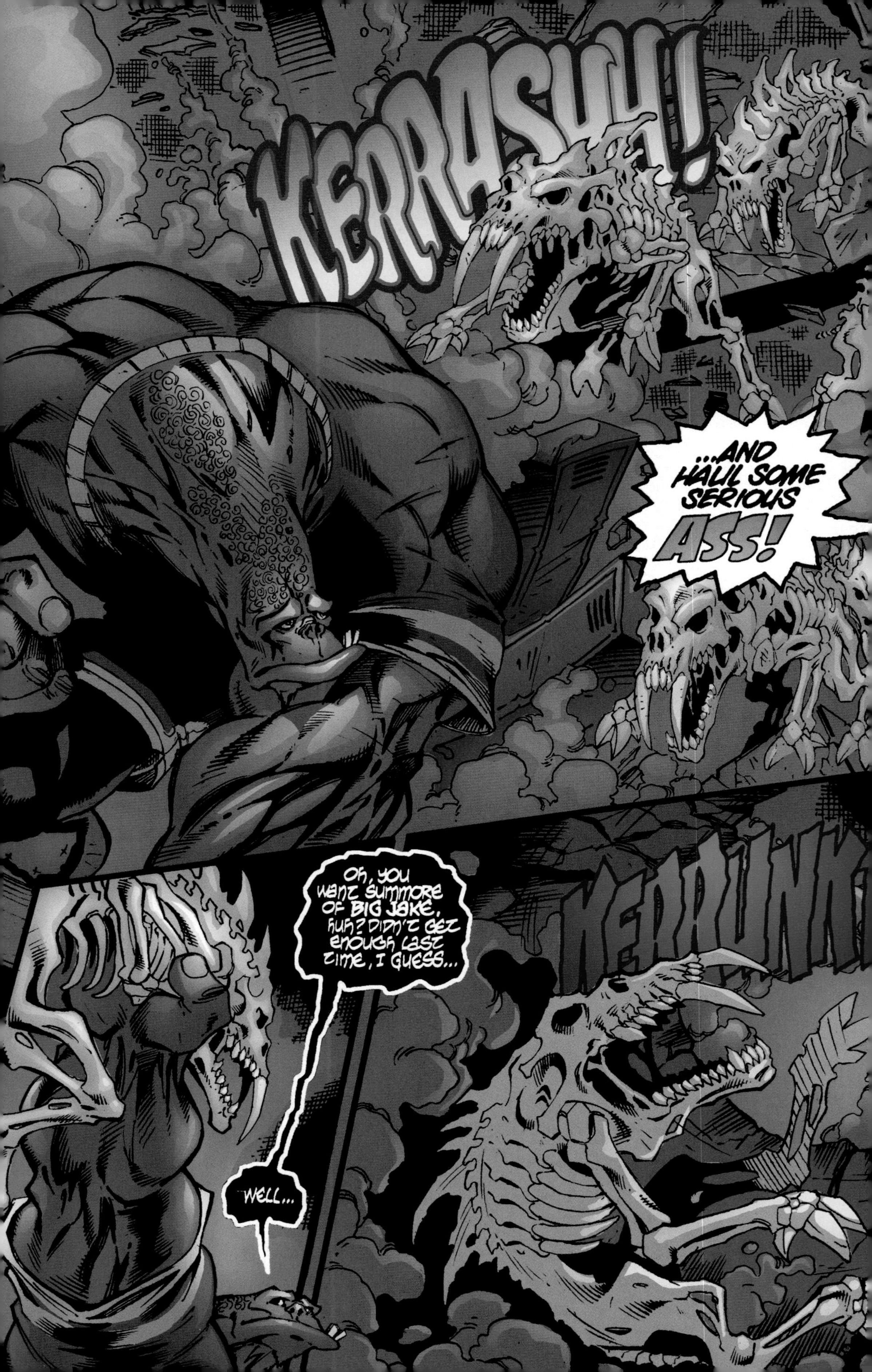
KERRASHH!
...AND HAUL SOME SERIOUS ASS!
OH, YOU WANT SUMMORE OF BIG JAKE, HUH? DIDN'T GET ENOUGH LAST TIME, I GUESS...
WELL...

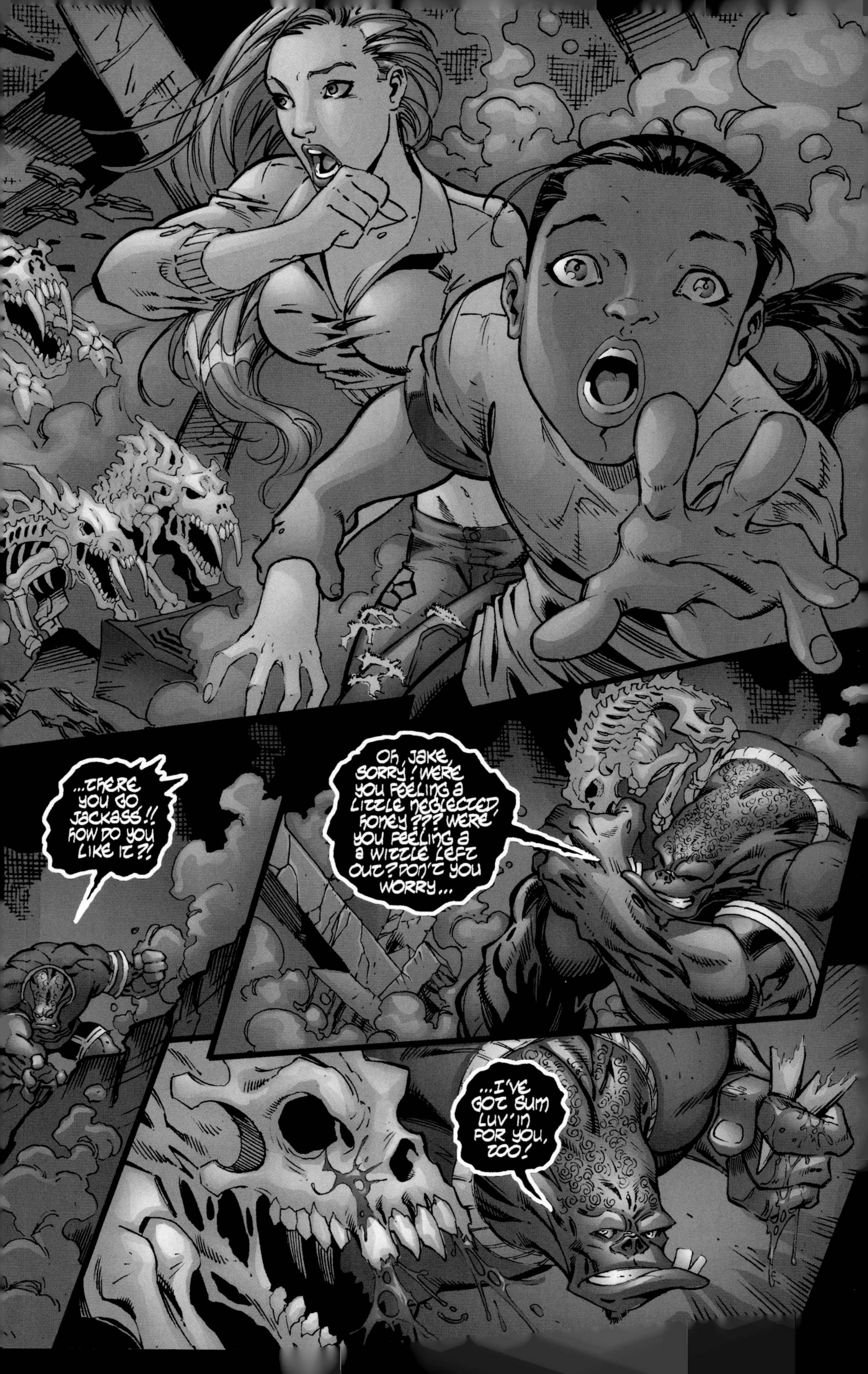
...THERE YOU GO JACKASS!! HOW DO YOU LIKE IT?!
OH, JAKE, SORRY! WERE YOU FEELING A LITTLE NEGLECTED, HONEY??? WERE YOU FEELING A A WITTLE LEFT OUT? DON'T YOU WORRY...
...I'VE GOT SUM LUV'IN FOR YOU, TOO!

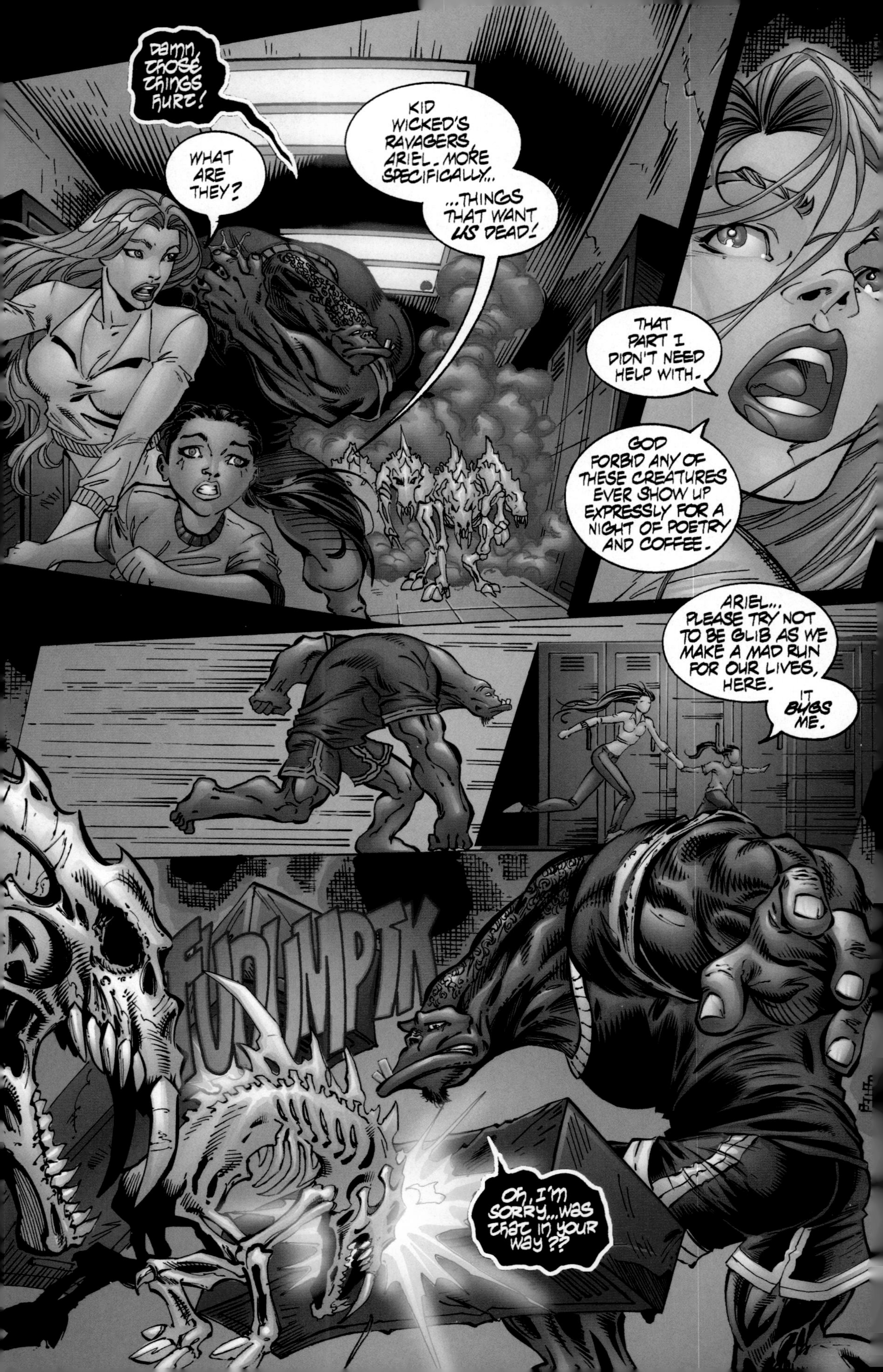
Damn, those things hurt!
WHAT ARE THEY?
KID WICKED'S RAVAGERS, ARIEL. MORE SPECIFICALLY...
...THINGS THAT WANT US DEAD!
THAT PART I DIDN'T NEED HELP WITH.
GOD FORBID ANY OF THESE CREATURES EVER SHOW UP EXPRESSLY FOR A NIGHT OF POETRY AND COFFEE.
ARIEL... PLEASE TRY NOT TO BE GLIB AS WE MAKE A MAD RUN FOR OUR LIVES, HERE.
IT BUGS ME.
FUDUMPTK
Oh, I'm sorry...was that in your way??

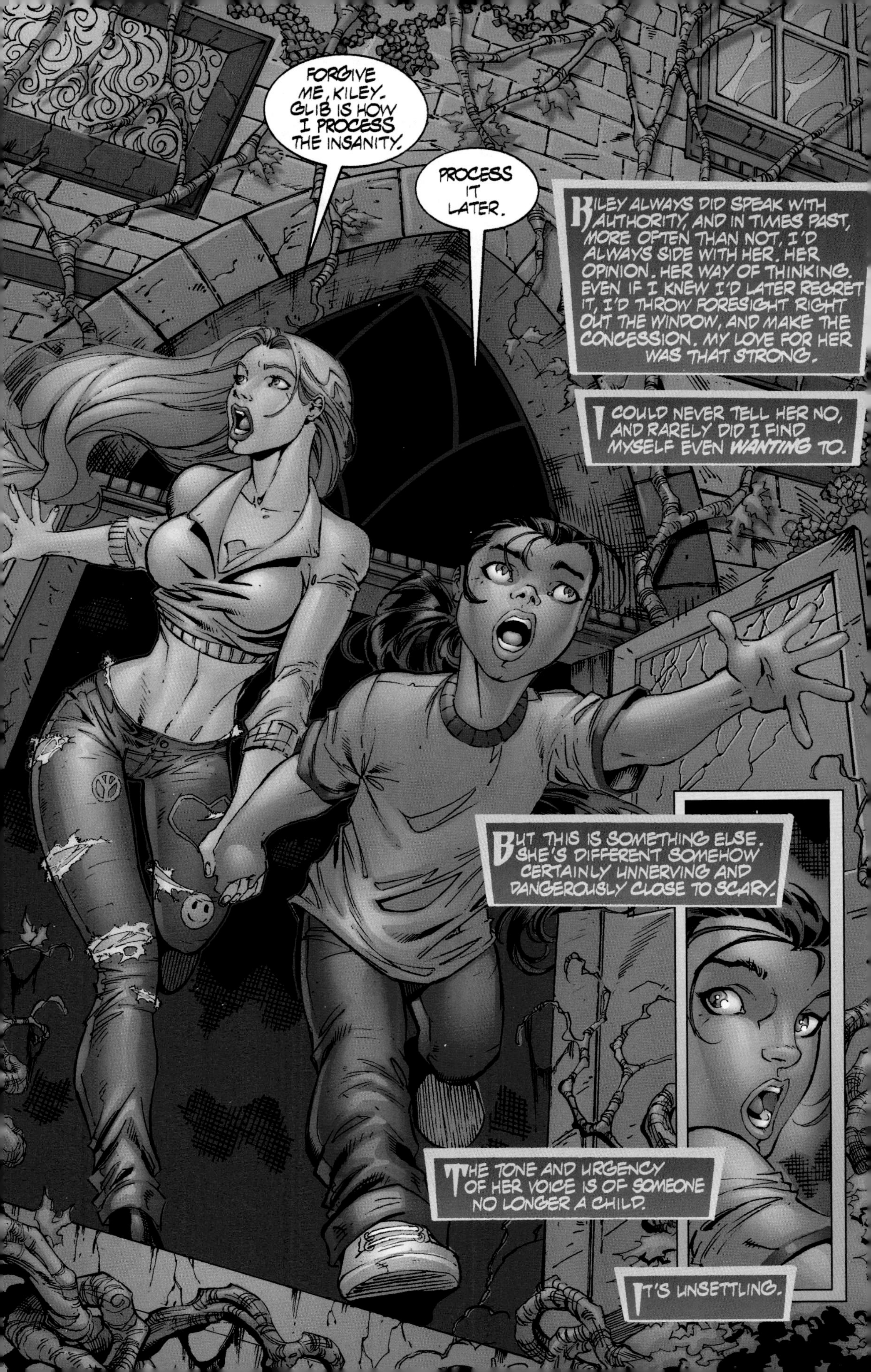
FORGIVE ME, KILEY. GLIB IS HOW I PROCESS THE INSANITY.
PROCESS IT LATER.
KILEY ALWAYS DID SPEAK WITH AUTHORITY, AND IN TIMES PAST, MORE OFTEN THAN NOT, I'D ALWAYS SIDE WITH HER. HER OPINION. HER WAY OF THINKING. EVEN IF I KNEW I'D LATER REGRET IT, I'D THROW FORESIGHT RIGHT OUT THE WINDOW, AND MAKE THE CONCESSION. MY LOVE FOR HER WAS THAT STRONG.
I COULD NEVER TELL HER NO, AND RARELY DID I FIND MYSELF EVEN WANTING TO.
BUT THIS IS SOMETHING ELSE. SHE'S DIFFERENT SOMEHOW CERTAINLY UNNERVING AND DANGEROUSLY CLOSE TO SCARY.
THE TONE AND URGENCY OF HER VOICE IS OF SOMEONE NO LONGER A CHILD.
IT'S UNSETTLING.

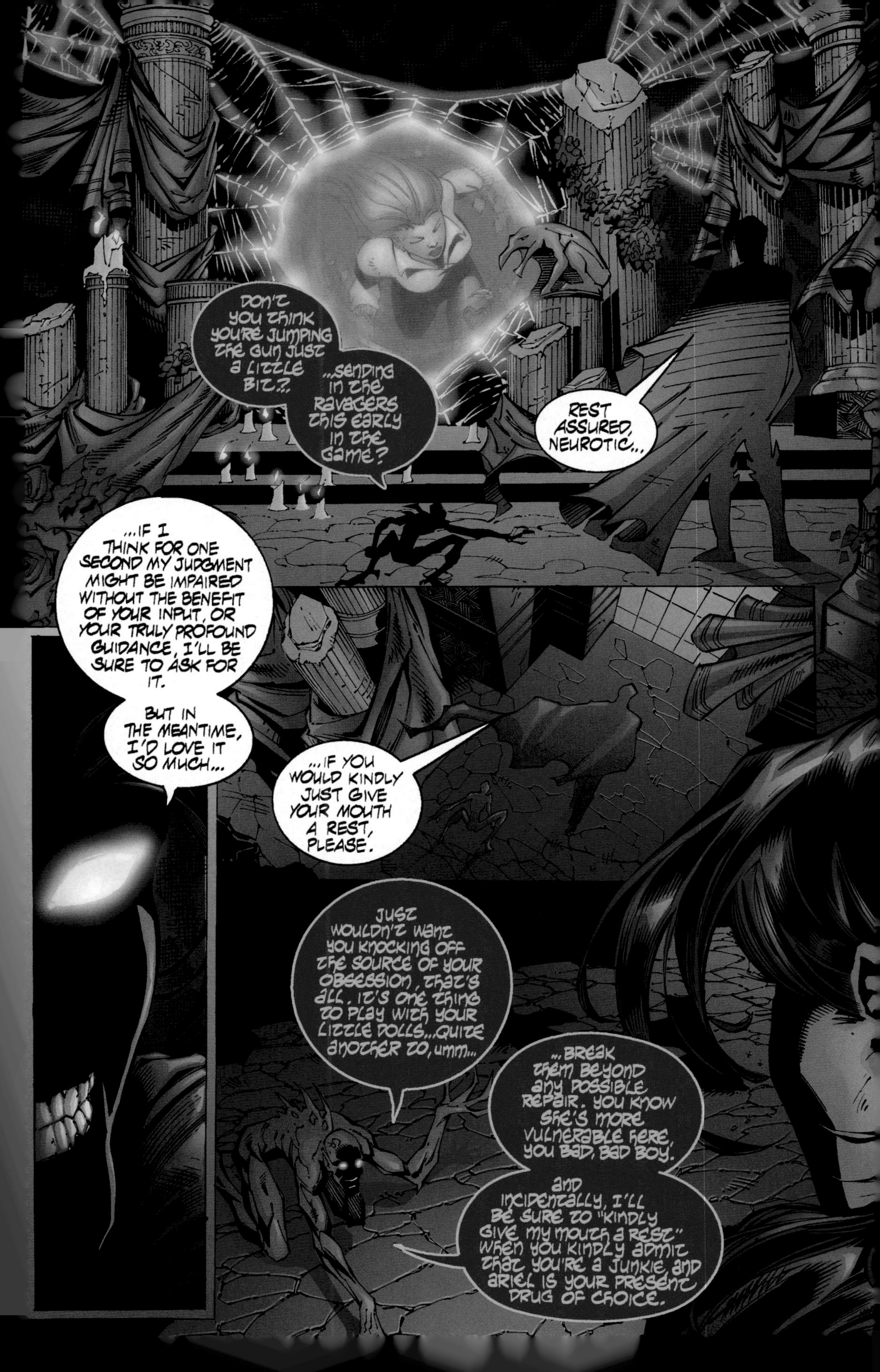
DON'T YOU THINK YOU'RE JUMPING THE GUN JUST A LITTLE BIT?!
...SENDING IN THE RAVAGERS THIS EARLY IN THE GAME?
REST ASSURED, NEUROTIC...
...IF I THINK FOR ONE SECOND MY JUDGMENT MIGHT BE IMPAIRED WITHOUT THE BENEFIT OF YOUR INPUT, OR YOUR TRULY PROFOUND GUIDANCE, I'LL BE SURE TO ASK FOR IT.
BUT IN THE MEANTIME, I'D LOVE IT SO MUCH...
...IF YOU WOULD KINDLY JUST GIVE YOUR MOUTH A REST, PLEASE.
JUST WOULDN'T WANT YOU KNOCKING OFF THE SOURCE OF YOUR OBSESSION, THAT'S ALL. IT'S ONE THING TO PLAY WITH YOUR LITTLE DOLLS... QUITE ANOTHER TO, UMM...
...BREAK THEM BEYOND ANY POSSIBLE REPAIR. YOU KNOW SHE'S MORE VULNERABLE HERE, YOU BAD, BAD BOY.
AND INCIDENTALLY, I'LL BE SURE TO "KINDLY GIVE MY MOUTH A REST" WHEN YOU KINDLY ADMIT THAT YOU'RE A JUNKIE, AND ARIEL IS YOUR PRESENT DRUG OF CHOICE.

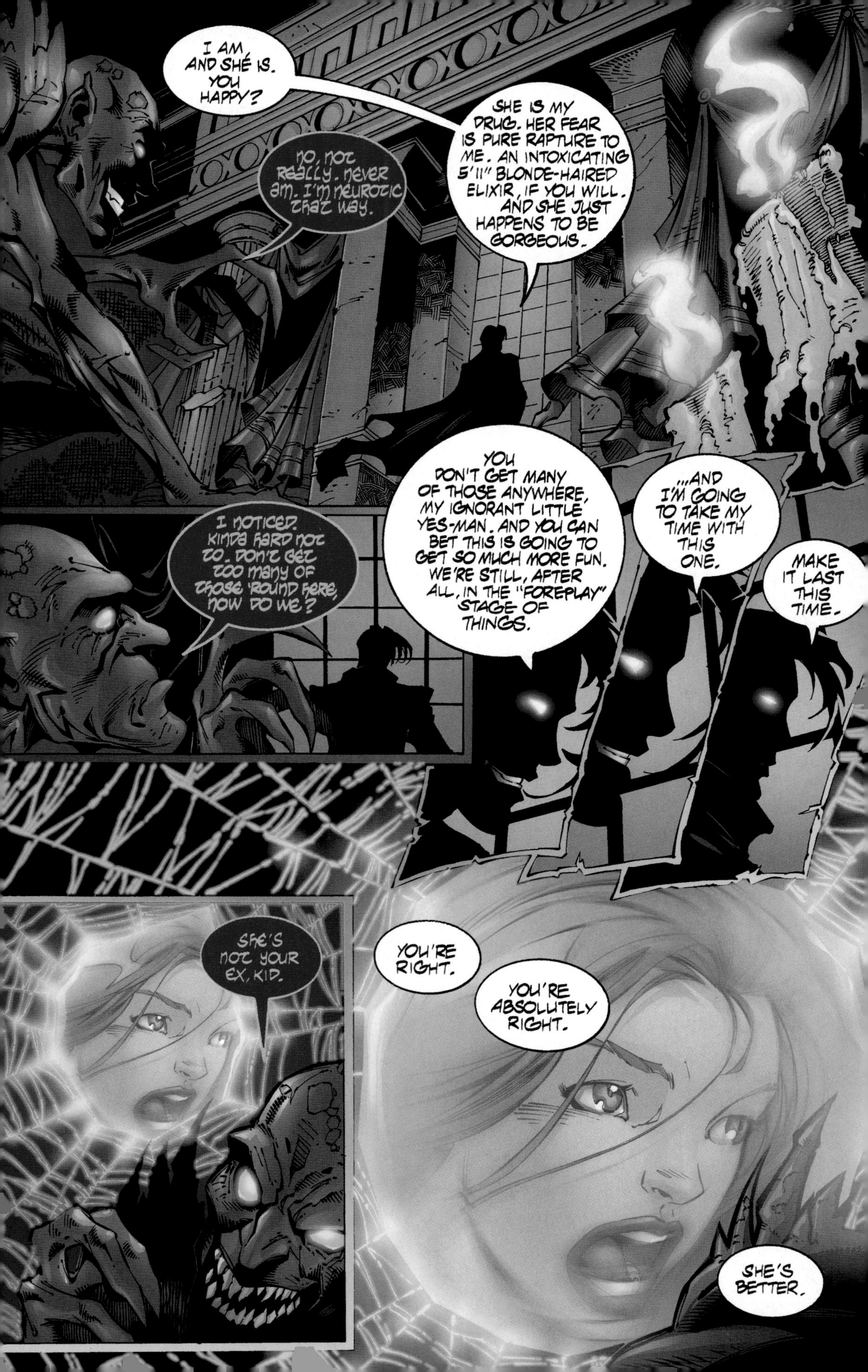
I AM AND SHÉ IS. YOU HAPPY?
no, not really. never am. I'm neurotic that way.
SHE IS MY DRUG. HER FEAR IS PURE RAPTURE TO ME. AN INTOXICATING 5'11" BLONDE-HAIRED ELIXIR, IF YOU WILL. AND SHE JUST HAPPENS TO BE GORGEOUS.
I noticed. kinda hard not to. Don't get too many of those 'round here, now do we?
YOU DON'T GET MANY OF THOSE ANYWHERE, MY IGNORANT LITTLE YES-MAN. AND YOU CAN BET THIS IS GOING TO GET SO MUCH MORE FUN. WE'RE STILL, AFTER ALL, IN THE "FOREPLAY" STAGE OF THINGS.
...AND I'M GOING TO TAKE MY TIME WITH THIS ONE.
MAKE IT LAST THIS TIME.
She's not your ex, kid.
YOU'RE RIGHT.
YOU'RE ABSOLUTELY RIGHT.
SHE'S BETTER.

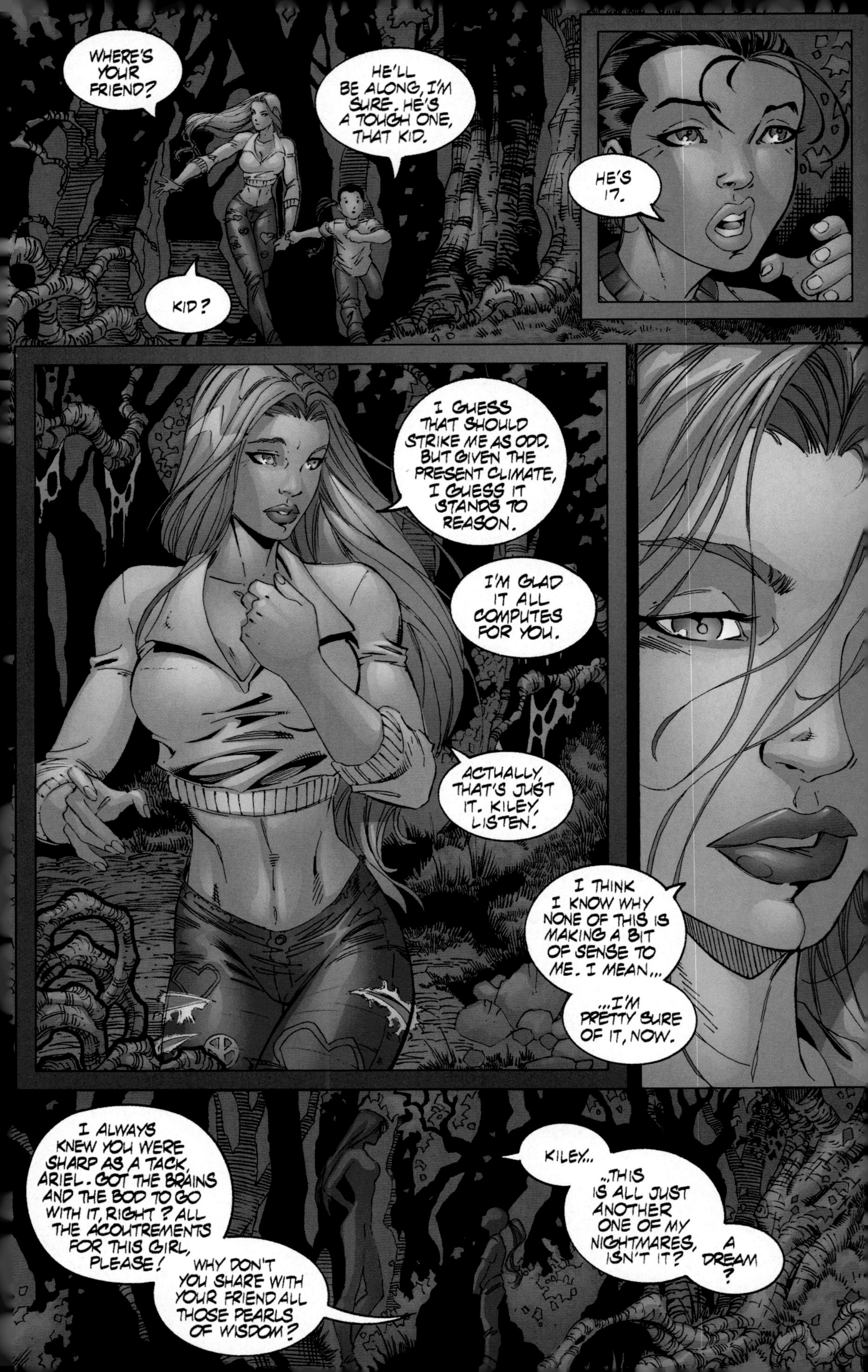
WHERE'S YOUR FRIEND?
HE'LL BE ALONG, I'M SURE. HE'S A TOUGH ONE, THAT KID.
KID?
HE'S 17.
I GUESS THAT SHOULD STRIKE ME AS ODD. BUT GIVEN THE PRESENT CLIMATE, I GUESS IT STANDS TO REASON.
I'M GLAD IT ALL COMPUTES FOR YOU.
ACTUALLY, THAT'S JUST IT. KILEY, LISTEN.
I THINK I KNOW WHY NONE OF THIS IS MAKING A BIT OF SENSE TO ME. I MEAN...
...I'M PRETTY SURE OF IT, NOW.
I ALWAYS KNEW YOU WERE SHARP AS A TACK, ARIEL. GOT THE BRAINS AND THE BOD TO GO WITH IT, RIGHT? ALL THE ACOUTREMENTS FOR THIS GIRL, PLEASE!
WHY DON'T YOU SHARE WITH YOUR FRIEND ALL THOSE PEARLS OF WISDOM?
KILEY...
...THIS IS ALL JUST ANOTHER ONE OF MY NIGHTMARES, ISN'T IT?
A DREAM?

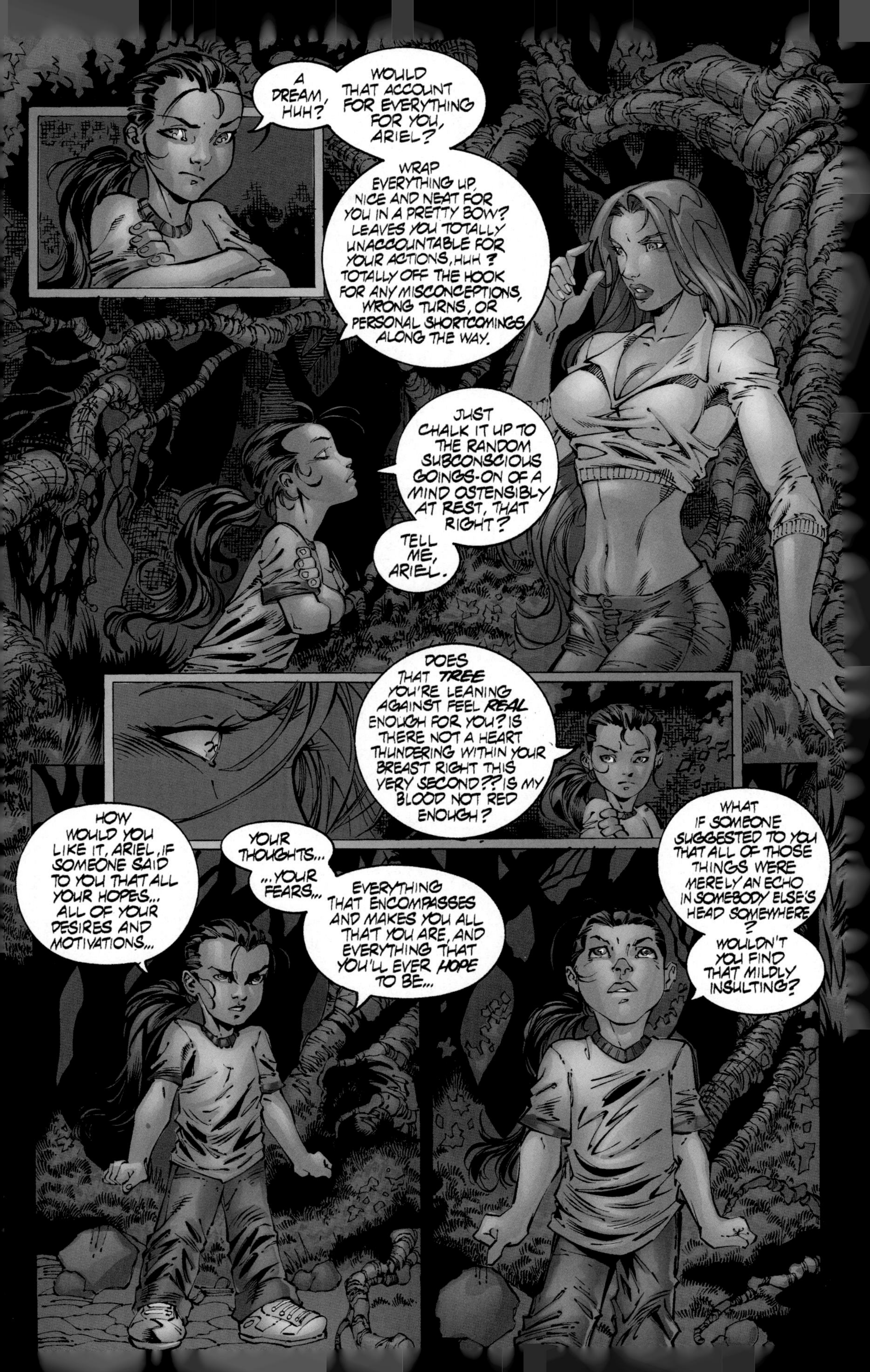
A DREAM, HUH?
WOULD THAT ACCOUNT FOR EVERYTHING FOR YOU, ARIEL?
WRAP EVERYTHING UP, NICE AND NEAT FOR YOU IN A PRETTY BOW? LEAVES YOU TOTALLY UNACCOUNTABLE FOR YOUR ACTIONS, HUH? TOTALLY OFF THE HOOK FOR ANY MISCONCEPTIONS, WRONG TURNS, OR PERSONAL SHORTCOMINGS ALONG THE WAY.
JUST CHALK IT UP TO THE RANDOM SUBCONSCIOUS GOINGS-ON OF A MIND OSTENSIBLY AT REST, THAT RIGHT?
TELL ME, ARIEL.
DOES THAT TREE YOU'RE LEANING AGAINST FEEL REAL ENOUGH FOR YOU? IS THERE NOT A HEART THUNDERING WITHIN YOUR BREAST RIGHT THIS VERY SECOND?? IS MY BLOOD NOT RED ENOUGH?
HOW WOULD YOU LIKE IT, ARIEL, IF SOMEONE SAID TO YOU THAT ALL YOUR HOPES... ALL OF YOUR DESIRES AND MOTIVATIONS...
YOUR THOUGHTS...
...YOUR FEARS...
EVERYTHING THAT ENCOMPASSES AND MAKES YOU ALL THAT YOU ARE, AND EVERYTHING THAT YOU'LL EVER HOPE TO BE...
WHAT IF SOMEONE SUGGESTED TO YOU THAT ALL OF THOSE THINGS WERE MERELY AN ECHO IN SOMEBODY ELSE'S HEAD SOMEWHERE?
WOULDN'T YOU FIND THAT MILDLY INSULTING?

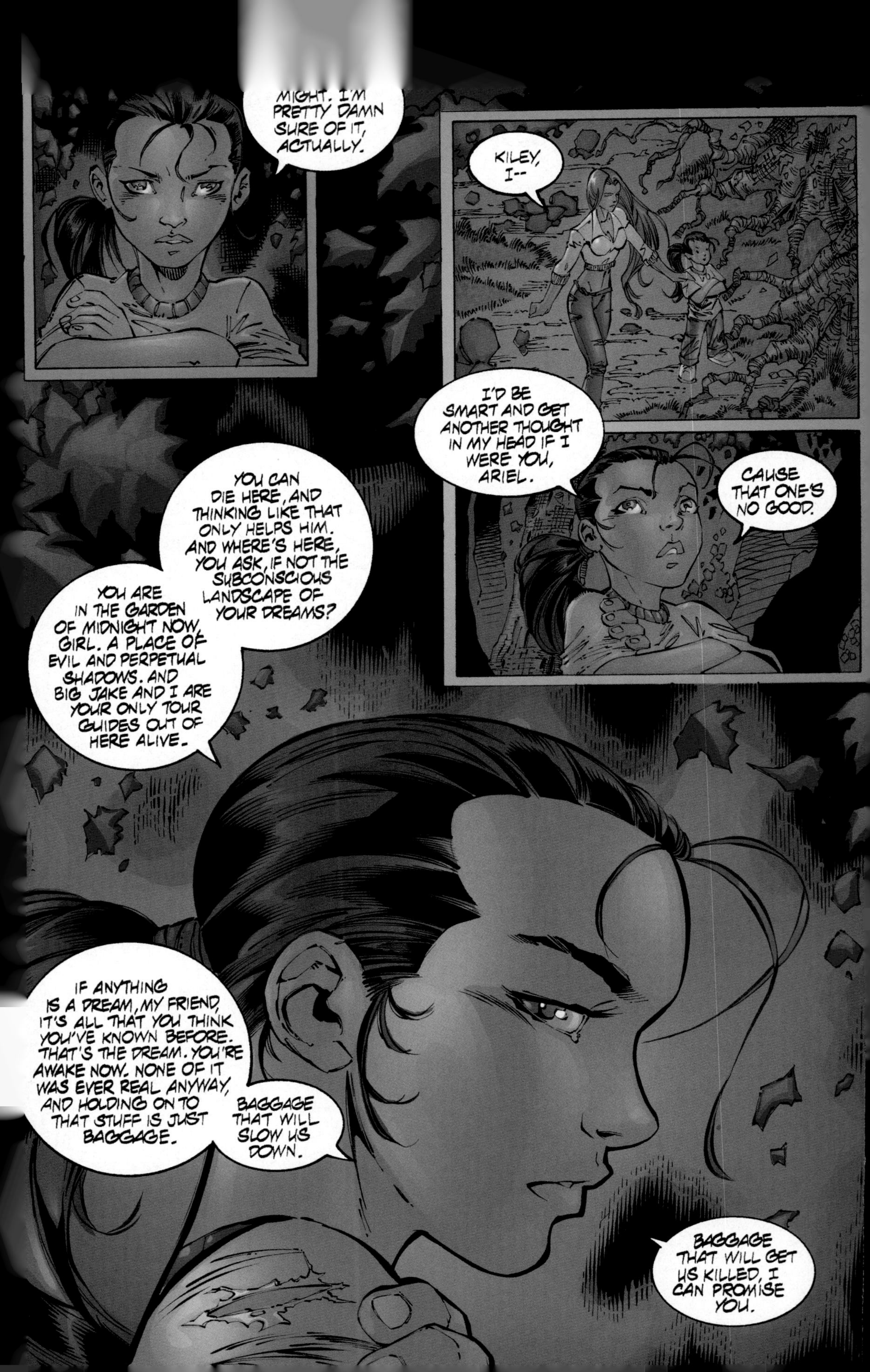
MIGHT. I'M PRETTY DAMN SURE OF IT, ACTUALLY.
KILEY, I--
I'D BE SMART AND GET ANOTHER THOUGHT IN MY HEAD IF I WERE YOU, ARIEL.
CAUSE THAT ONE'S NO GOOD.
YOU CAN DIE HERE, AND THINKING LIKE THAT ONLY HELPS HIM. AND WHERE'S HERE, YOU ASK, IF NOT THE SUBCONSCIOUS LANDSCAPE OF YOUR DREAMS?
YOU ARE IN THE GARDEN OF MIDNIGHT NOW, GIRL. A PLACE OF EVIL AND PERPETUAL SHADOWS. AND BIG JAKE AND I ARE YOUR ONLY TOUR GUIDES OUT OF HERE ALIVE.
IF ANYTHING IS A DREAM, MY FRIEND, IT'S ALL THAT YOU THINK YOU'VE KNOWN BEFORE. THAT'S THE DREAM. YOU'RE AWAKE NOW. NONE OF IT WAS EVER REAL ANYWAY, AND HOLDING ON TO THAT STUFF IS JUST BAGGAGE.
BAGGAGE THAT WILL SLOW US DOWN.
BAGGAGE THAT WILL GET US KILLED, I CAN PROMISE YOU.

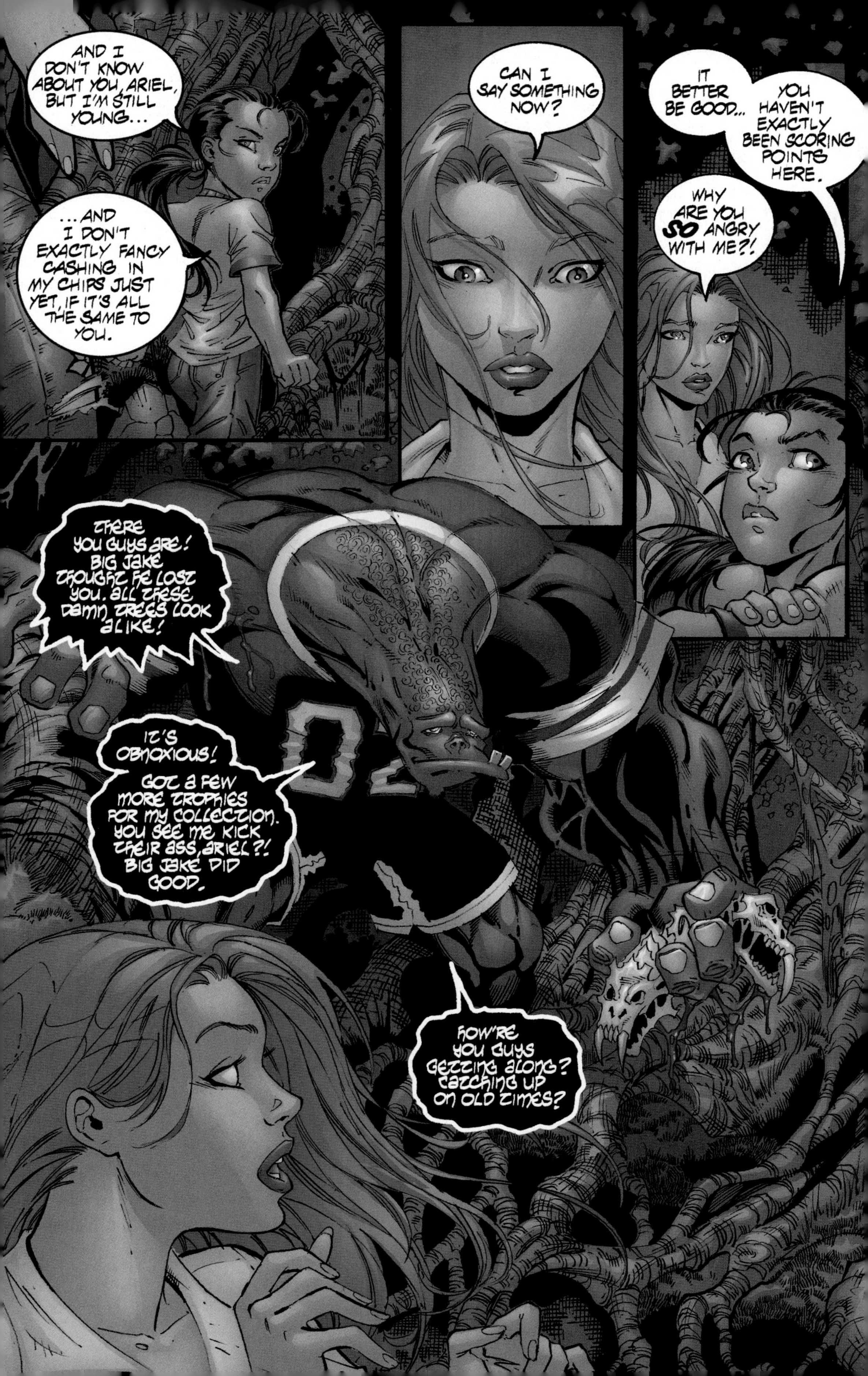
AND I DON'T KNOW ABOUT YOU, ARIEL, BUT I'M STILL YOUNG...
...AND I DON'T EXACTLY FANCY CASHING IN MY CHIPS JUST YET, IF IT'S ALL THE SAME TO YOU.
CAN I SAY SOMETHING NOW?
IT BETTER BE GOOD...
YOU HAVEN'T EXACTLY BEEN SCORING POINTS HERE.
WHY ARE YOU SO ANGRY WITH ME?!
THERE YOU GUYS ARE! BIG JAKE THOUGHT HE LOST YOU. ALL THESE DAMN TREES LOOK ALIKE!
IT'S OBNOXIOUS!
GOT A FEW MORE TROPHIES FOR MY COLLECTION. YOU SEE ME KICK THEIR ASS, ARIEL?! BIG JAKE DID GOOD.
HOW'RE YOU GUYS GETTING ALONG? CATCHING UP ON OLD TIMES?

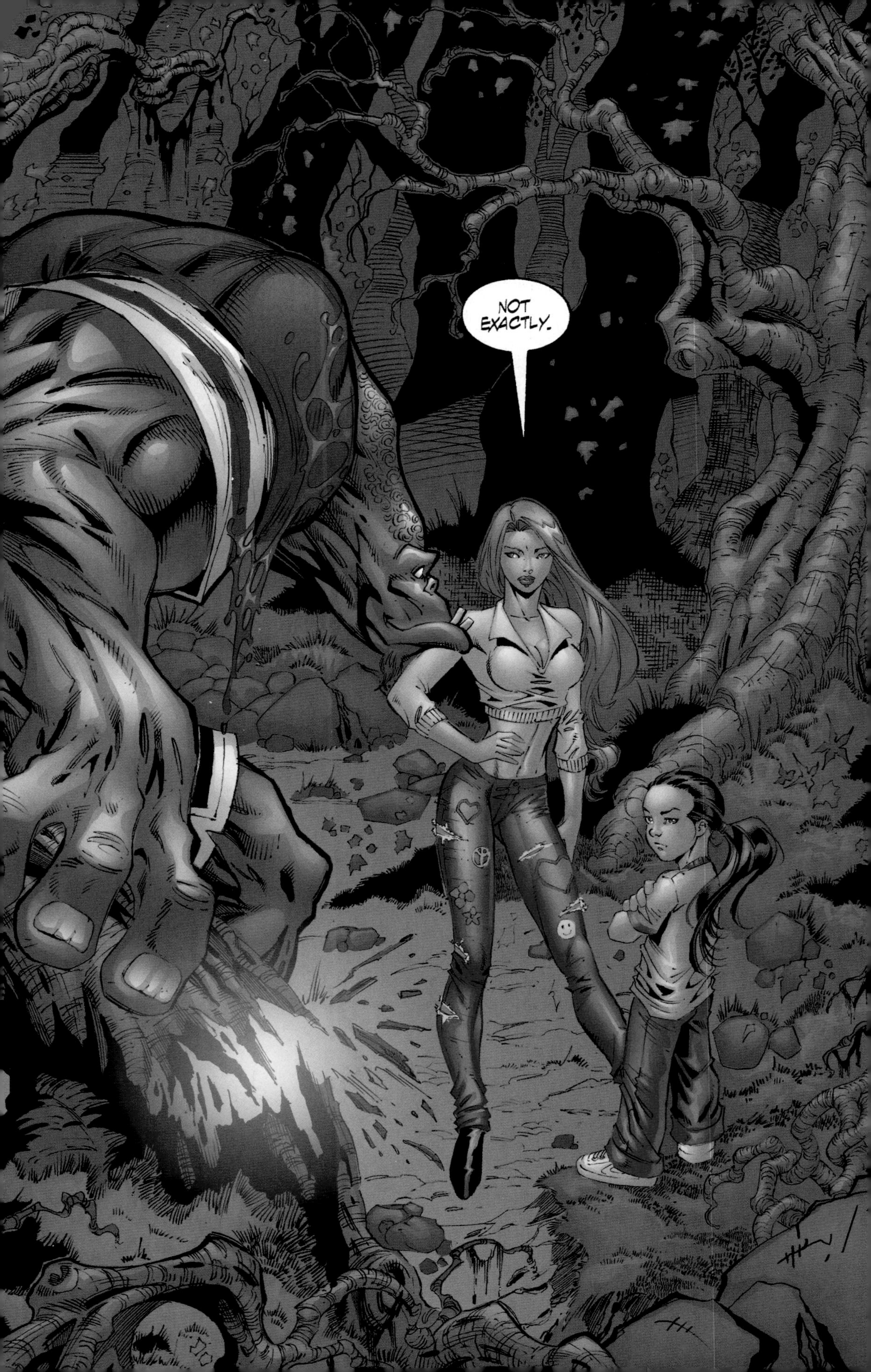
NOT EXACTLY.

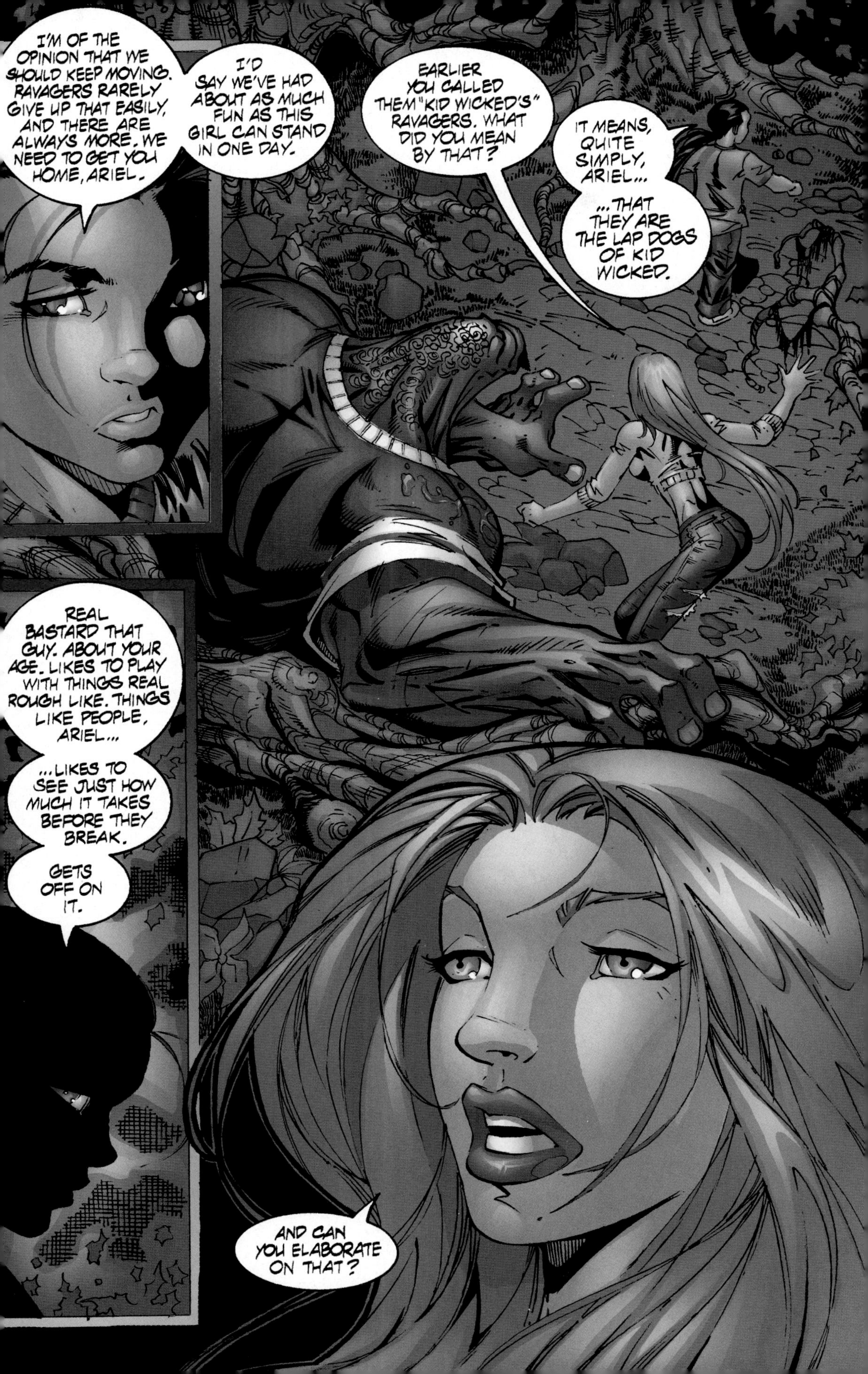
I'M OF THE OPINION THAT WE SHOULD KEEP MOVING. RAVAGERS RARELY GIVE UP THAT EASILY, AND THERE ARE ALWAYS MORE. WE NEED TO GET YOU HOME, ARIEL.
I'D SAY WE'VE HAD ABOUT AS MUCH FUN AS THIS GIRL CAN STAND IN ONE DAY.
EARLIER YOU CALLED THEM "KID WICKED'S" RAVAGERS. WHAT DID YOU MEAN BY THAT?
IT MEANS, QUITE SIMPLY, ARIEL...
...THAT THEY ARE THE LAP DOGS OF KID WICKED.
REAL BASTARD THAT GUY. ABOUT YOUR AGE. LIKES TO PLAY WITH THINGS REAL ROUGH LIKE. THINGS LIKE PEOPLE, ARIEL...
...LIKES TO SEE JUST HOW MUCH IT TAKES BEFORE THEY BREAK.
GETS OFF ON IT.
AND CAN YOU ELABORATE ON THAT?

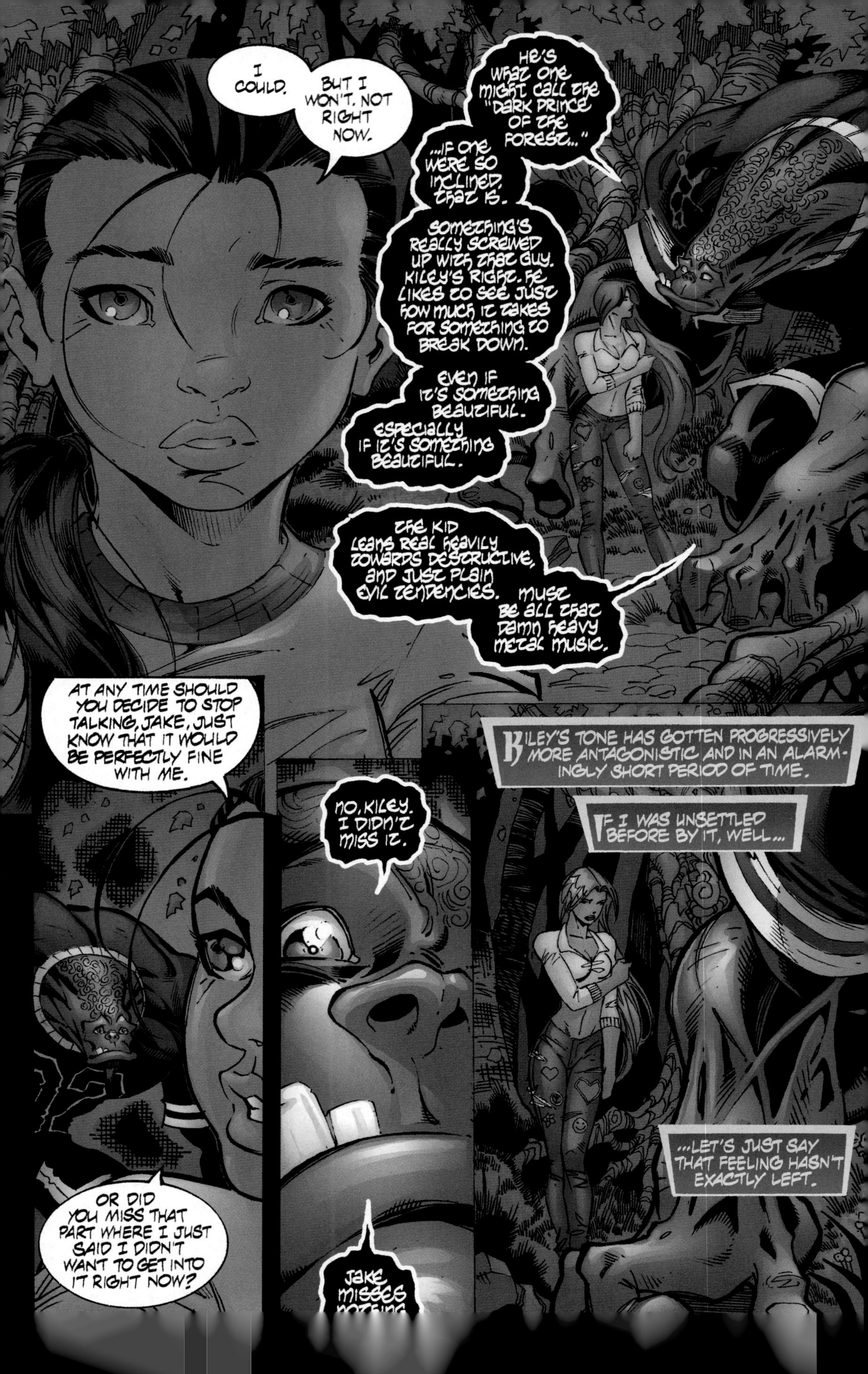
I COULD.
BUT I WON'T. NOT RIGHT NOW.
HE'S WHAT ONE MIGHT CALL THE "DARK PRINCE OF THE FOREST..."
...IF ONE WERE SO INCLINED, THAT IS.
SOMETHING'S REALLY SCREWED UP WITH THAT GUY. KILEY'S RIGHT. HE LIKES TO SEE JUST HOW MUCH IT TAKES FOR SOMETHING TO BREAK DOWN.
EVEN IF IT'S SOMETHING BEAUTIFUL.
ESPECIALLY IF IT'S SOMETHING BEAUTIFUL.
THE KID LEANS REAL HEAVILY TOWARDS DESTRUCTIVE, AND JUST PLAIN EVIL TENDENCIES.
MUST BE ALL THAT DAMN HEAVY METAL MUSIC.
AT ANY TIME SHOULD YOU DECIDE TO STOP TALKING, JAKE, JUST KNOW THAT IT WOULD BE PERFECTLY FINE WITH ME.
OR DID YOU MISS THAT PART WHERE I JUST SAID I DIDN'T WANT TO GET INTO IT RIGHT NOW?
NO, KILEY. I DIDN'T MISS IT.
JAKE MISSES
KILEY'S TONE HAS GOTTEN PROGRESSIVELY MORE ANTAGONISTIC AND IN AN ALARMINGLY SHORT PERIOD OF TIME.
IF I WAS UNSETTLED BEFORE BY IT, WELL...
...LET'S JUST SAY THAT FEELING HASN'T EXACTLY LEFT.

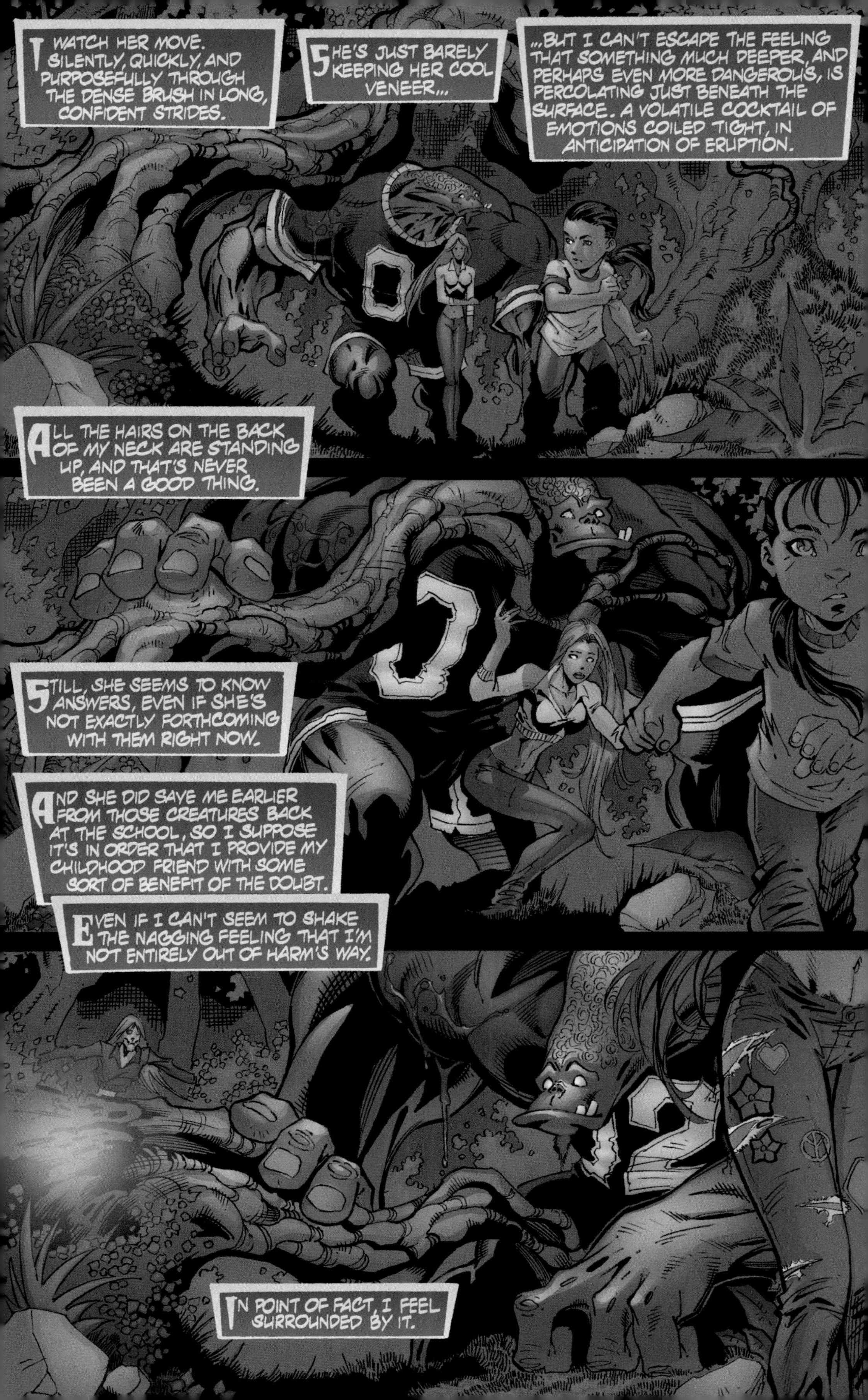
I WATCH HER MOVE. SILENTLY, QUICKLY, AND PURPOSEFULLY THROUGH THE DENSE BRUSH IN LONG, CONFIDENT STRIDES.
SHE'S JUST BARELY KEEPING HER COOL VENEER...
...BUT I CAN'T ESCAPE THE FEELING THAT SOMETHING MUCH DEEPER, AND PERHAPS EVEN MORE DANGEROUS, IS PERCOLATING JUST BENEATH THE SURFACE. A VOLATILE COCKTAIL OF EMOTIONS COILED TIGHT, IN ANTICIPATION OF ERUPTION.
ALL THE HAIRS ON THE BACK OF MY NECK ARE STANDING UP, AND THAT'S NEVER BEEN A GOOD THING.
STILL, SHE SEEMS TO KNOW ANSWERS, EVEN IF SHE'S NOT EXACTLY FORTHCOMING WITH THEM RIGHT NOW.
AND SHE DID SAVE ME EARLIER FROM THOSE CREATURES BACK AT THE SCHOOL, SO I SUPPOSE IT'S IN ORDER THAT I PROVIDE MY CHILDHOOD FRIEND WITH SOME SORT OF BENEFIT OF THE DOUBT.
EVEN IF I CAN'T SEEM TO SHAKE THE NAGGING FEELING THAT I'M NOT ENTIRELY OUT OF HARM'S WAY.
IN POINT OF FACT, I FEEL SURROUNDED BY IT.

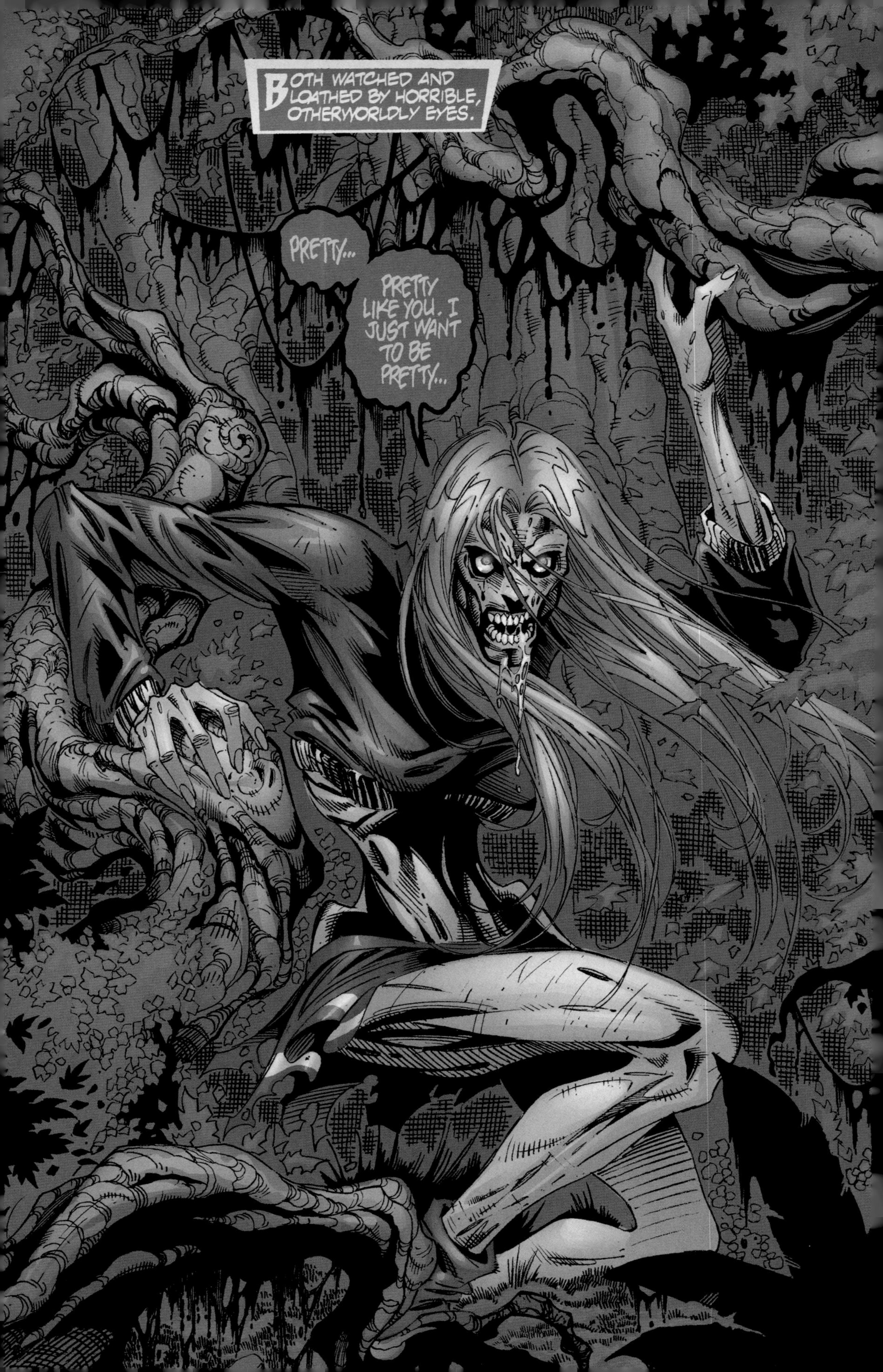
BOTH WATCHED AND LOATHED BY HORRIBLE, OTHERWORLDLY EYES.
PRETTY...
PRETTY LIKE YOU. I JUST WANT TO BE PRETTY...

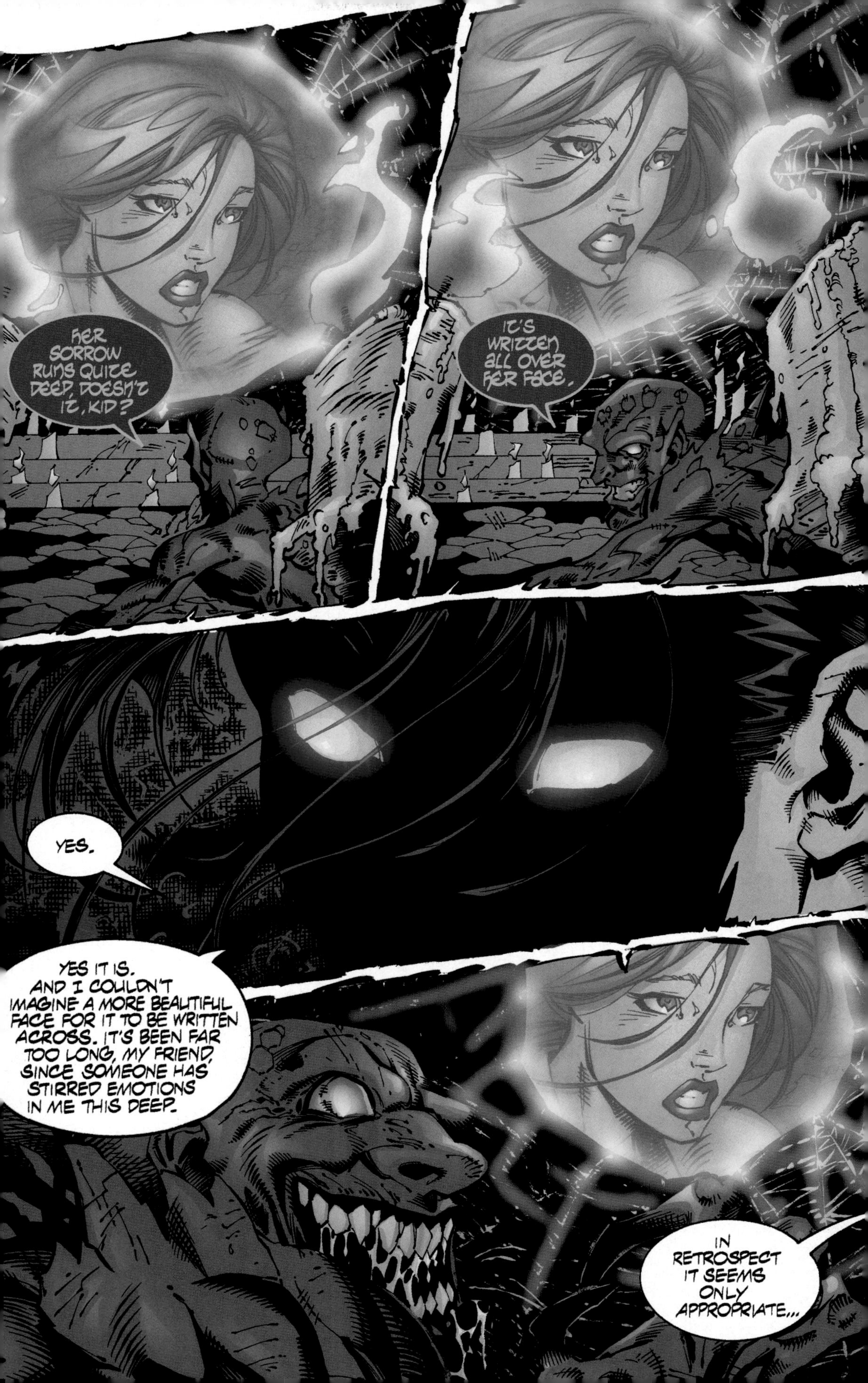
HER SORROW RUNS QUITE DEEP, DOESN'T IT, KID?
IT'S WRITTEN ALL OVER HER FACE.
YES.
YES IT IS. AND I COULDN'T IMAGINE A MORE BEAUTIFUL FACE FOR IT TO BE WRITTEN ACROSS. IT'S BEEN FAR TOO LONG, MY FRIEND, SINCE SOMEONE HAS STIRRED EMOTIONS IN ME THIS DEEP.
IN RETROSPECT IT SEEMS ONLY APPROPRIATE...

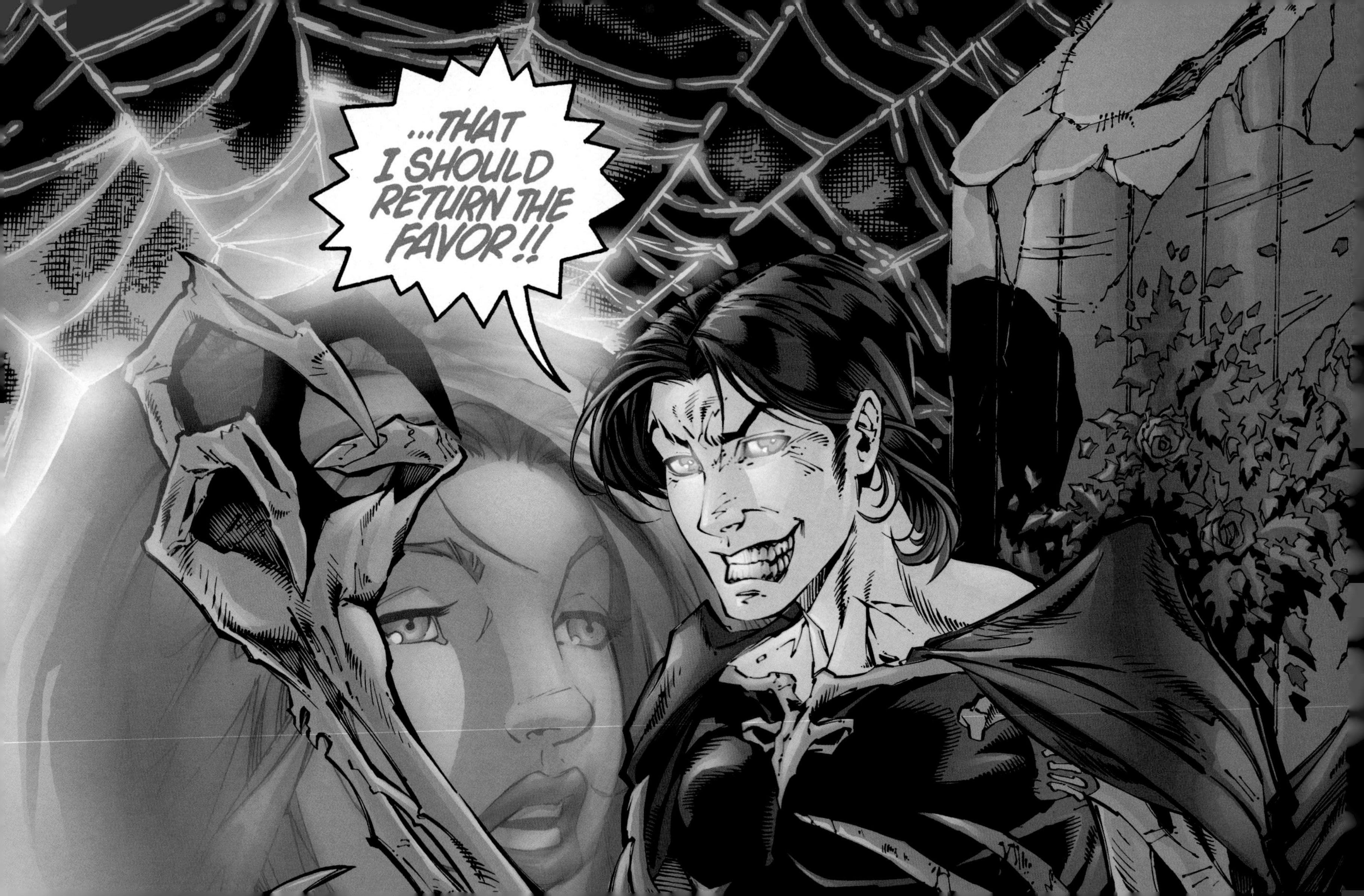
...THAT I SHOULD RETURN THE FAVOR!!

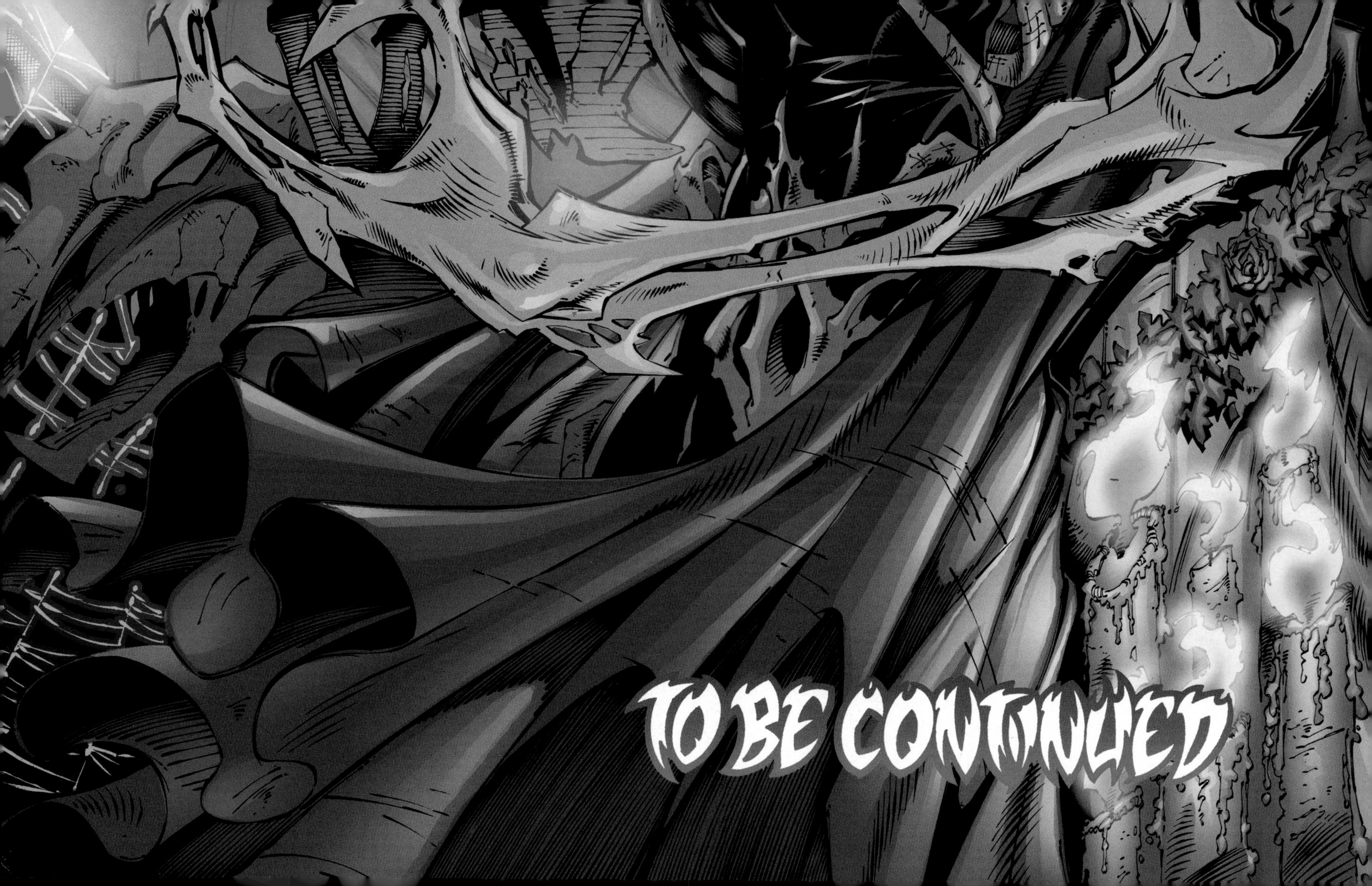
TO BE CONTINUED

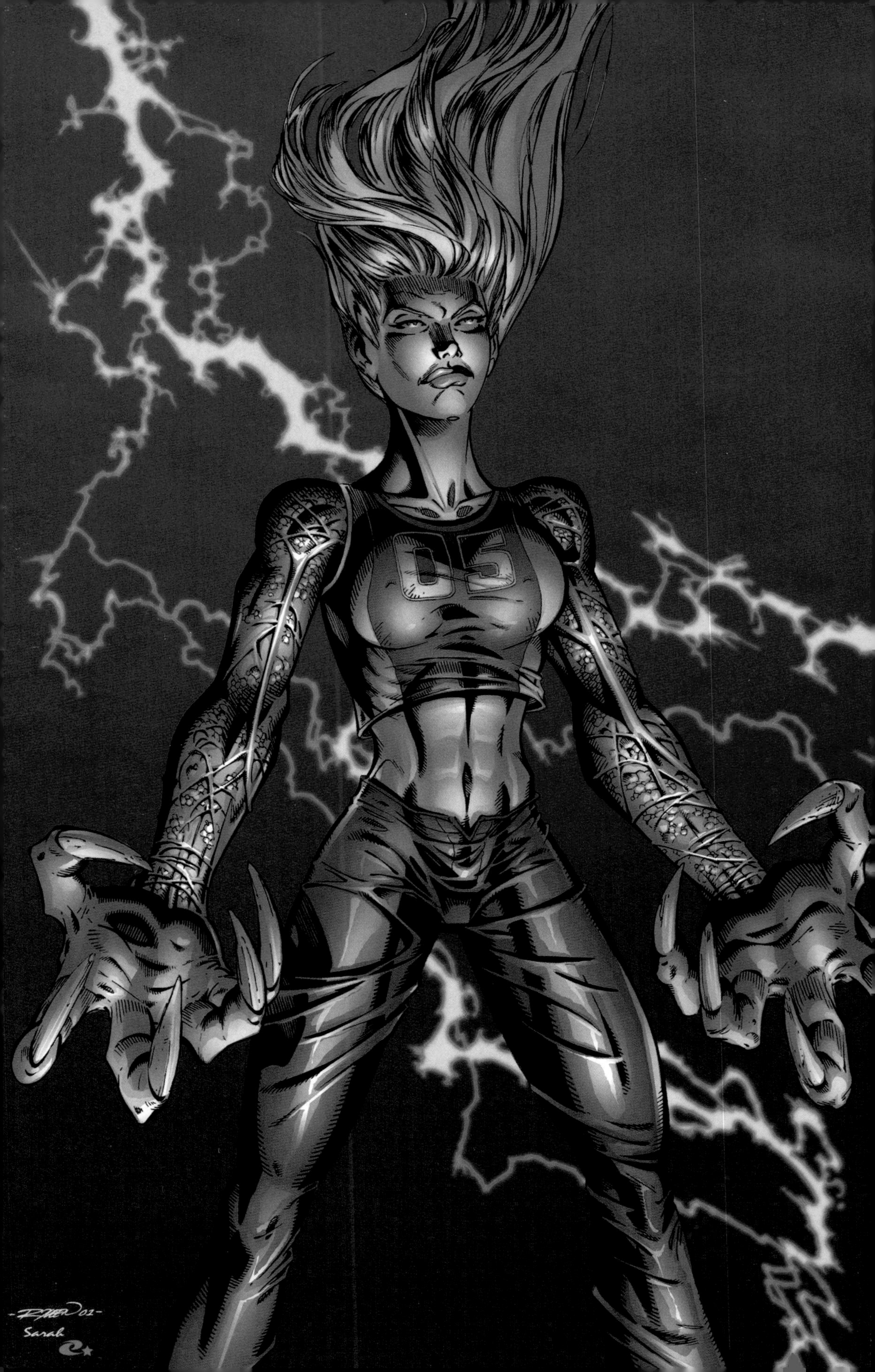
05
Sarah

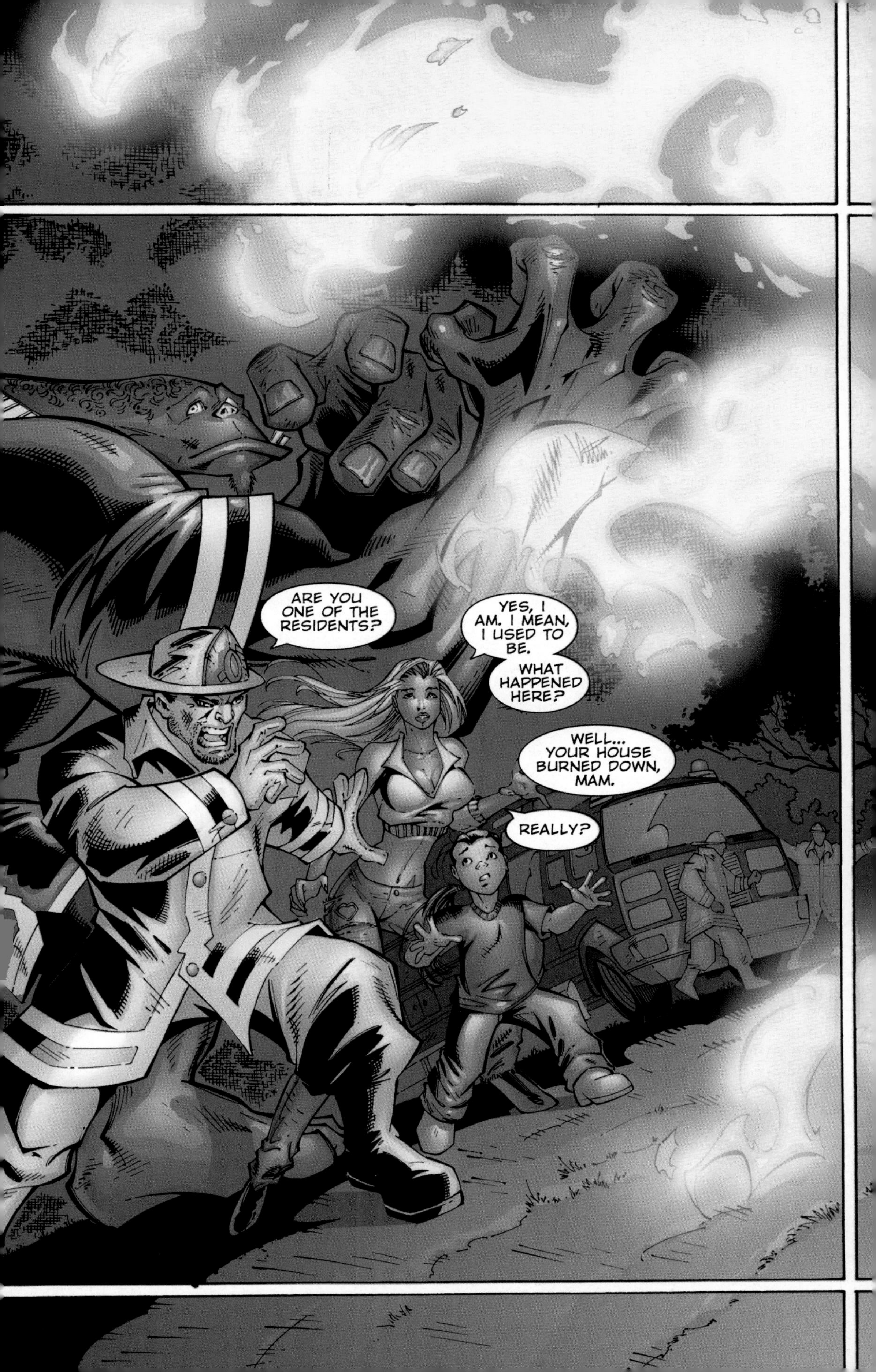
ARE YOU ONE OF THE RESIDENTS?
YES, I AM. I MEAN, I USED TO BE.
WHAT HAPPENED HERE?
WELL... YOUR HOUSE BURNED DOWN, MAM.
REALLY?

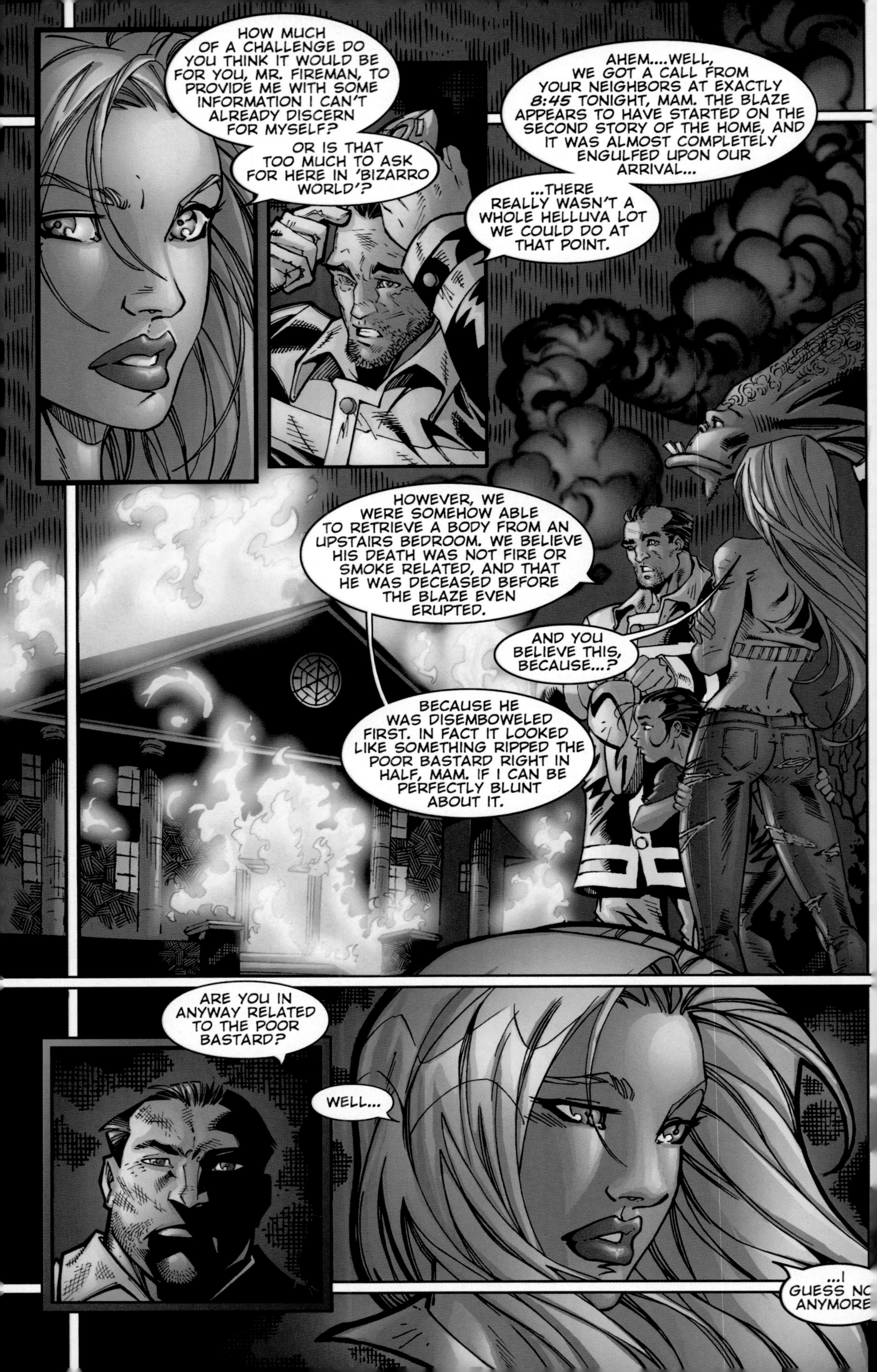
HOW MUCH OF A CHALLENGE DO YOU THINK IT WOULD BE FOR YOU, MR. FIREMAN, TO PROVIDE ME WITH SOME INFORMATION I CAN'T ALREADY DISCERN FOR MYSELF?
OR IS THAT TOO MUCH TO ASK FOR HERE IN 'BIZARRO WORLD'?
AHEM....WELL, WE GOT A CALL FROM YOUR NEIGHBORS AT EXACTLY 8:45 TONIGHT, MAM. THE BLAZE APPEARS TO HAVE STARTED ON THE SECOND STORY OF THE HOME, AND IT WAS ALMOST COMPLETELY ENGULFED UPON OUR ARRIVAL...
...THERE REALLY WASN'T A WHOLE HELLUVA LOT WE COULD DO AT THAT POINT.
HOWEVER, WE WERE SOMEHOW ABLE TO RETRIEVE A BODY FROM AN UPSTAIRS BEDROOM. WE BELIEVE HIS DEATH WAS NOT FIRE OR SMOKE RELATED, AND THAT HE WAS DECEASED BEFORE THE BLAZE EVEN ERUPTED.
AND YOU BELIEVE THIS, BECAUSE...?
BECAUSE HE WAS DISEMBOWELED FIRST. IN FACT IT LOOKED LIKE SOMETHING RIPPED THE POOR BASTARD RIGHT IN HALF, MAM. IF I CAN BE PERFECTLY BLUNT ABOUT IT.
ARE YOU IN ANYWAY RELATED TO THE POOR BASTARD?
WELL...
...I GUESS NO ANYMORE

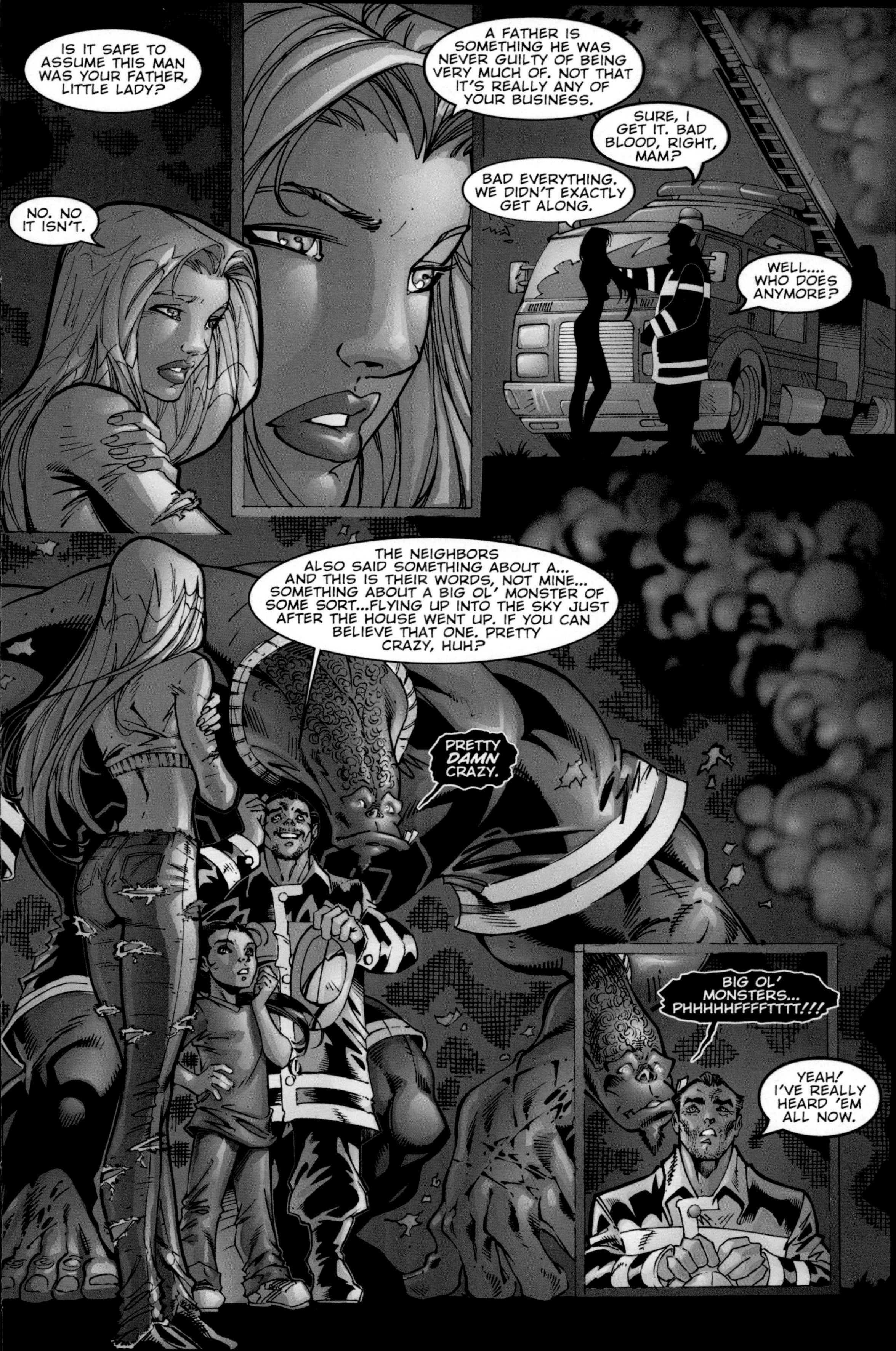
IS IT SAFE TO ASSUME THIS MAN WAS YOUR FATHER, LITTLE LADY?
NO. NO IT ISN'T.
A FATHER IS SOMETHING HE WAS NEVER GUILTY OF BEING VERY MUCH OF. NOT THAT IT'S REALLY ANY OF YOUR BUSINESS.
SURE, I GET IT. BAD BLOOD, RIGHT, MAM?
BAD EVERYTHING. WE DIDN'T EXACTLY GET ALONG.
WELL.... WHO DOES ANYMORE?
THE NEIGHBORS ALSO SAID SOMETHING ABOUT A... AND THIS IS THEIR WORDS, NOT MINE... SOMETHING ABOUT A BIG OL' MONSTER OF SOME SORT...FLYING UP INTO THE SKY JUST AFTER THE HOUSE WENT UP. IF YOU CAN BELIEVE THAT ONE. PRETTY CRAZY, HUH?
PRETTY *DAMN* CRAZY.
BIG OL' MONSTERS... PHHHHHFFFFTTTT!!!
YEAH! I'VE REALLY HEARD 'EM ALL NOW.

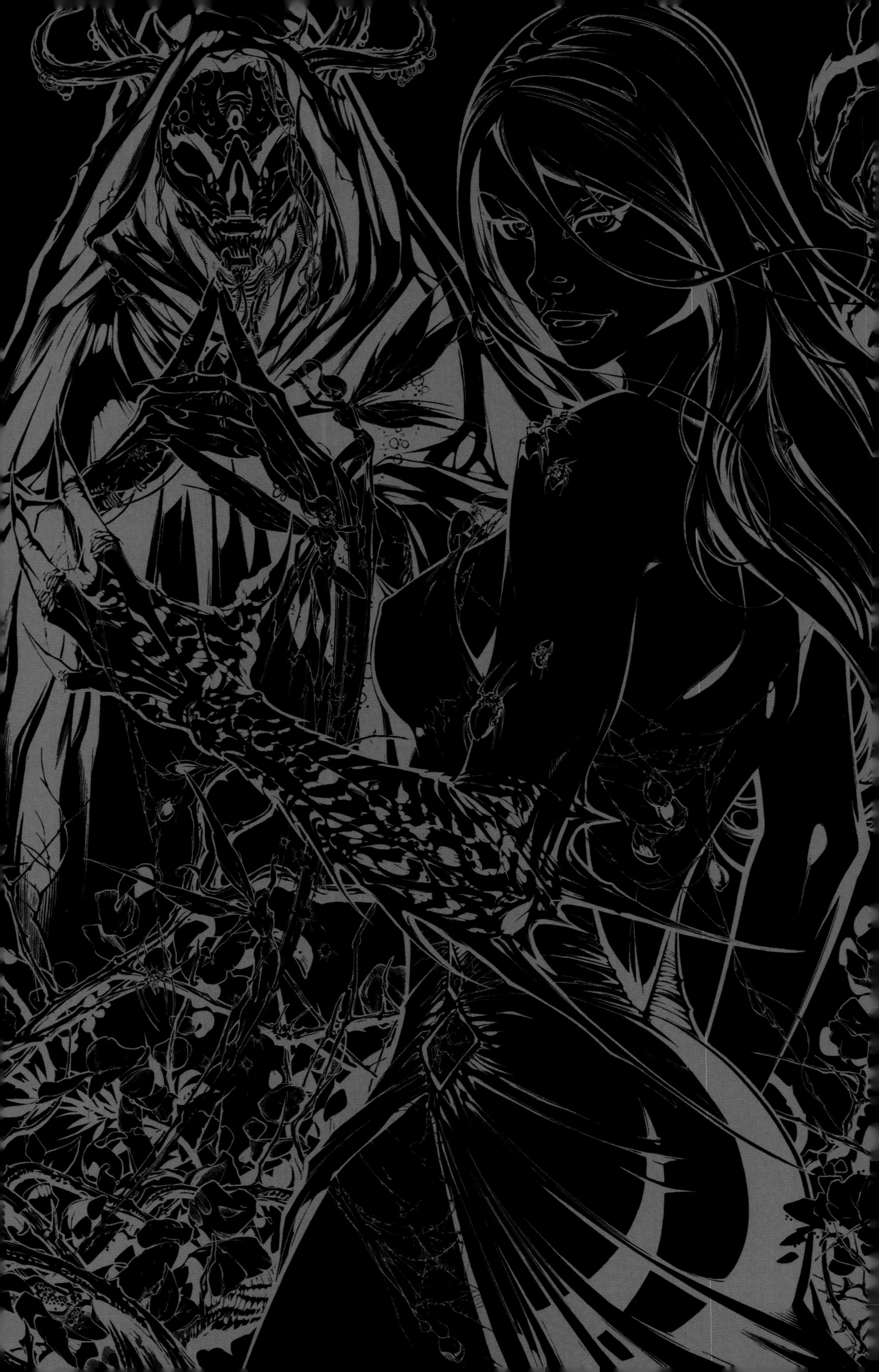

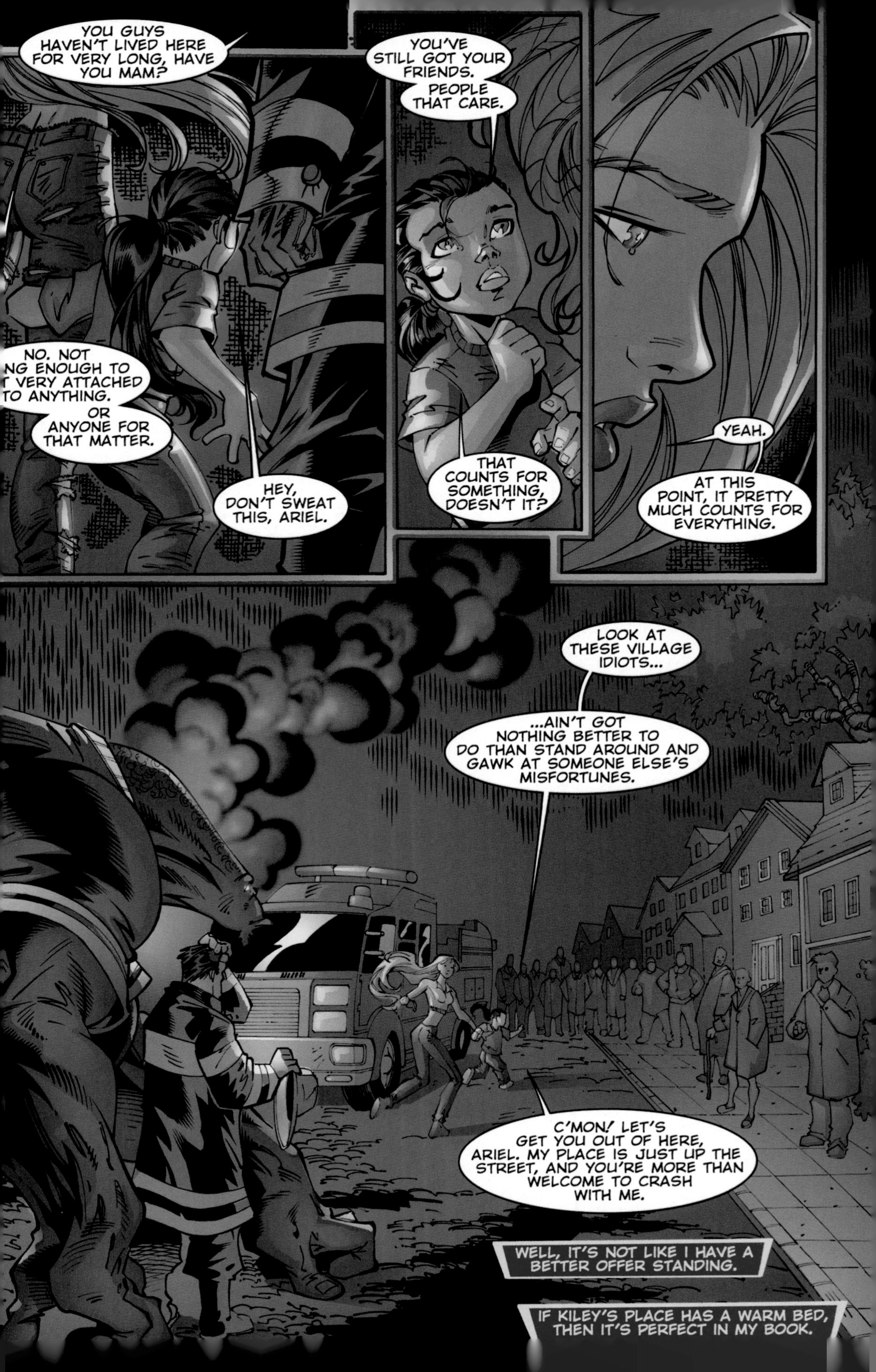
YOU GUYS HAVEN'T LIVED HERE FOR VERY LONG, HAVE YOU MAM?
NO. NOT
NG ENOUGH TO
T VERY ATTACHED TO ANYTHING.
OR ANYONE FOR THAT MATTER.
HEY, DON'T SWEAT THIS, ARIEL.
YOU'VE STILL GOT YOUR FRIENDS.
PEOPLE THAT CARE.
THAT COUNTS FOR SOMETHING, DOESN'T IT?
YEAH.
AT THIS POINT, IT PRETTY MUCH COUNTS FOR EVERYTHING.
LOOK AT THESE VILLAGE IDIOTS...
...AIN'T GOT NOTHING BETTER TO DO THAN STAND AROUND AND GAWK AT SOMEONE ELSE'S MISFORTUNES.
C'MON! LET'S GET YOU OUT OF HERE, ARIEL. MY PLACE IS JUST UP THE STREET, AND YOU'RE MORE THAN WELCOME TO CRASH WITH ME.
WELL, IT'S NOT LIKE I HAVE A BETTER OFFER STANDING.
IF KILEY'S PLACE HAS A WARM BED, THEN IT'S PERFECT IN MY BOOK.

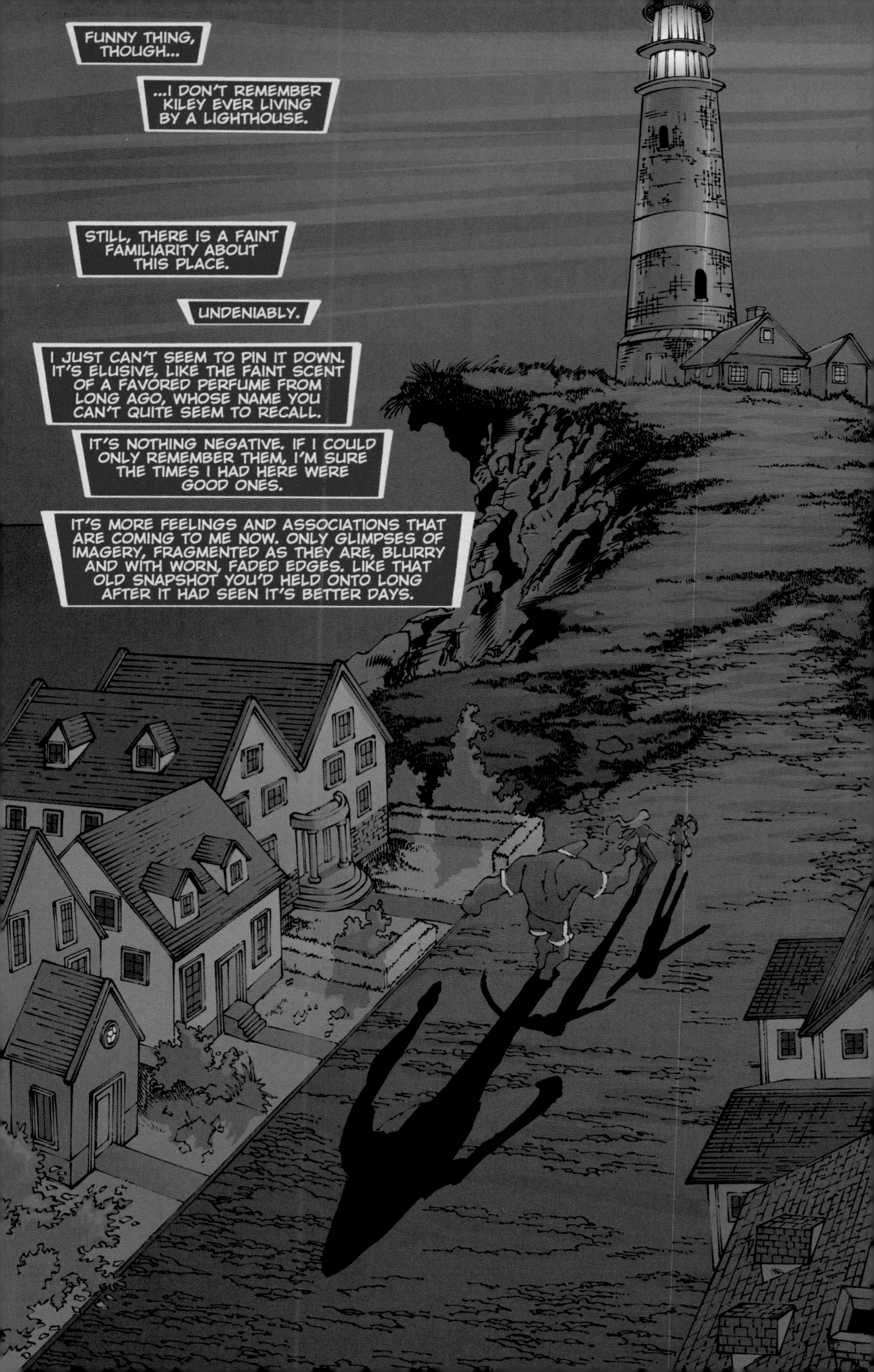
FUNNY THING, THOUGH...
...I DON'T REMEMBER KILEY EVER LIVING BY A LIGHTHOUSE.
STILL, THERE IS A FAINT FAMILIARITY ABOUT THIS PLACE.
UNDENIABLY.
I JUST CAN'T SEEM TO PIN IT DOWN. IT'S ELUSIVE, LIKE THE FAINT SCENT OF A FAVORED PERFUME FROM LONG AGO, WHOSE NAME YOU CAN'T QUITE SEEM TO RECALL.
IT'S NOTHING NEGATIVE. IF I COULD ONLY REMEMBER THEM, I'M SURE THE TIMES I HAD HERE WERE GOOD ONES.
IT'S MORE FEELINGS AND ASSOCIATIONS THAT ARE COMING TO ME NOW. ONLY GLIMPSES OF IMAGERY, FRAGMENTED AS THEY ARE, BLURRY AND WITH WORN, FADED EDGES. LIKE THAT OLD SNAPSHOT YOU'D HELD ONTO LONG AFTER IT HAD SEEN IT'S BETTER DAYS.

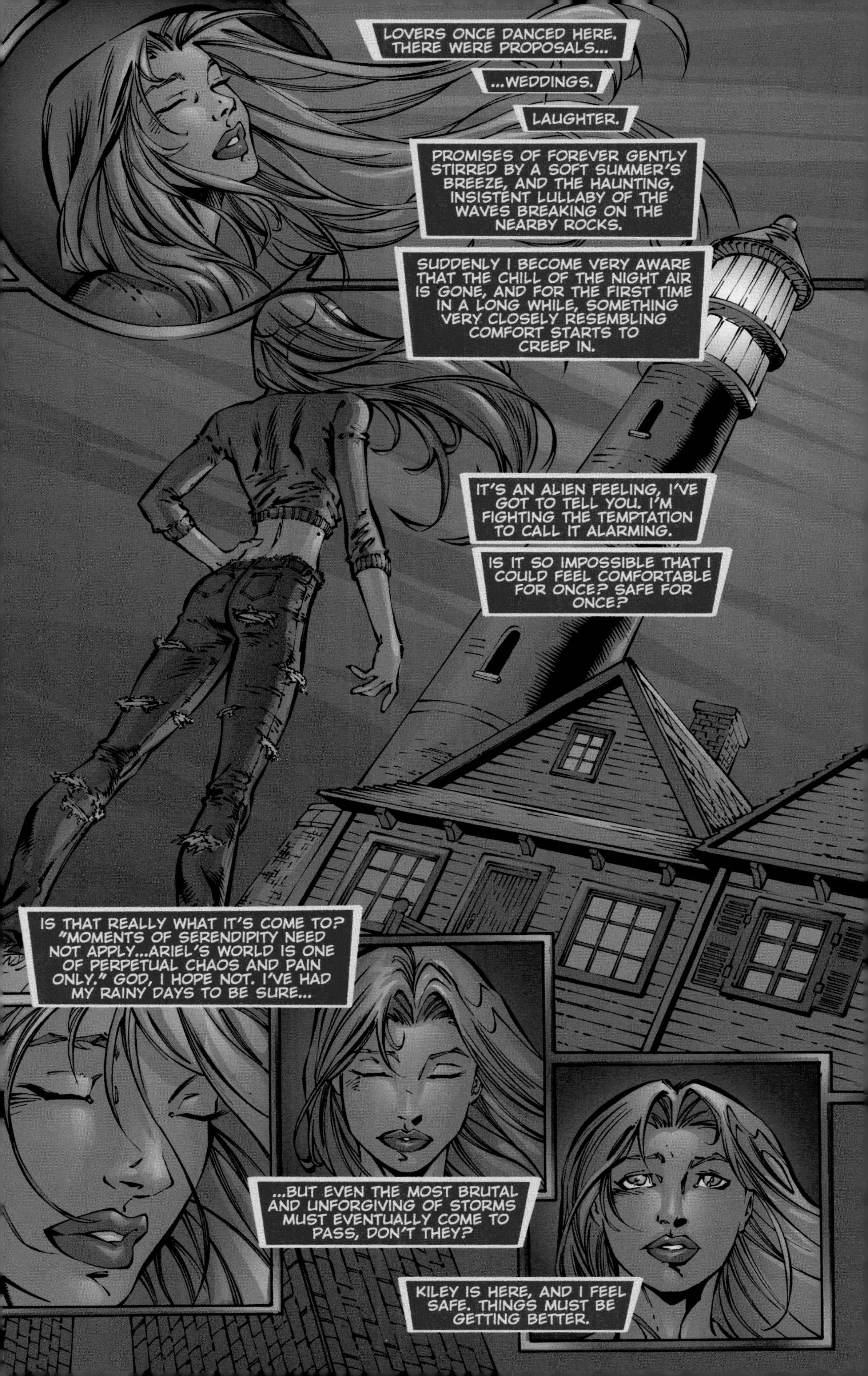
LOVERS ONCE DANCED HERE. THERE WERE PROPOSALS...
...WEDDINGS.
LAUGHTER.
PROMISES OF FOREVER GENTLY STIRRED BY A SOFT SUMMER'S BREEZE, AND THE HAUNTING, INSISTENT LULLABY OF THE WAVES BREAKING ON THE NEARBY ROCKS.
SUDDENLY I BECOME VERY AWARE THAT THE CHILL OF THE NIGHT AIR IS GONE, AND FOR THE FIRST TIME IN A LONG WHILE, SOMETHING VERY CLOSELY RESEMBLING COMFORT STARTS TO CREEP IN.
IT'S AN ALIEN FEELING, I'VE GOT TO TELL YOU. I'M FIGHTING THE TEMPTATION TO CALL IT ALARMING.
IS IT SO IMPOSSIBLE THAT I COULD FEEL COMFORTABLE FOR ONCE? SAFE FOR ONCE?
IS THAT REALLY WHAT IT'S COME TO? "MOMENTS OF SERENDIPITY NEED NOT APPLY...ARIEL'S WORLD IS ONE OF PERPETUAL CHAOS AND PAIN ONLY." GOD, I HOPE NOT. I'VE HAD MY RAINY DAYS TO BE SURE...
...BUT EVEN THE MOST BRUTAL AND UNFORGIVING OF STORMS MUST EVENTUALLY COME TO PASS, DON'T THEY?
KILEY IS HERE, AND I FEEL SAFE. THINGS MUST BE GETTING BETTER.

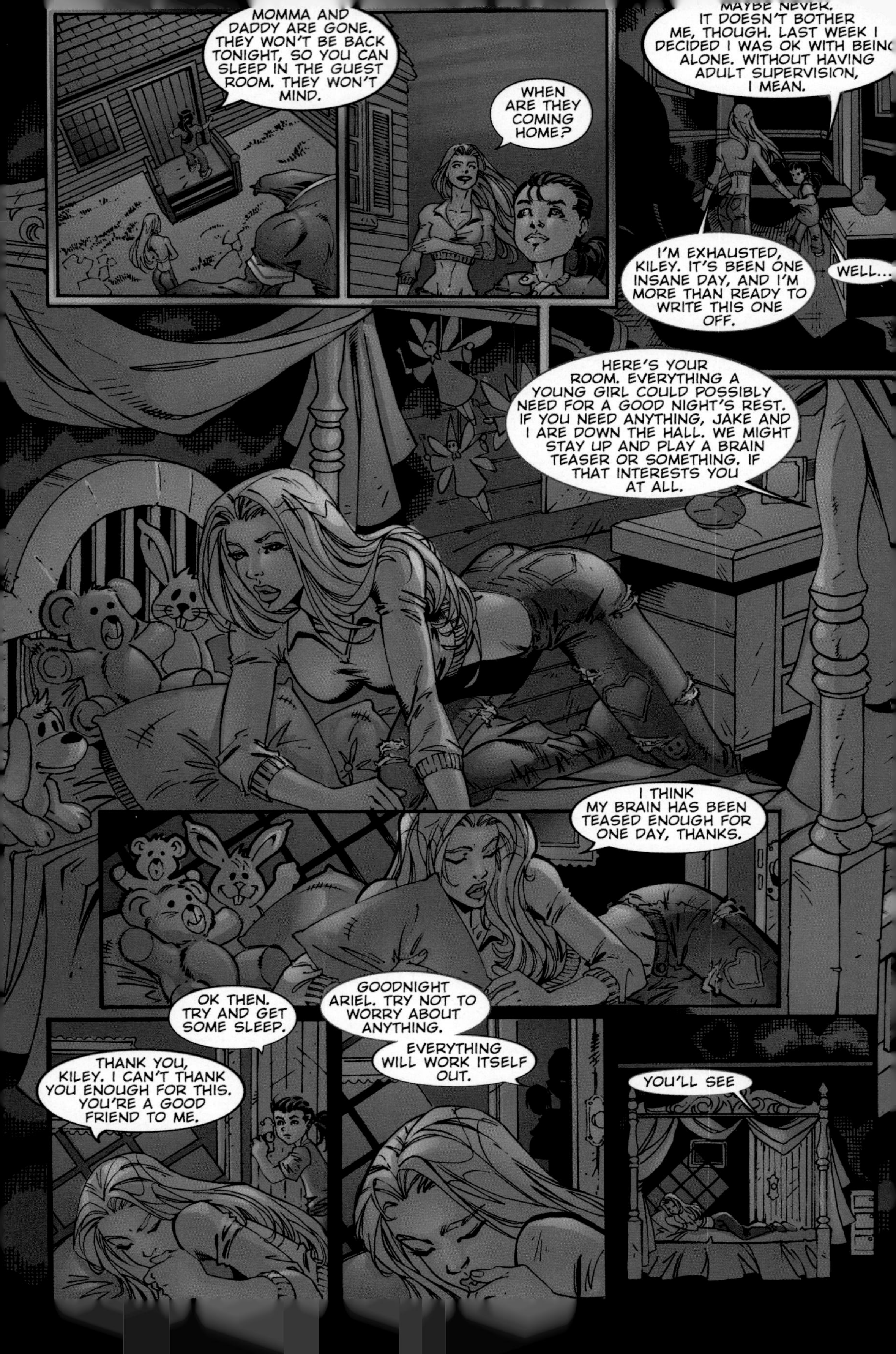
MOMMA AND DADDY ARE GONE. THEY WON'T BE BACK TONIGHT, SO YOU CAN SLEEP IN THE GUEST ROOM. THEY WON'T MIND.
WHEN ARE THEY COMING HOME?
MAYBE NEVER. IT DOESN'T BOTHER ME, THOUGH. LAST WEEK I DECIDED I WAS OK WITH BEING ALONE. WITHOUT HAVING ADULT SUPERVISION, I MEAN.
WELL...
I'M EXHAUSTED, KILEY. IT'S BEEN ONE INSANE DAY, AND I'M MORE THAN READY TO WRITE THIS ONE OFF.
HERE'S YOUR ROOM. EVERYTHING A YOUNG GIRL COULD POSSIBLY NEED FOR A GOOD NIGHT'S REST. IF YOU NEED ANYTHING, JAKE AND I ARE DOWN THE HALL. WE MIGHT STAY UP AND PLAY A BRAIN TEASER OR SOMETHING. IF THAT INTERESTS YOU AT ALL.
I THINK MY BRAIN HAS BEEN TEASED ENOUGH FOR ONE DAY, THANKS.
OK THEN. TRY AND GET SOME SLEEP.
THANK YOU, KILEY. I CAN'T THANK YOU ENOUGH FOR THIS. YOU'RE A GOOD FRIEND TO ME.
GOODNIGHT ARIEL. TRY NOT TO WORRY ABOUT ANYTHING.
EVERYTHING WILL WORK ITSELF OUT.
YOU'LL SEE

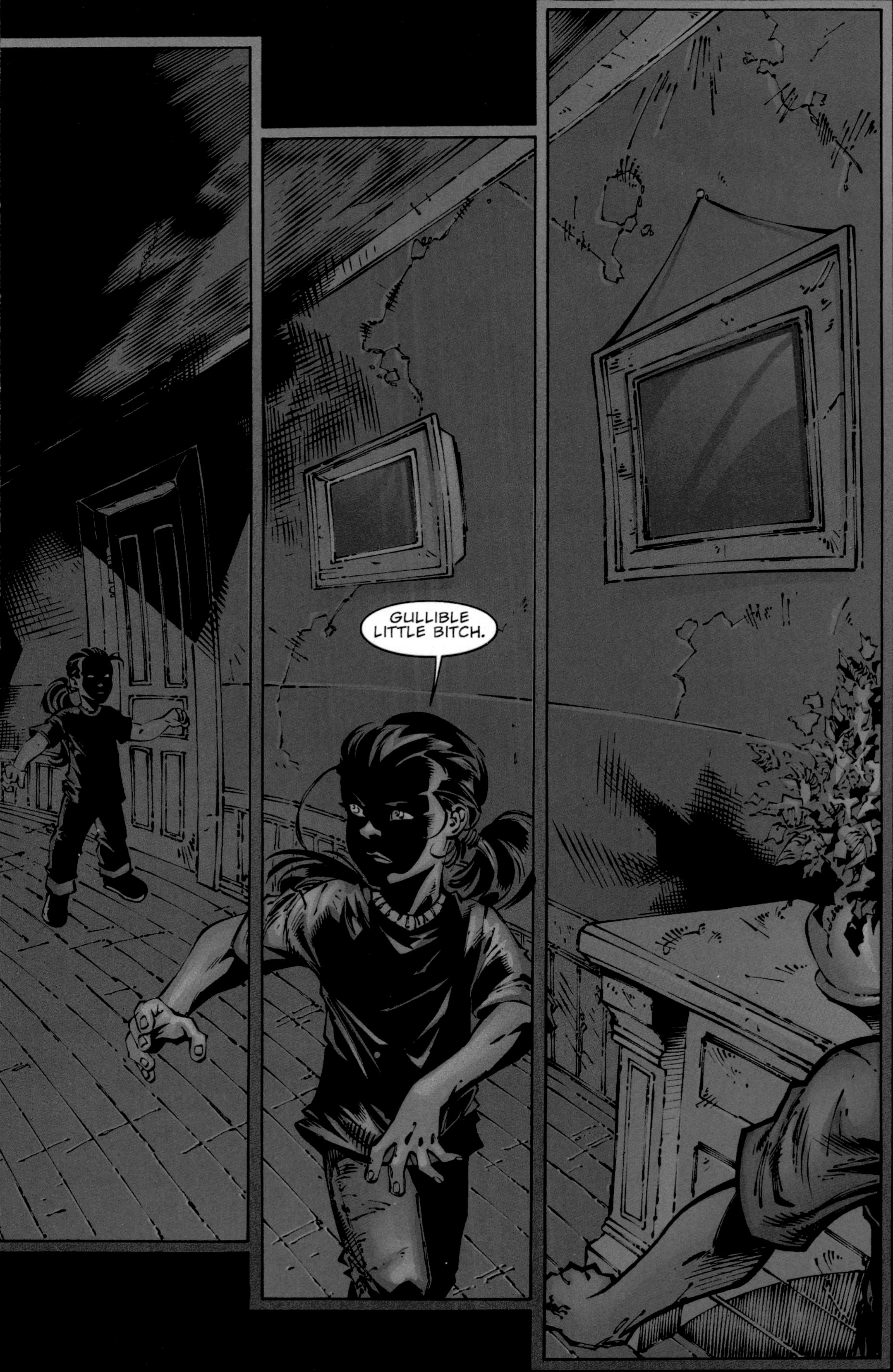
GULLIBLE LITTLE BITCH.

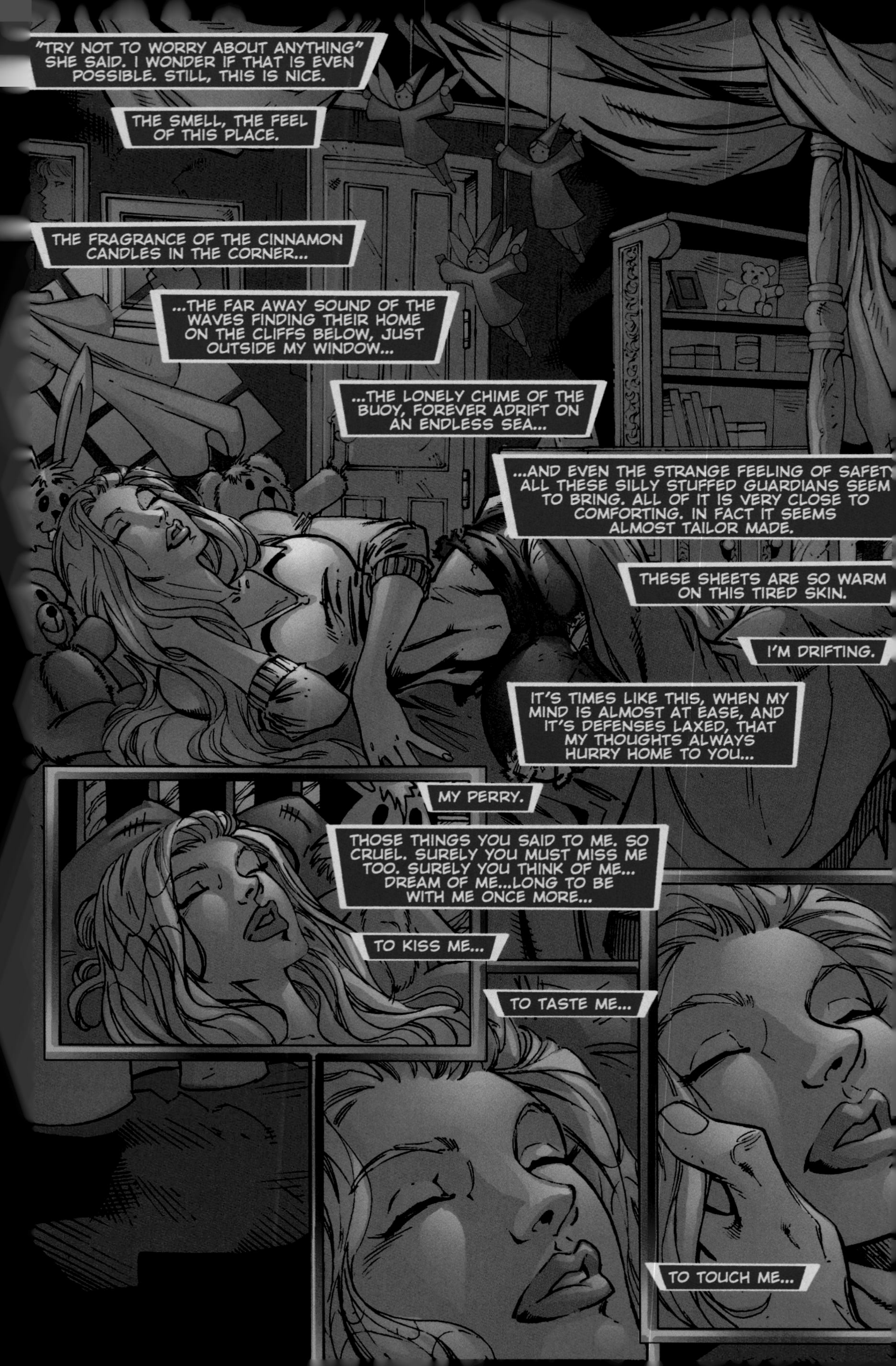
"TRY NOT TO WORRY ABOUT ANYTHING" SHE SAID. I WONDER IF THAT IS EVEN POSSIBLE. STILL, THIS IS NICE.
THE SMELL, THE FEEL OF THIS PLACE.
THE FRAGRANCE OF THE CINNAMON CANDLES IN THE CORNER...
...THE FAR AWAY SOUND OF THE WAVES FINDING THEIR HOME ON THE CLIFFS BELOW, JUST OUTSIDE MY WINDOW...
...THE LONELY CHIME OF THE BUOY, FOREVER ADRIFT ON AN ENDLESS SEA...
...AND EVEN THE STRANGE FEELING OF SAFETY ALL THESE SILLY STUFFED GUARDIANS SEEM TO BRING. ALL OF IT IS VERY CLOSE TO COMFORTING. IN FACT IT SEEMS ALMOST TAILOR MADE.
THESE SHEETS ARE SO WARM ON THIS TIRED SKIN.
I'M DRIFTING.
IT'S TIMES LIKE THIS, WHEN MY MIND IS ALMOST AT EASE, AND IT'S DEFENSES LAXED, THAT MY THOUGHTS ALWAYS HURRY HOME TO YOU...
MY PERRY.
THOSE THINGS YOU SAID TO ME. SO CRUEL. SURELY YOU MUST MISS ME TOO. SURELY YOU THINK OF ME... DREAM OF ME...LONG TO BE WITH ME ONCE MORE...
TO KISS ME...
TO TASTE ME...
TO TOUCH ME...

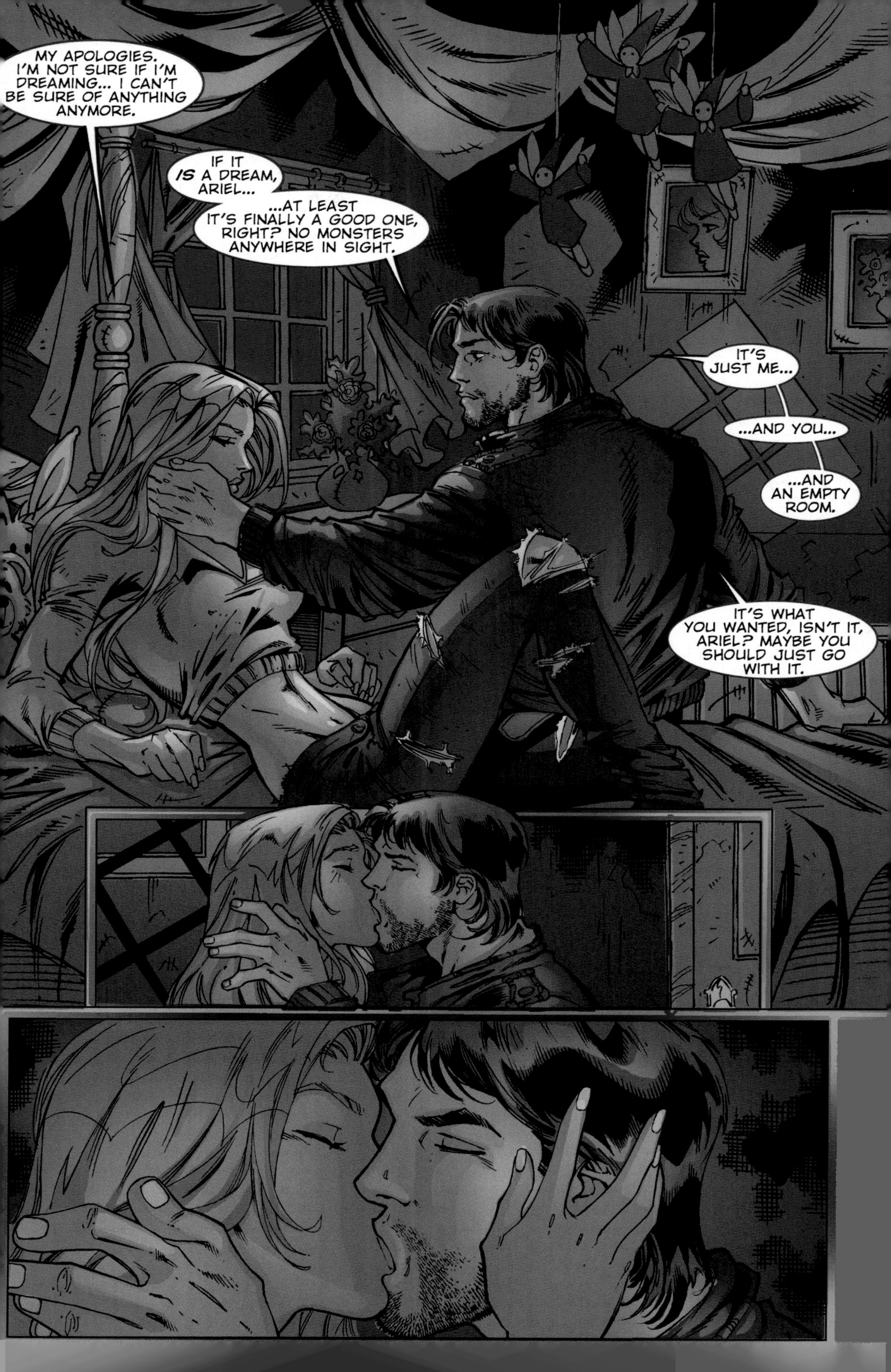
MY APOLOGIES. I'M NOT SURE IF I'M DREAMING... I CAN'T BE SURE OF ANYTHING ANYMORE.
IF IT *IS* A DREAM, ARIEL...
...AT LEAST IT'S FINALLY A *GOOD* ONE, RIGHT? NO MONSTERS ANYWHERE IN SIGHT.
IT'S JUST ME...
...AND YOU...
...AND AN EMPTY ROOM.
IT'S WHAT YOU WANTED, ISN'T IT, ARIEL? MAYBE YOU SHOULD JUST GO WITH IT.

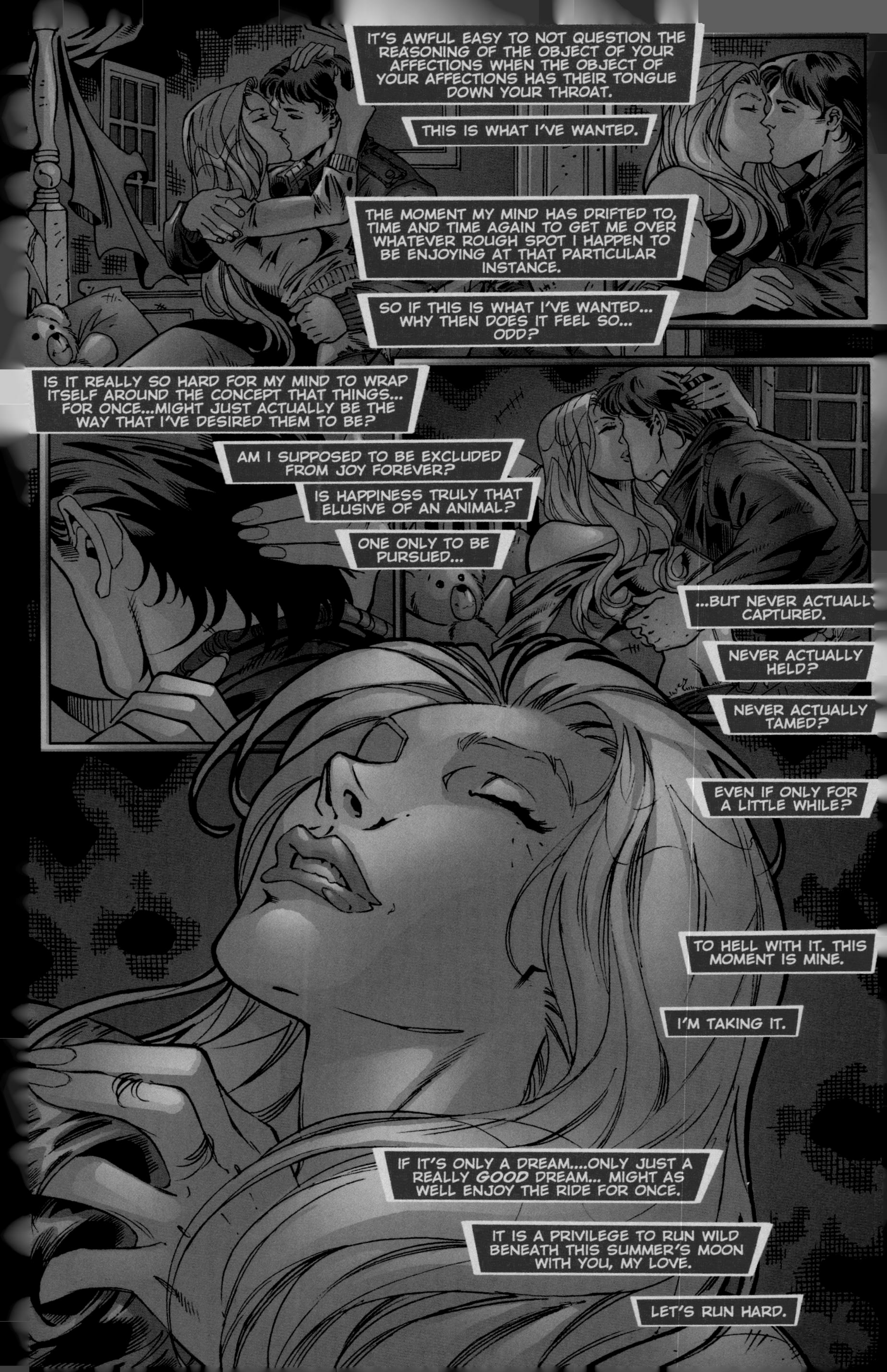
IT'S AWFUL EASY TO NOT QUESTION THE REASONING OF THE OBJECT OF YOUR AFFECTIONS WHEN THE OBJECT OF YOUR AFFECTIONS HAS THEIR TONGUE DOWN YOUR THROAT.
THIS IS WHAT I'VE WANTED.
THE MOMENT MY MIND HAS DRIFTED TO, TIME AND TIME AGAIN TO GET ME OVER WHATEVER ROUGH SPOT I HAPPEN TO BE ENJOYING AT THAT PARTICULAR INSTANCE.
SO IF THIS IS WHAT I'VE WANTED... WHY THEN DOES IT FEEL SO... ODD?
IS IT REALLY SO HARD FOR MY MIND TO WRAP ITSELF AROUND THE CONCEPT THAT THINGS... FOR ONCE...MIGHT JUST ACTUALLY BE THE WAY THAT I'VE DESIRED THEM TO BE?
AM I SUPPOSED TO BE EXCLUDED FROM JOY FOREVER?
IS HAPPINESS TRULY THAT ELUSIVE OF AN ANIMAL?
ONE ONLY TO BE PURSUED...
...BUT NEVER ACTUALLY CAPTURED.
NEVER ACTUALLY HELD?
NEVER ACTUALLY TAMED?
EVEN IF ONLY FOR A LITTLE WHILE?
TO HELL WITH IT. THIS MOMENT IS MINE.
I'M TAKING IT.
IF IT'S ONLY A DREAM....ONLY JUST A REALLY *GOOD* DREAM... MIGHT AS WELL ENJOY THE RIDE FOR ONCE.
IT IS A PRIVILEGE TO RUN WILD BENEATH THIS SUMMER'S MOON WITH YOU, MY LOVE.
LET'S RUN HARD.

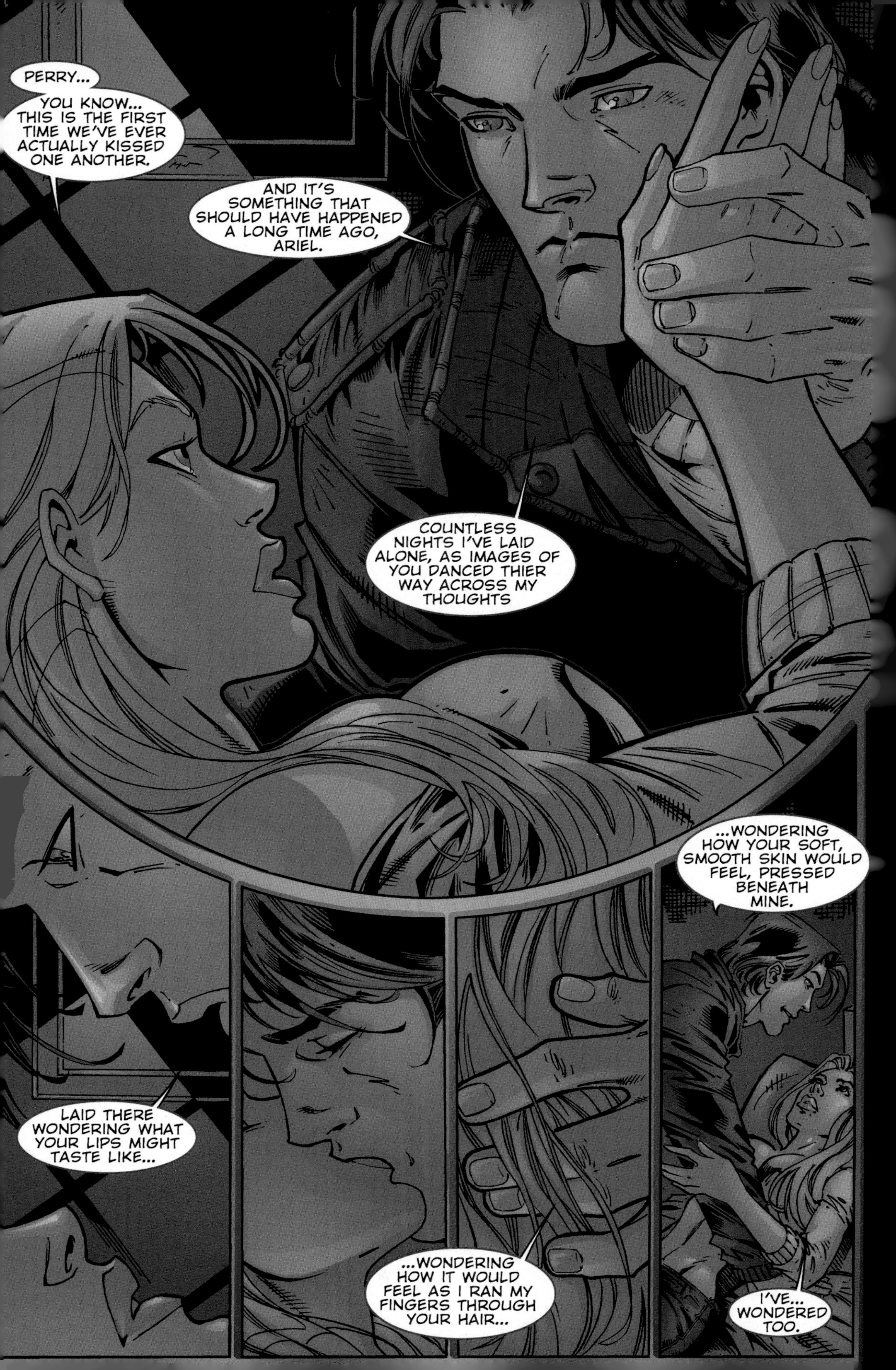
PERRY...
YOU KNOW... THIS IS THE FIRST TIME WE'VE EVER ACTUALLY KISSED ONE ANOTHER.
AND IT'S SOMETHING THAT SHOULD HAVE HAPPENED A LONG TIME AGO, ARIEL.
COUNTLESS NIGHTS I'VE LAID ALONE, AS IMAGES OF YOU DANCED THIER WAY ACROSS MY THOUGHTS
LAID THERE WONDERING WHAT YOUR LIPS MIGHT TASTE LIKE...
...WONDERING HOW IT WOULD FEEL AS I RAN MY FINGERS THROUGH YOUR HAIR...
...WONDERING HOW YOUR SOFT, SMOOTH SKIN WOULD FEEL, PRESSED BENEATH MINE.
I'VE... WONDERED TOO.

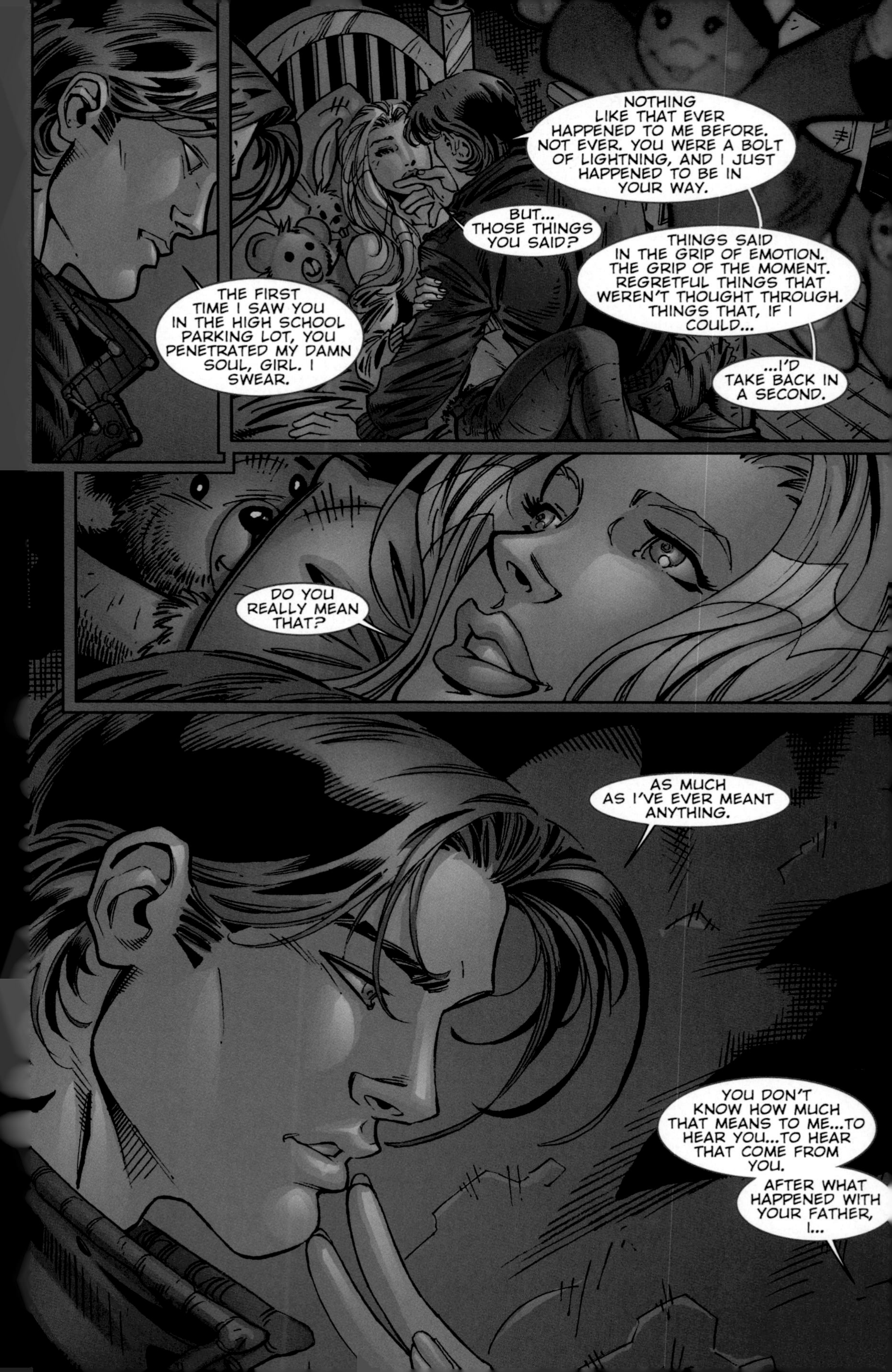
NOTHING LIKE THAT EVER HAPPENED TO ME BEFORE. NOT EVER. YOU WERE A BOLT OF LIGHTNING, AND I JUST HAPPENED TO BE IN YOUR WAY.
BUT... THOSE THINGS YOU SAID?
THINGS SAID IN THE GRIP OF EMOTION. THE GRIP OF THE MOMENT. REGRETFUL THINGS THAT WEREN'T THOUGHT THROUGH. THINGS THAT, IF I COULD...
...I'D TAKE BACK IN A SECOND.
THE FIRST TIME I SAW YOU IN THE HIGH SCHOOL PARKING LOT, YOU PENETRATED MY DAMN SOUL, GIRL. I SWEAR.
DO YOU REALLY MEAN THAT?
AS MUCH AS I'VE EVER MEANT ANYTHING.
YOU DON'T KNOW HOW MUCH THAT MEANS TO ME...TO HEAR YOU...TO HEAR THAT COME FROM YOU.
AFTER WHAT HAPPENED WITH YOUR FATHER, I...

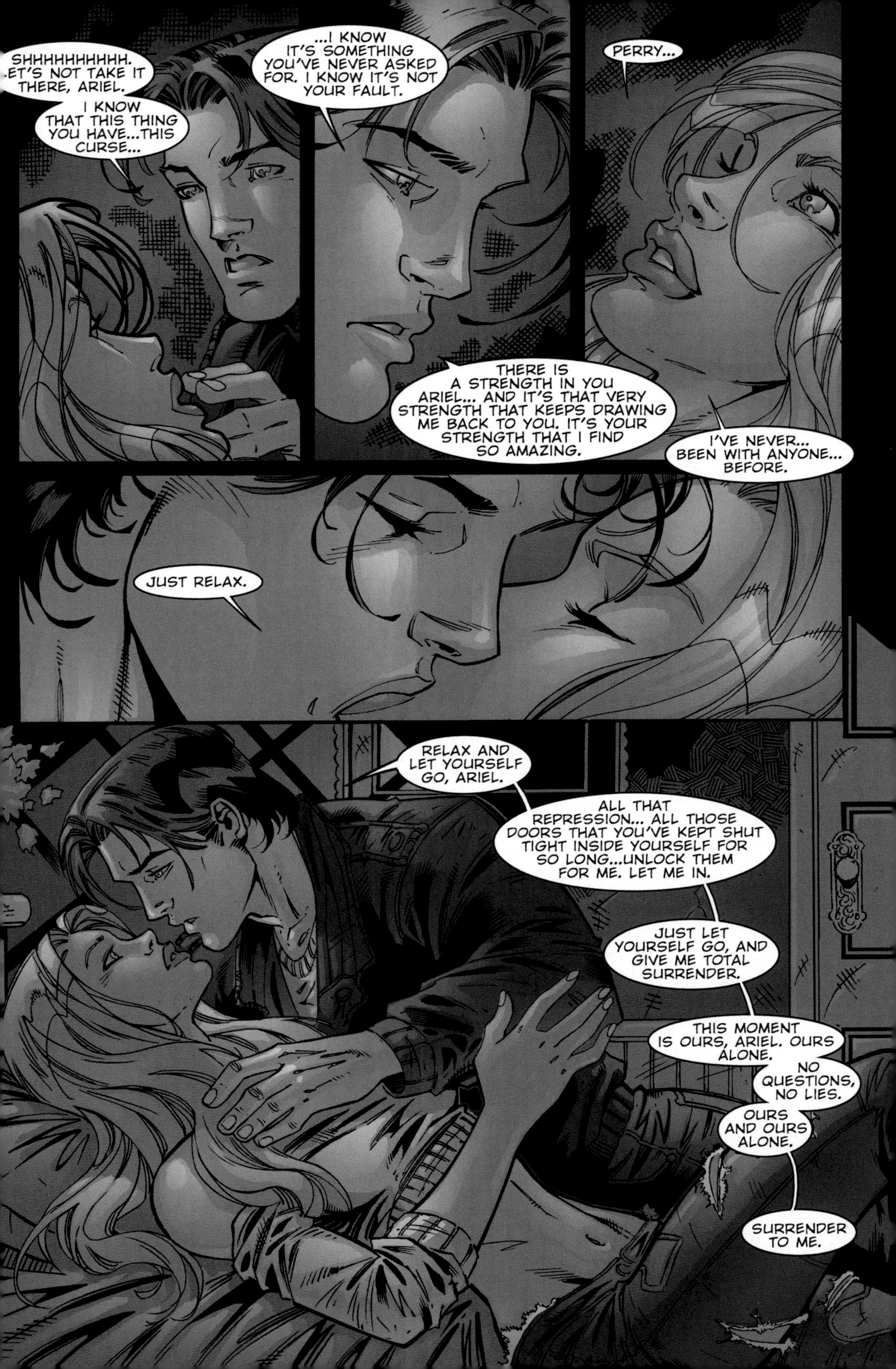
SHHHHHHHHHH. LET'S NOT TAKE IT THERE, ARIEL.
I KNOW THAT THIS THING YOU HAVE...THIS CURSE...
...I KNOW IT'S SOMETHING YOU'VE NEVER ASKED FOR. I KNOW IT'S NOT YOUR FAULT.
PERRY...
THERE IS A STRENGTH IN YOU ARIEL... AND IT'S THAT VERY STRENGTH THAT KEEPS DRAWING ME BACK TO YOU. IT'S YOUR STRENGTH THAT I FIND SO AMAZING.
I'VE NEVER... BEEN WITH ANYONE... BEFORE.
JUST RELAX.
RELAX AND LET YOURSELF GO, ARIEL.
ALL THAT REPRESSION... ALL THOSE DOORS THAT YOU'VE KEPT SHUT TIGHT INSIDE YOURSELF FOR SO LONG...UNLOCK THEM FOR ME. LET ME IN.
JUST LET YOURSELF GO, AND GIVE ME TOTAL SURRENDER.
THIS MOMENT IS OURS, ARIEL. OURS ALONE.
NO QUESTIONS, NO LIES.
OURS AND OURS ALONE.
SURRENDER TO ME.

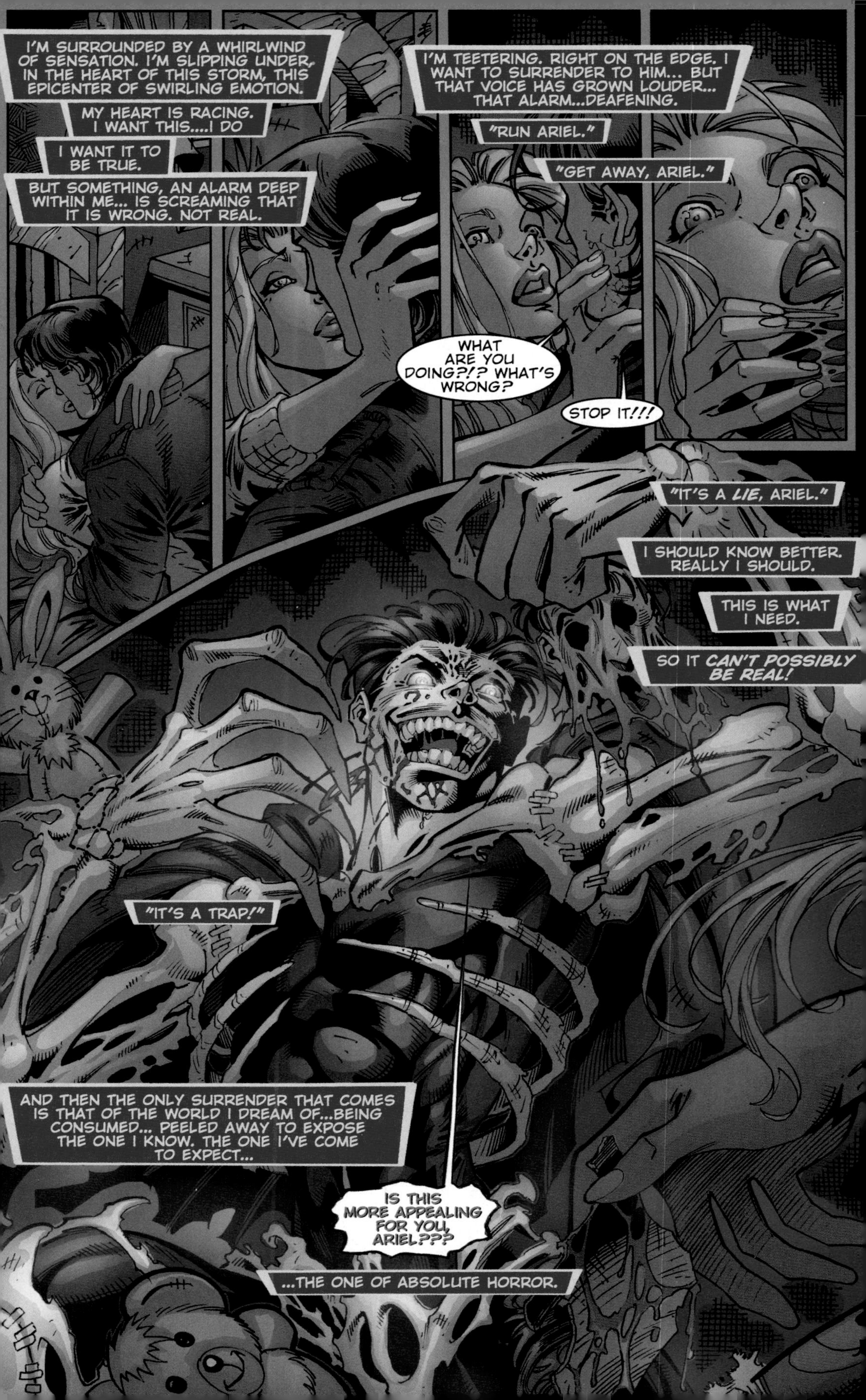
I'M SURROUNDED BY A WHIRLWIND OF SENSATION. I'M SLIPPING UNDER, IN THE HEART OF THIS STORM, THIS EPICENTER OF SWIRLING EMOTION.
MY HEART IS RACING. I WANT THIS....I DO
I WANT IT TO BE TRUE.
BUT SOMETHING, AN ALARM DEEP WITHIN ME... IS SCREAMING THAT IT IS WRONG. NOT REAL.
I'M TEETERING. RIGHT ON THE EDGE. I WANT TO SURRENDER TO HIM... BUT THAT VOICE HAS GROWN LOUDER... THAT ALARM...DEAFENING.
"RUN ARIEL."
"GET AWAY, ARIEL."
WHAT ARE YOU DOING?!? WHAT'S WRONG?
STOP IT!!!
"IT'S A LIE, ARIEL."
I SHOULD KNOW BETTER. REALLY I SHOULD.
THIS IS WHAT I NEED.
SO IT CAN'T POSSIBLY BE REAL!
"IT'S A TRAP!"
AND THEN THE ONLY SURRENDER THAT COMES IS THAT OF THE WORLD I DREAM OF...BEING CONSUMED... PEELED AWAY TO EXPOSE THE ONE I KNOW. THE ONE I'VE COME TO EXPECT...
IS THIS MORE APPEALING FOR YOU, ARIEL???
...THE ONE OF ABSOLUTE HORROR.

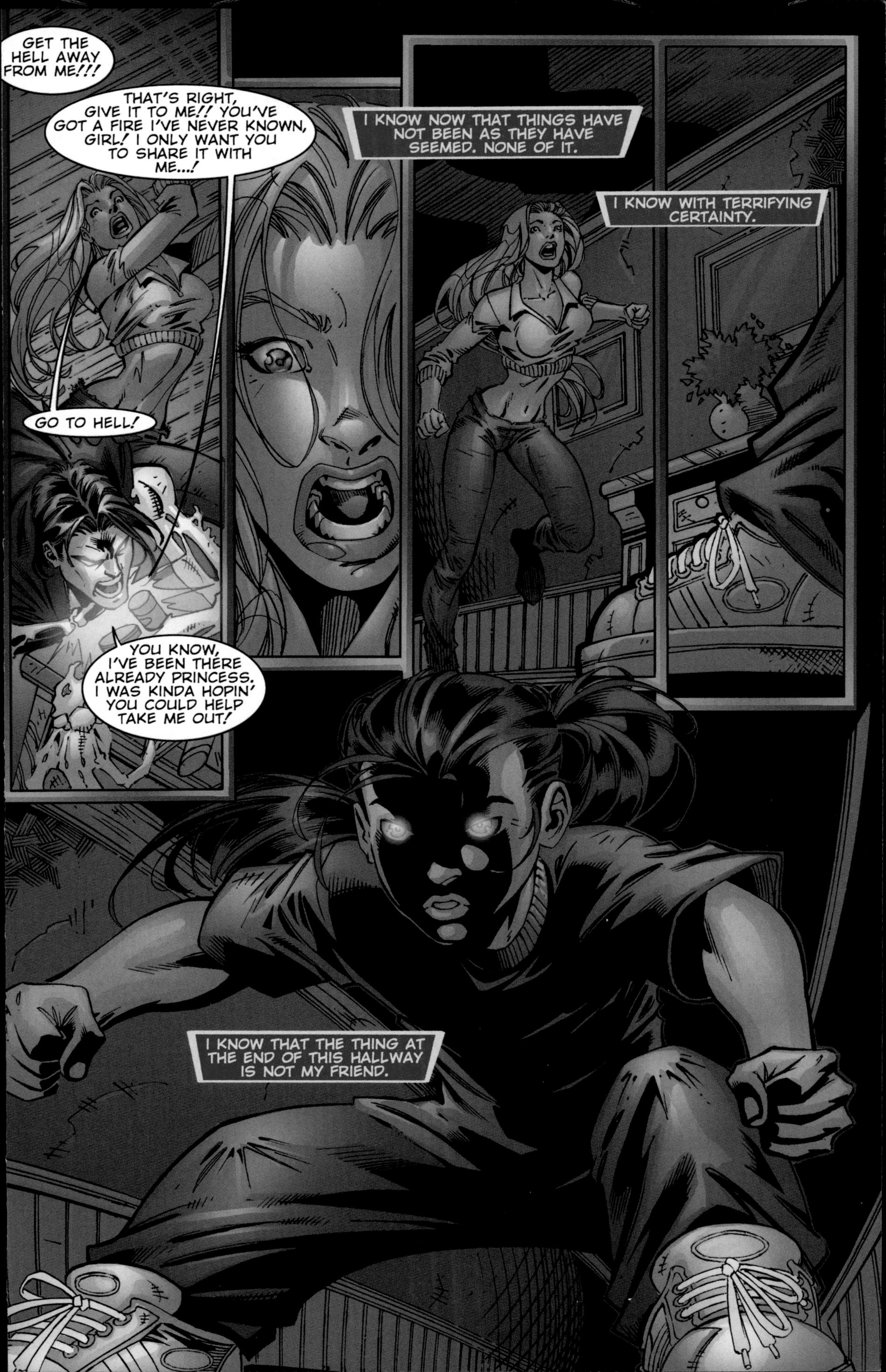
GET THE HELL AWAY FROM ME!!!
THAT'S RIGHT, GIVE IT TO ME!! YOU'VE GOT A FIRE I'VE NEVER KNOWN, GIRL! I ONLY WANT YOU TO SHARE IT WITH ME...!
GO TO HELL!
YOU KNOW, I'VE BEEN THERE ALREADY PRINCESS. I WAS KINDA HOPIN' YOU COULD HELP TAKE ME OUT!
I KNOW NOW THAT THINGS HAVE NOT BEEN AS THEY HAVE SEEMED. NONE OF IT.
I KNOW WITH TERRIFYING CERTAINTY.
I KNOW THAT THE THING AT THE END OF THIS HALLWAY IS NOT MY FRIEND.

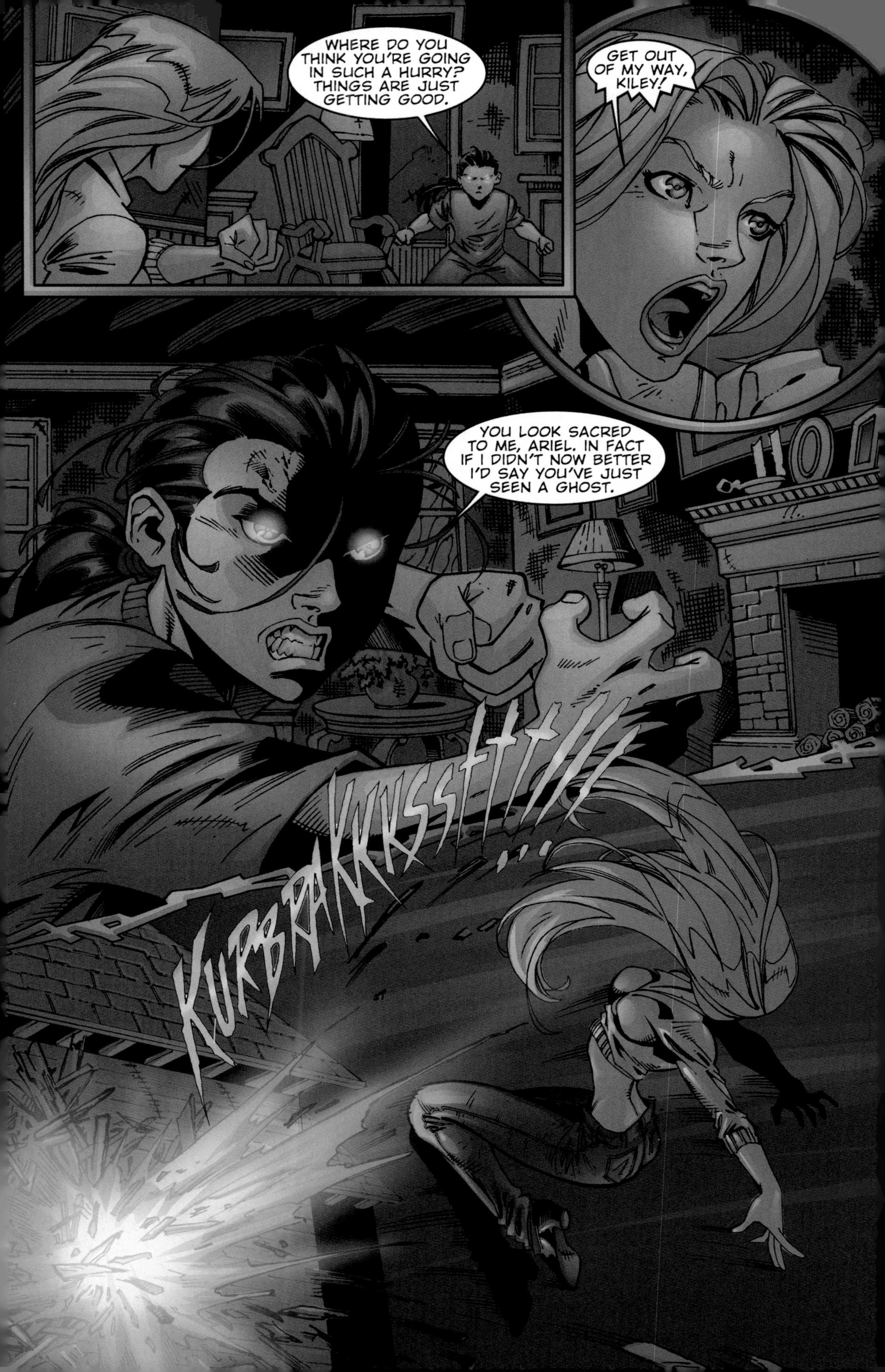
WHERE DO YOU THINK YOU'RE GOING IN SUCH A HURRY? THINGS ARE JUST GETTING GOOD.
GET OUT OF MY WAY, KILEY!
YOU LOOK SACRED TO ME, ARIEL. IN FACT IF I DIDN'T NOW BETTER I'D SAY YOU'VE JUST SEEN A GHOST.
KURBRAKKKRSSSTTT!!

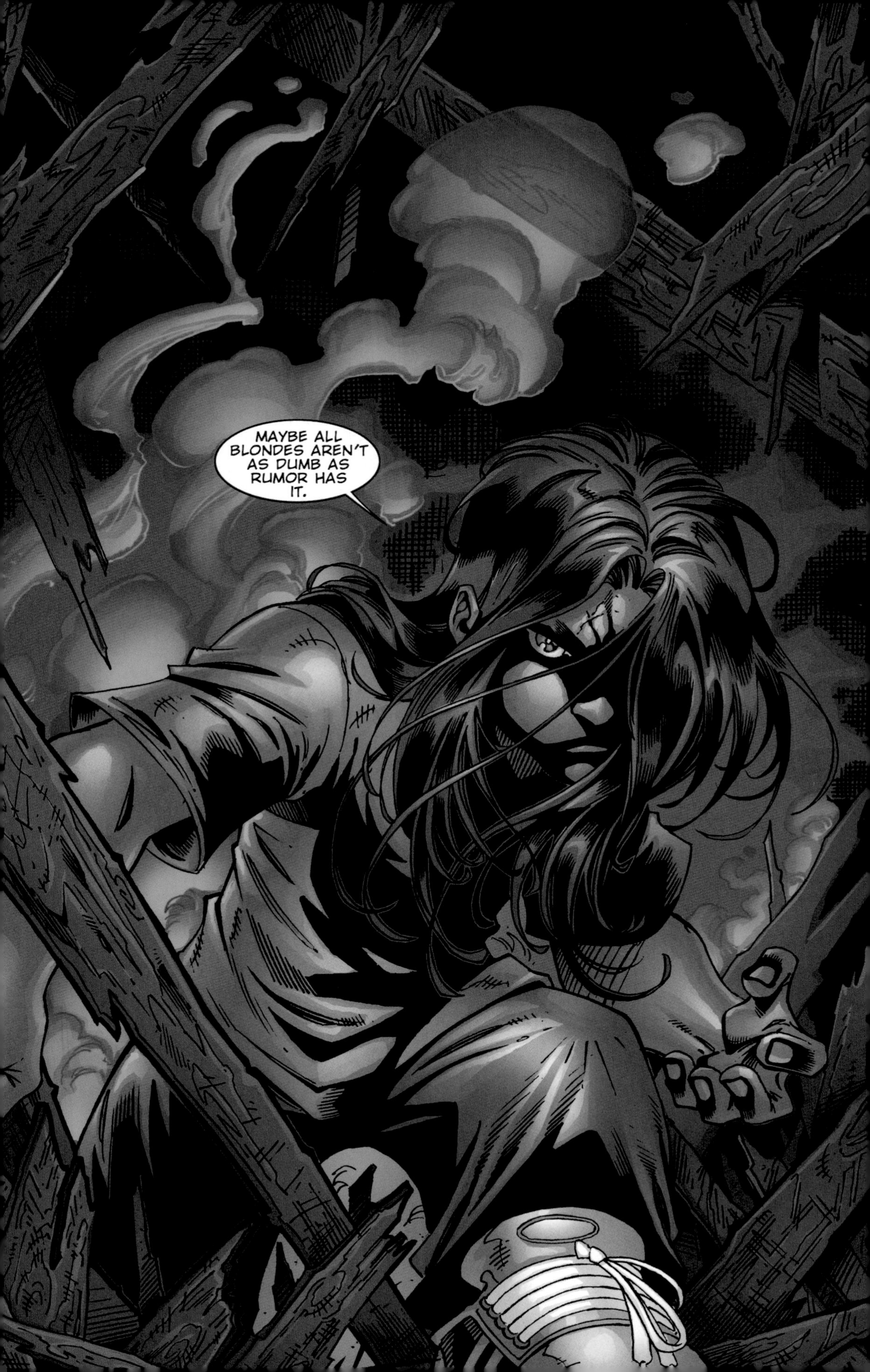
MAYBE ALL BLONDES AREN'T AS DUMB AS RUMOR HAS IT.

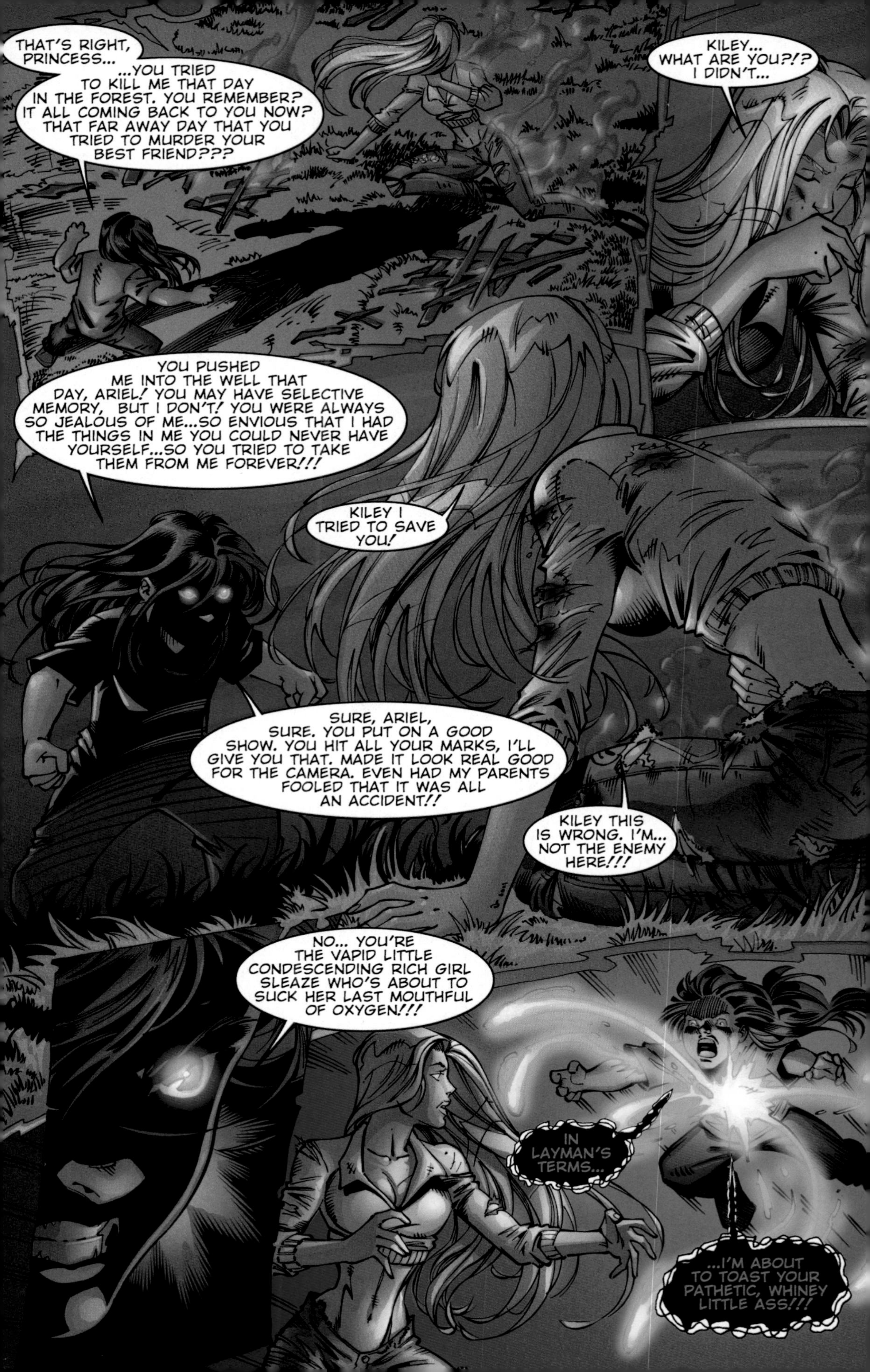
THAT'S RIGHT, PRINCESS...
...YOU TRIED TO KILL ME THAT DAY IN THE FOREST. YOU REMEMBER? IT ALL COMING BACK TO YOU NOW? THAT FAR AWAY DAY THAT YOU TRIED TO MURDER YOUR BEST FRIEND???
KILEY... WHAT ARE YOU?!? I DIDN'T...
YOU PUSHED ME INTO THE WELL THAT DAY, ARIEL! YOU MAY HAVE SELECTIVE MEMORY, BUT I DON'T! YOU WERE ALWAYS SO JEALOUS OF ME...SO ENVIOUS THAT I HAD THE THINGS IN ME YOU COULD NEVER HAVE YOURSELF...SO YOU TRIED TO TAKE THEM FROM ME FOREVER!!!
KILEY I TRIED TO SAVE YOU!
SURE, ARIEL, SURE. YOU PUT ON A GOOD SHOW. YOU HIT ALL YOUR MARKS, I'LL GIVE YOU THAT. MADE IT LOOK REAL GOOD FOR THE CAMERA. EVEN HAD MY PARENTS FOOLED THAT IT WAS ALL AN ACCIDENT!!
KILEY THIS IS WRONG. I'M... NOT THE ENEMY HERE!!!
NO... YOU'RE THE VAPID LITTLE CONDESCENDING RICH GIRL SLEAZE WHO'S ABOUT TO SUCK HER LAST MOUTHFUL OF OXYGEN!!!
IN LAYMAN'S TERMS...
...I'M ABOUT TO TOAST YOUR PATHETIC, WHINEY LITTLE ASS!!!

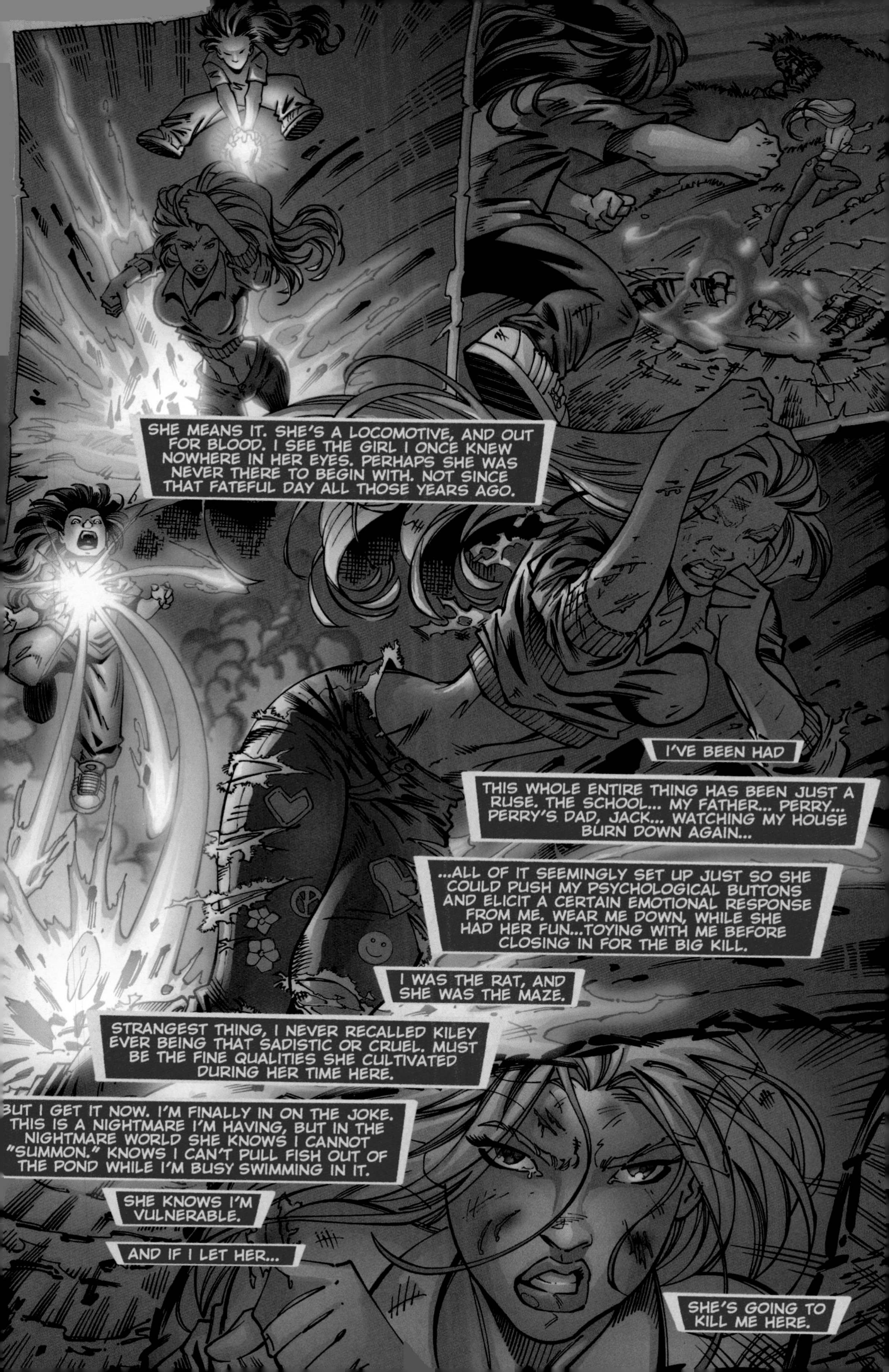
SHE MEANS IT. SHE'S A LOCOMOTIVE, AND OUT FOR BLOOD. I SEE THE GIRL I ONCE KNEW NOWHERE IN HER EYES. PERHAPS SHE WAS NEVER THERE TO BEGIN WITH. NOT SINCE THAT FATEFUL DAY ALL THOSE YEARS AGO.
I'VE BEEN HAD
THIS WHOLE ENTIRE THING HAS BEEN JUST A RUSE. THE SCHOOL... MY FATHER... PERRY... PERRY'S DAD, JACK... WATCHING MY HOUSE BURN DOWN AGAIN...
...ALL OF IT SEEMINGLY SET UP JUST SO SHE COULD PUSH MY PSYCHOLOGICAL BUTTONS AND ELICIT A CERTAIN EMOTIONAL RESPONSE FROM ME. WEAR ME DOWN, WHILE SHE HAD HER FUN...TOYING WITH ME BEFORE CLOSING IN FOR THE BIG KILL.
I WAS THE RAT, AND SHE WAS THE MAZE.
STRANGEST THING, I NEVER RECALLED KILEY EVER BEING THAT SADISTIC OR CRUEL. MUST BE THE FINE QUALITIES SHE CULTIVATED DURING HER TIME HERE.
BUT I GET IT NOW. I'M FINALLY IN ON THE JOKE. THIS IS A NIGHTMARE I'M HAVING, BUT IN THE NIGHTMARE WORLD SHE KNOWS I CANNOT "SUMMON." KNOWS I CAN'T PULL FISH OUT OF THE POND WHILE I'M BUSY SWIMMING IN IT.
SHE KNOWS I'M VULNERABLE.
AND IF I LET HER...
SHE'S GOING TO KILL ME HERE.

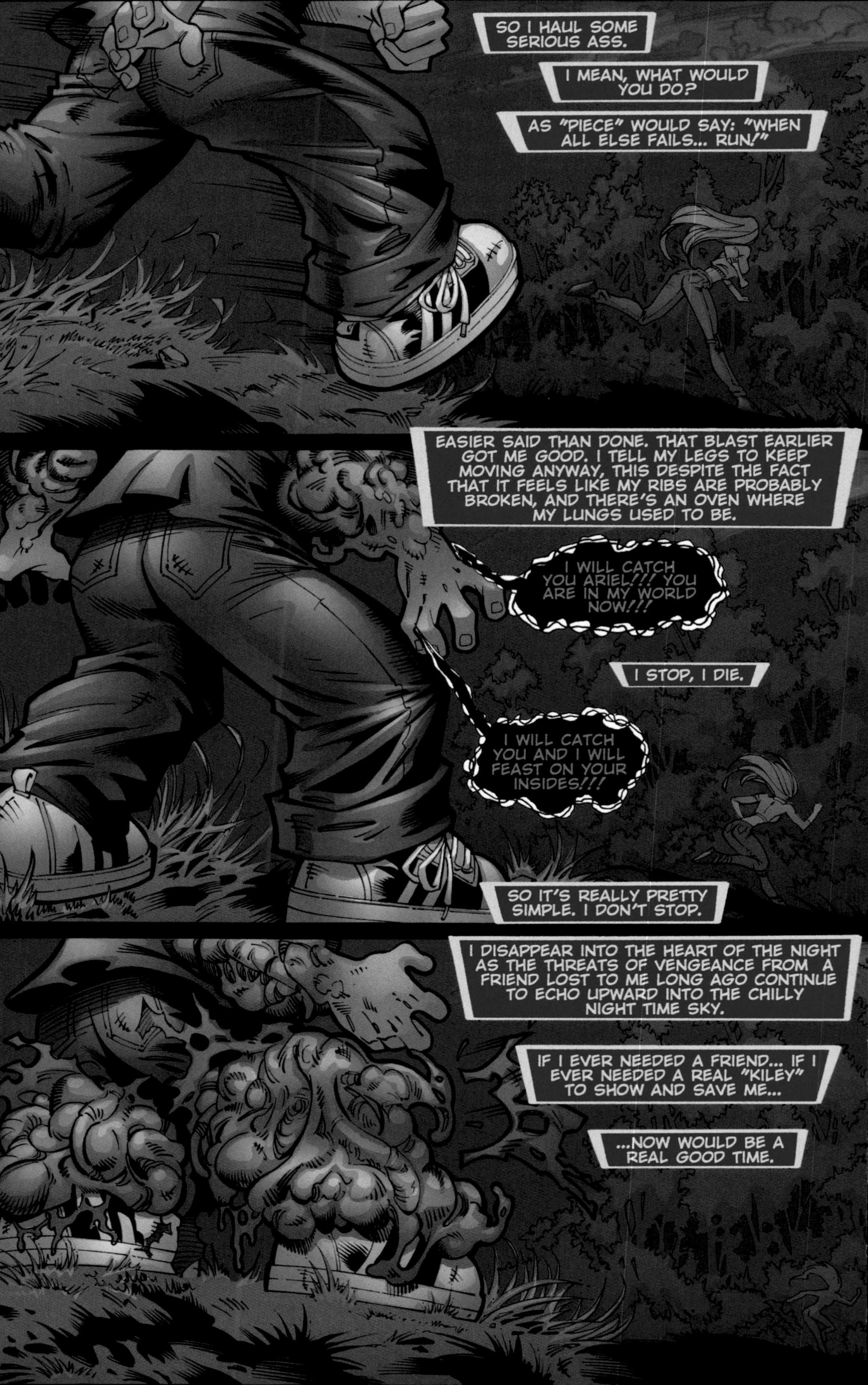
SO I HAUL SOME SERIOUS ASS.
I MEAN, WHAT WOULD YOU DO?
AS "PIECE" WOULD SAY: "WHEN ALL ELSE FAILS... RUN!"
EASIER SAID THAN DONE. THAT BLAST EARLIER GOT ME GOOD. I TELL MY LEGS TO KEEP MOVING ANYWAY, THIS DESPITE THE FACT THAT IT FEELS LIKE MY RIBS ARE PROBABLY BROKEN, AND THERE'S AN OVEN WHERE MY LUNGS USED TO BE.
I WILL CATCH YOU ARIEL!!! YOU ARE IN MY WORLD NOW!!!
I STOP, I DIE.
I WILL CATCH YOU AND I WILL FEAST ON YOUR INSIDES!!!
SO IT'S REALLY PRETTY SIMPLE. I DON'T STOP.
I DISAPPEAR INTO THE HEART OF THE NIGHT AS THE THREATS OF VENGEANCE FROM A FRIEND LOST TO ME LONG AGO CONTINUE TO ECHO UPWARD INTO THE CHILLY NIGHT TIME SKY.
IF I EVER NEEDED A FRIEND... IF I EVER NEEDED A REAL "KILEY" TO SHOW AND SAVE ME...
...NOW WOULD BE A REAL GOOD TIME.

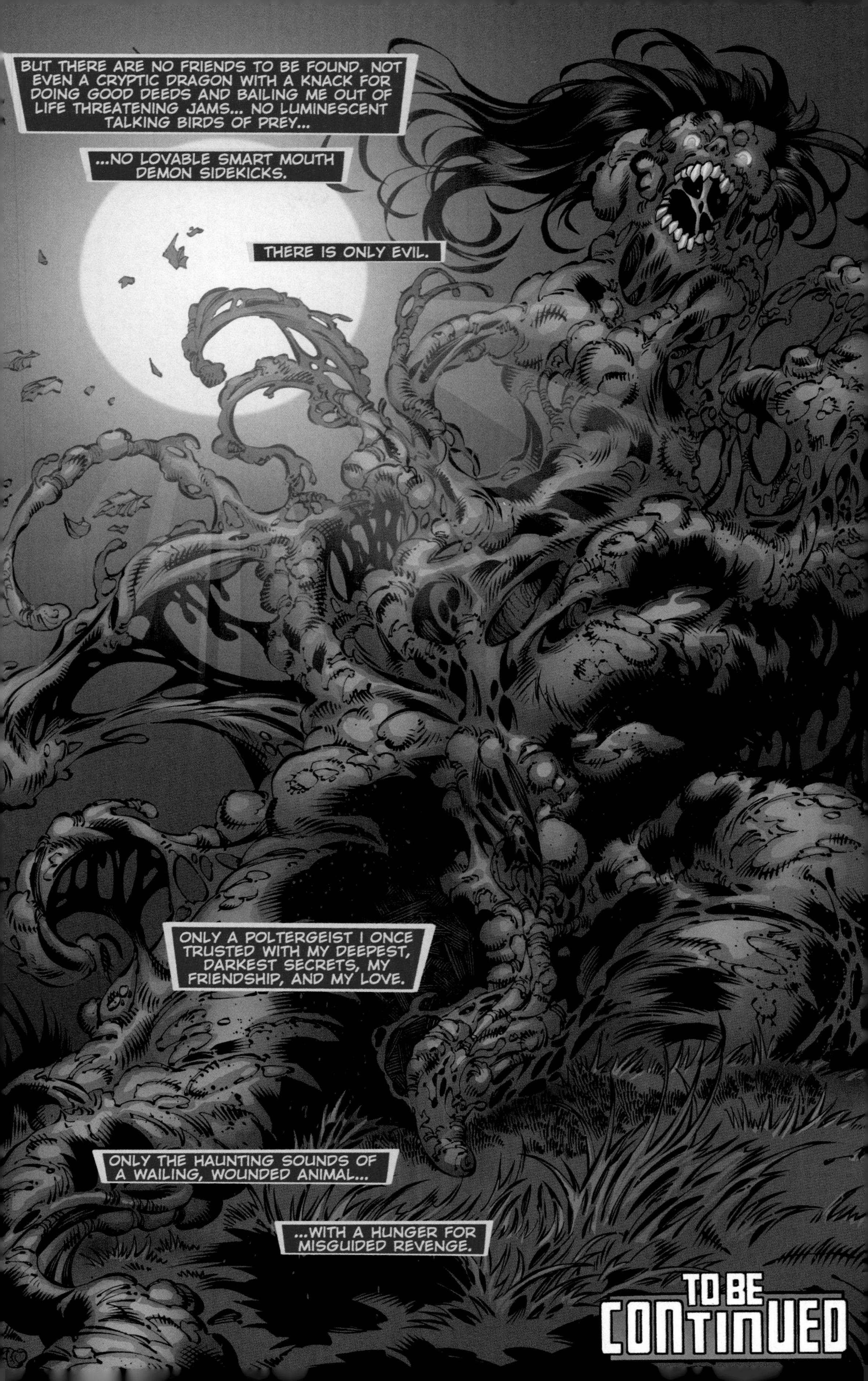
BUT THERE ARE NO FRIENDS TO BE FOUND. NOT EVEN A CRYPTIC DRAGON WITH A KNACK FOR DOING GOOD DEEDS AND BAILING ME OUT OF LIFE THREATENING JAMS... NO LUMINESCENT TALKING BIRDS OF PREY...
...NO LOVABLE SMART MOUTH DEMON SIDEKICKS.
THERE IS ONLY EVIL.
ONLY A POLTERGEIST I ONCE TRUSTED WITH MY DEEPEST, DARKEST SECRETS, MY FRIENDSHIP, AND MY LOVE.
ONLY THE HAUNTING SOUNDS OF A WAILING, WOUNDED ANIMAL...
...WITH A HUNGER FOR MISGUIDED REVENGE.
TO BE CONTINUED

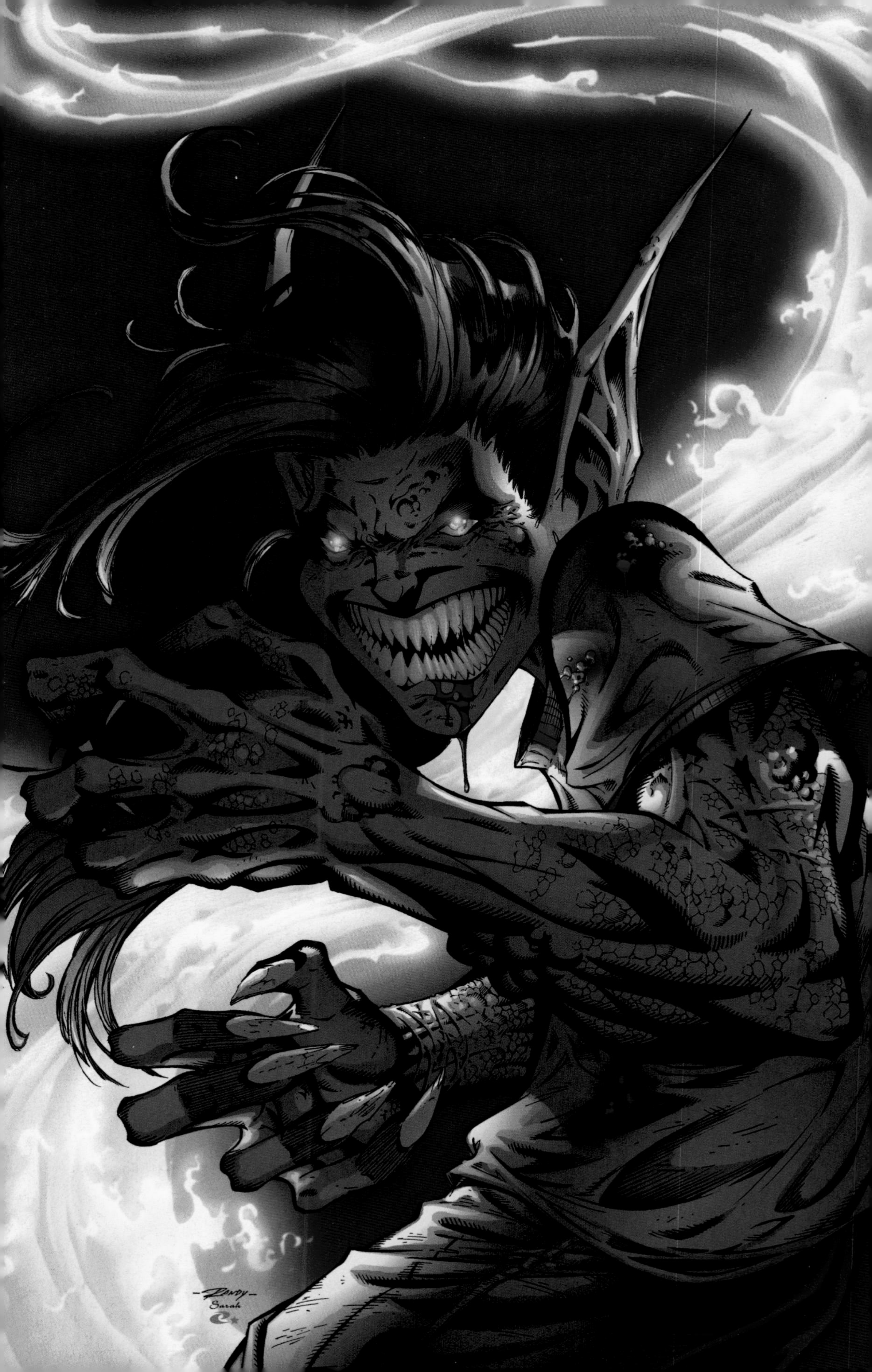

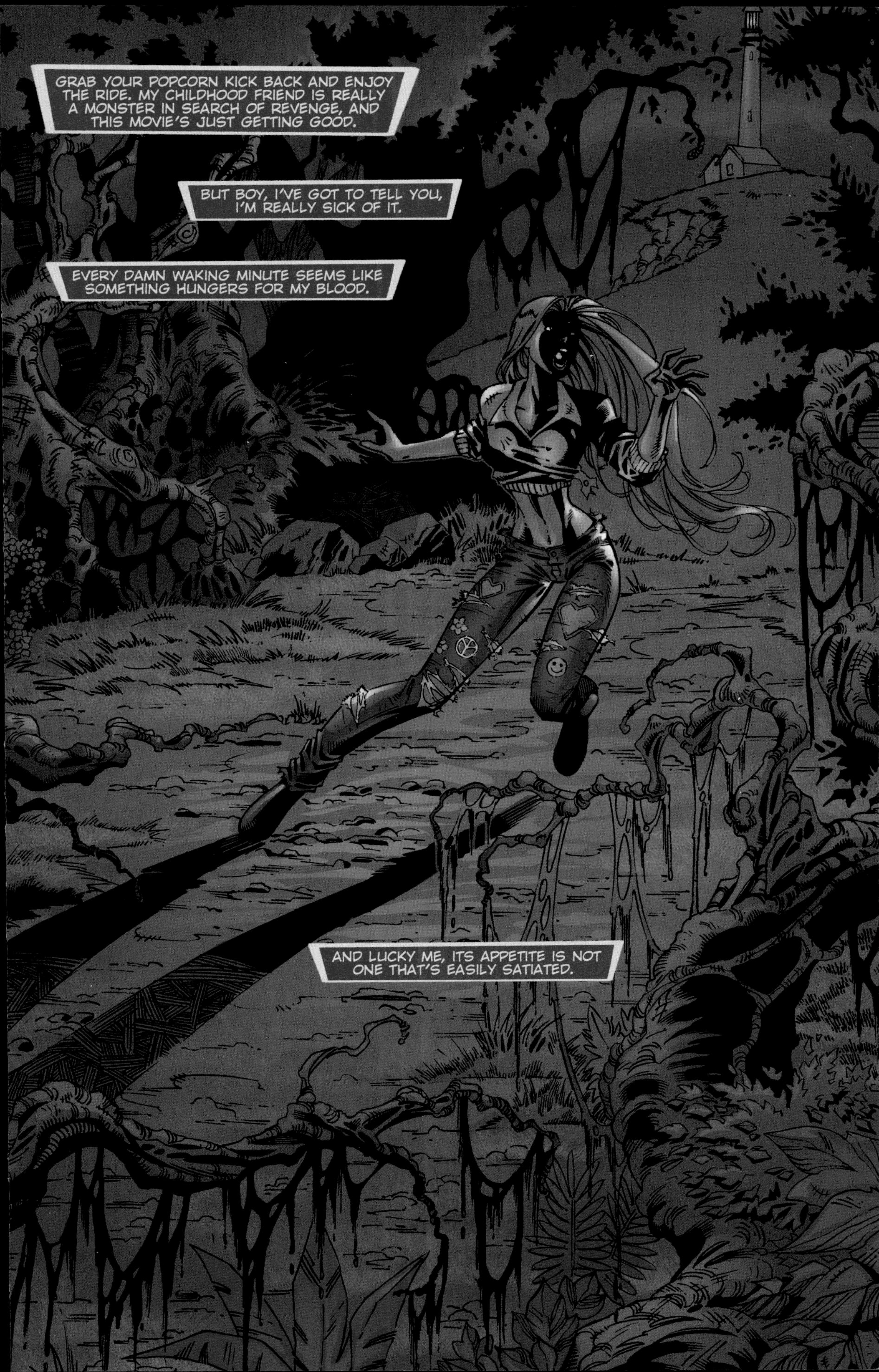
GRAB YOUR POPCORN KICK BACK AND ENJOY THE RIDE. MY CHILDHOOD FRIEND IS REALLY A MONSTER IN SEARCH OF REVENGE, AND THIS MOVIE'S JUST GETTING GOOD.
BUT BOY, I'VE GOT TO TELL YOU, I'M REALLY SICK OF IT.
EVERY DAMN WAKING MINUTE SEEMS LIKE SOMETHING HUNGERS FOR MY BLOOD.
AND LUCKY ME, ITS APPETITE IS NOT ONE THAT'S EASILY SATIATED.

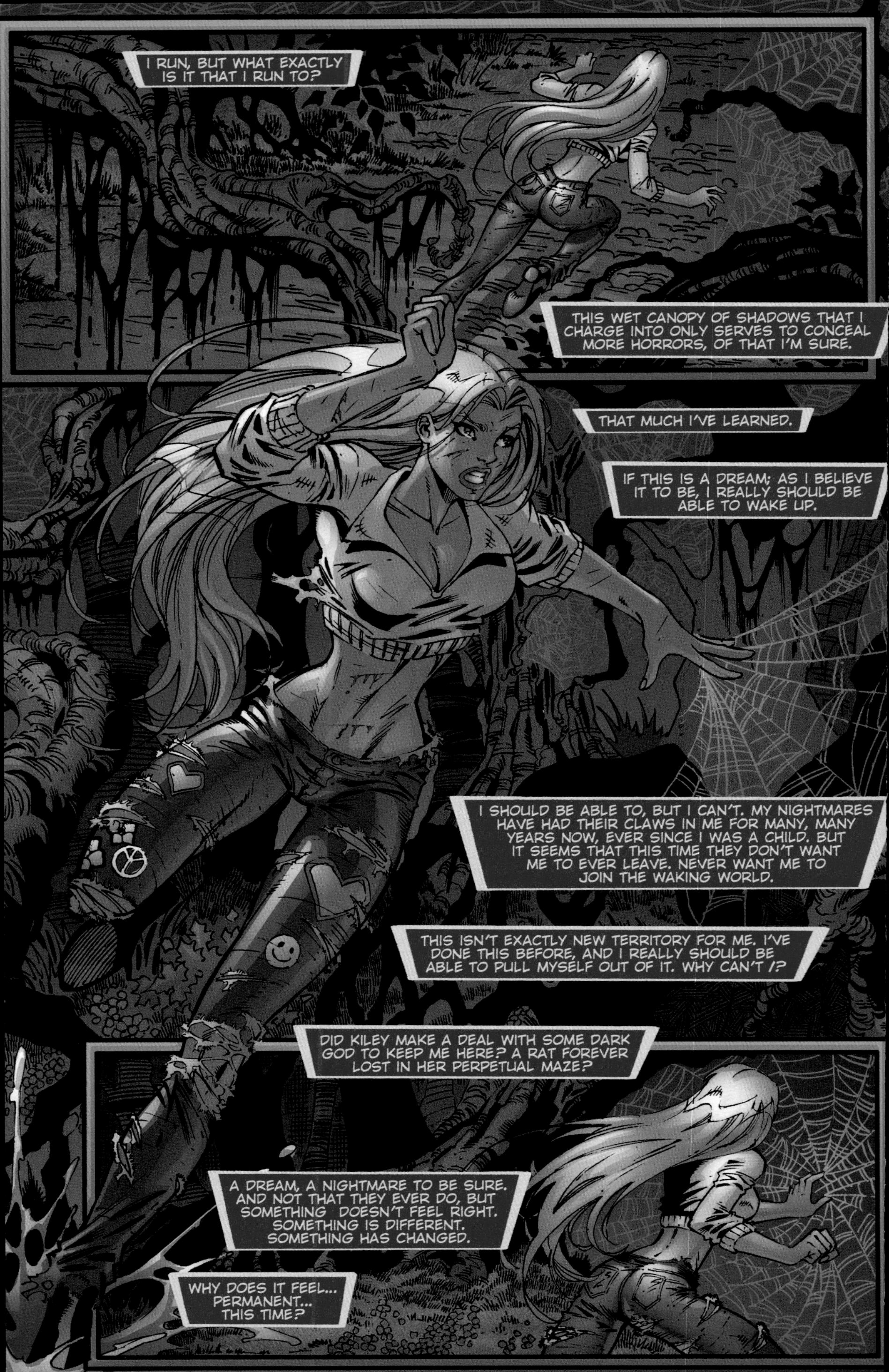
I RUN, BUT WHAT EXACTLY IS IT THAT I RUN TO?
THIS WET CANOPY OF SHADOWS THAT I CHARGE INTO ONLY SERVES TO CONCEAL MORE HORRORS, OF THAT I'M SURE.
THAT MUCH I'VE LEARNED.
IF THIS IS A DREAM; AS I BELIEVE IT TO BE, I REALLY SHOULD BE ABLE TO WAKE UP.
I SHOULD BE ABLE TO, BUT I CAN'T. MY NIGHTMARES HAVE HAD THEIR CLAWS IN ME FOR MANY, MANY YEARS NOW, EVER SINCE I WAS A CHILD. BUT IT SEEMS THAT THIS TIME THEY DON'T WANT ME TO EVER LEAVE. NEVER WANT ME TO JOIN THE WAKING WORLD.
THIS ISN'T EXACTLY NEW TERRITORY FOR ME. I'VE DONE THIS BEFORE, AND I REALLY SHOULD BE ABLE TO PULL MYSELF OUT OF IT. WHY CAN'T *I*?
DID KILEY MAKE A DEAL WITH SOME DARK GOD TO KEEP ME HERE? A RAT FOREVER LOST IN HER PERPETUAL MAZE?
A DREAM, A NIGHTMARE TO BE SURE. AND NOT THAT THEY EVER DO, BUT SOMETHING DOESN'T FEEL RIGHT. SOMETHING IS DIFFERENT. SOMETHING HAS CHANGED.
WHY DOES IT FEEL... PERMANENT... THIS TIME?

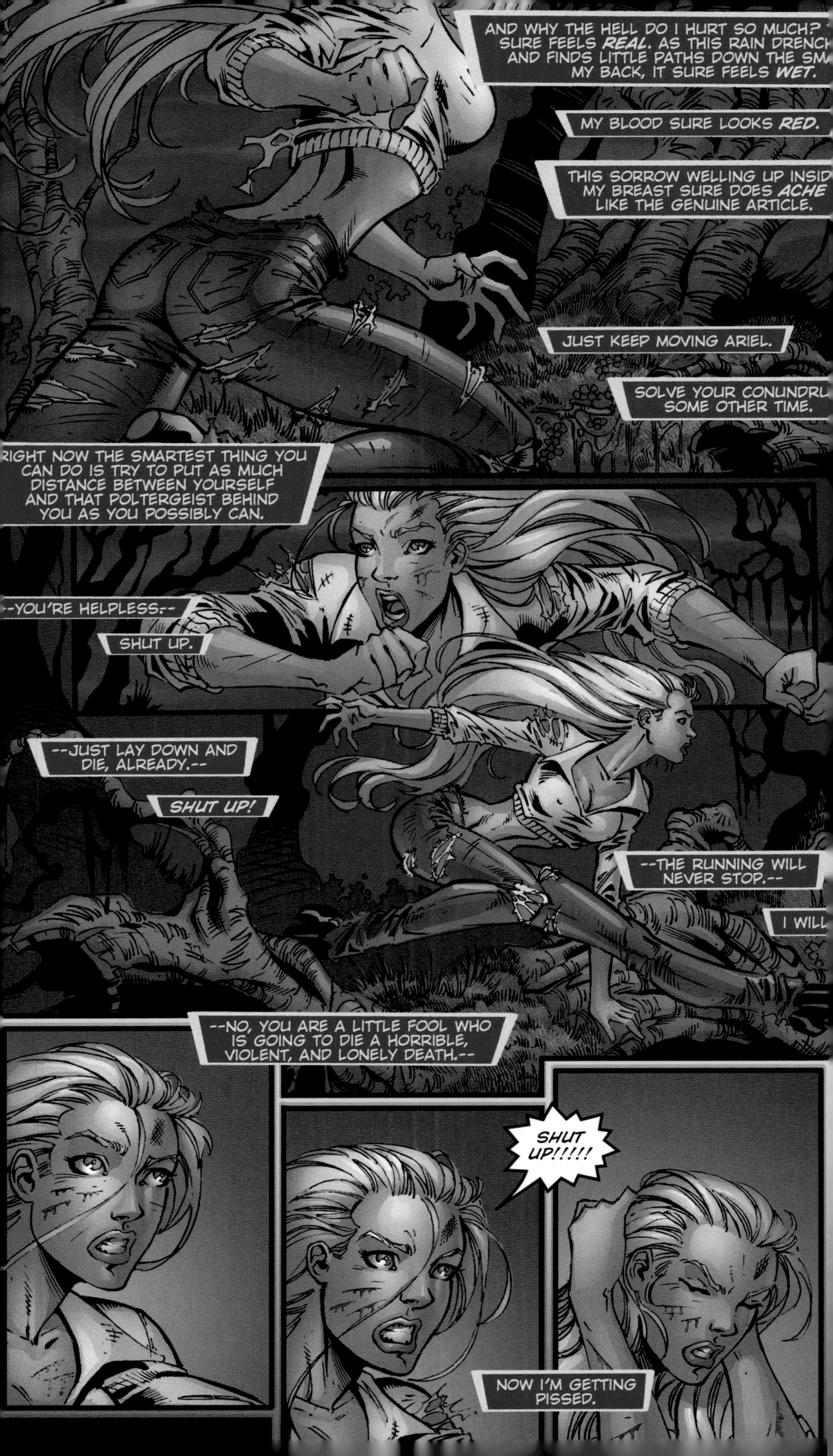
AND WHY THE HELL DO I HURT SO MUCH? SURE FEELS REAL. AS THIS RAIN DRENCH AND FINDS LITTLE PATHS DOWN THE SMA MY BACK, IT SURE FEELS WET.
MY BLOOD SURE LOOKS RED.
THIS SORROW WELLING UP INSID MY BREAST SURE DOES ACHE LIKE THE GENUINE ARTICLE.
JUST KEEP MOVING ARIEL.
SOLVE YOUR CONUNDRU SOME OTHER TIME.
RIGHT NOW THE SMARTEST THING YOU CAN DO IS TRY TO PUT AS MUCH DISTANCE BETWEEN YOURSELF AND THAT POLTERGEIST BEHIND YOU AS YOU POSSIBLY CAN.
--YOU'RE HELPLESS.--
SHUT UP.
--JUST LAY DOWN AND DIE, ALREADY.--
SHUT UP!
--THE RUNNING WILL NEVER STOP.--
I WILL
--NO, YOU ARE A LITTLE FOOL WHO IS GOING TO DIE A HORRIBLE, VIOLENT, AND LONELY DEATH.--
SHUT UP!!!!!
NOW I'M GETTING PISSED.

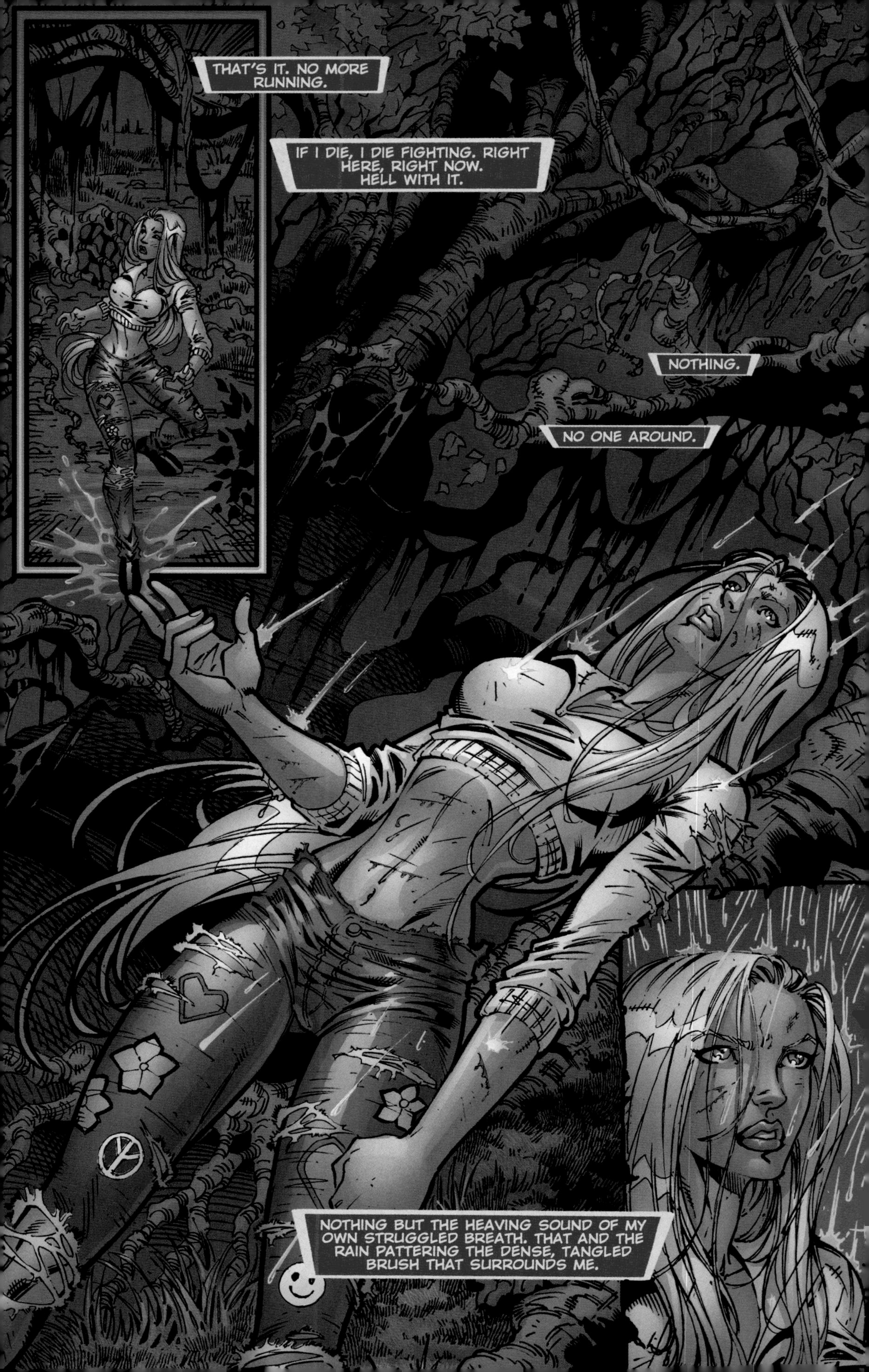
THAT'S IT. NO MORE RUNNING.
IF I DIE, I DIE FIGHTING. RIGHT HERE, RIGHT NOW. HELL WITH IT.
NOTHING.
NO ONE AROUND.
NOTHING BUT THE HEAVING SOUND OF MY OWN STRUGGLED BREATH. THAT AND THE RAIN PATTERING THE DENSE, TANGLED BRUSH THAT SURROUNDS ME.

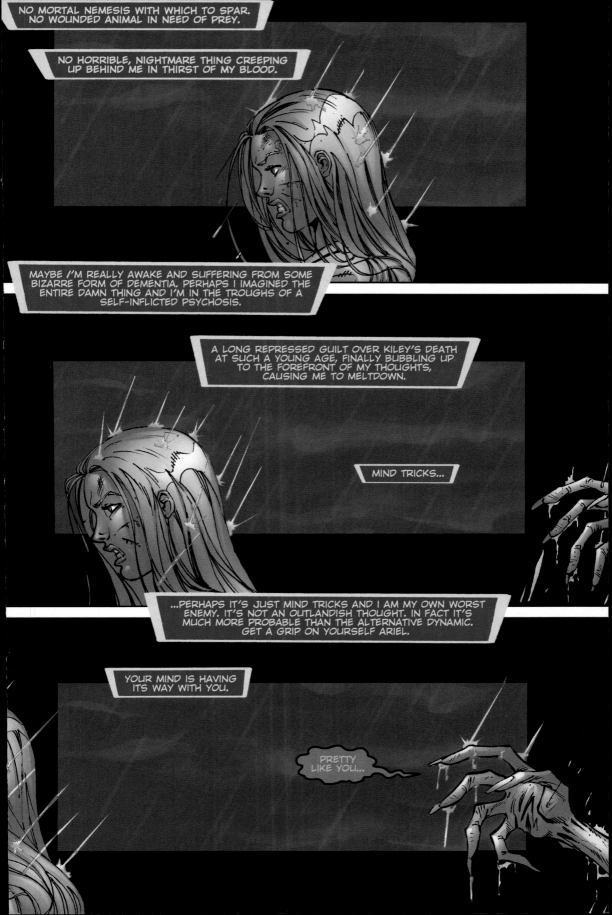

NO MORTAL NEMESIS WITH WHICH TO SPAR. NO WOUNDED ANIMAL IN NEED OF PREY.

NO HORRIBLE, NIGHTMARE THING CREEPING UP BEHIND ME IN THIRST OF MY BLOOD.

MAYBE I'M REALLY AWAKE AND SUFFERING FROM SOME BIZARRE FORM OF DEMENTIA. PERHAPS I IMAGINED THE ENTIRE DAMN THING AND I'M IN THE TROUGHS OF A SELF-INFLICTED PSYCHOSIS.

A LONG REPRESSED GUILT OVER KILEY'S DEATH AT SUCH A YOUNG AGE, FINALLY BUBBLING UP. TO THE FOREFRONT OF MY THOUGHTS, CAUSING ME TO MELTDOWN.

MIND TRICKS...

...PERHAPS IT'S JUST MIND TRICKS AND I AM MY OWN WORST ENEMY. IT'S NOT AN OUTLANDISH THOUGHT. IN FACT IT'S MUCH MORE PROBABLE THAN THE ALTERNATIVE DYNAMIC. GET A GRIP ON YOURSELF ARIEL.

YOUR MIND IS HAVING ITS WAY WITH YOU.

PRETTY LIKE YOU...

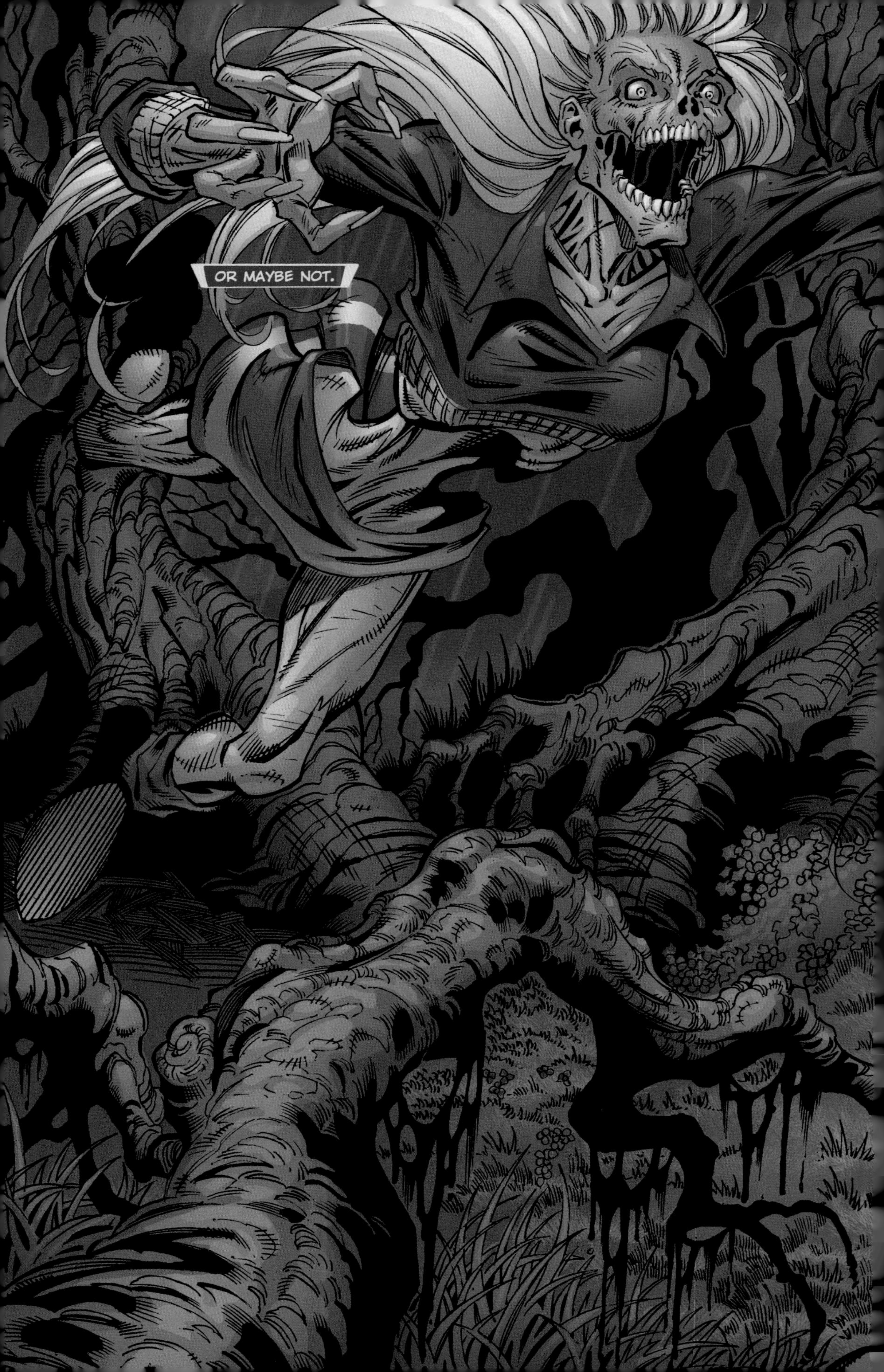
OR MAYBE NOT.

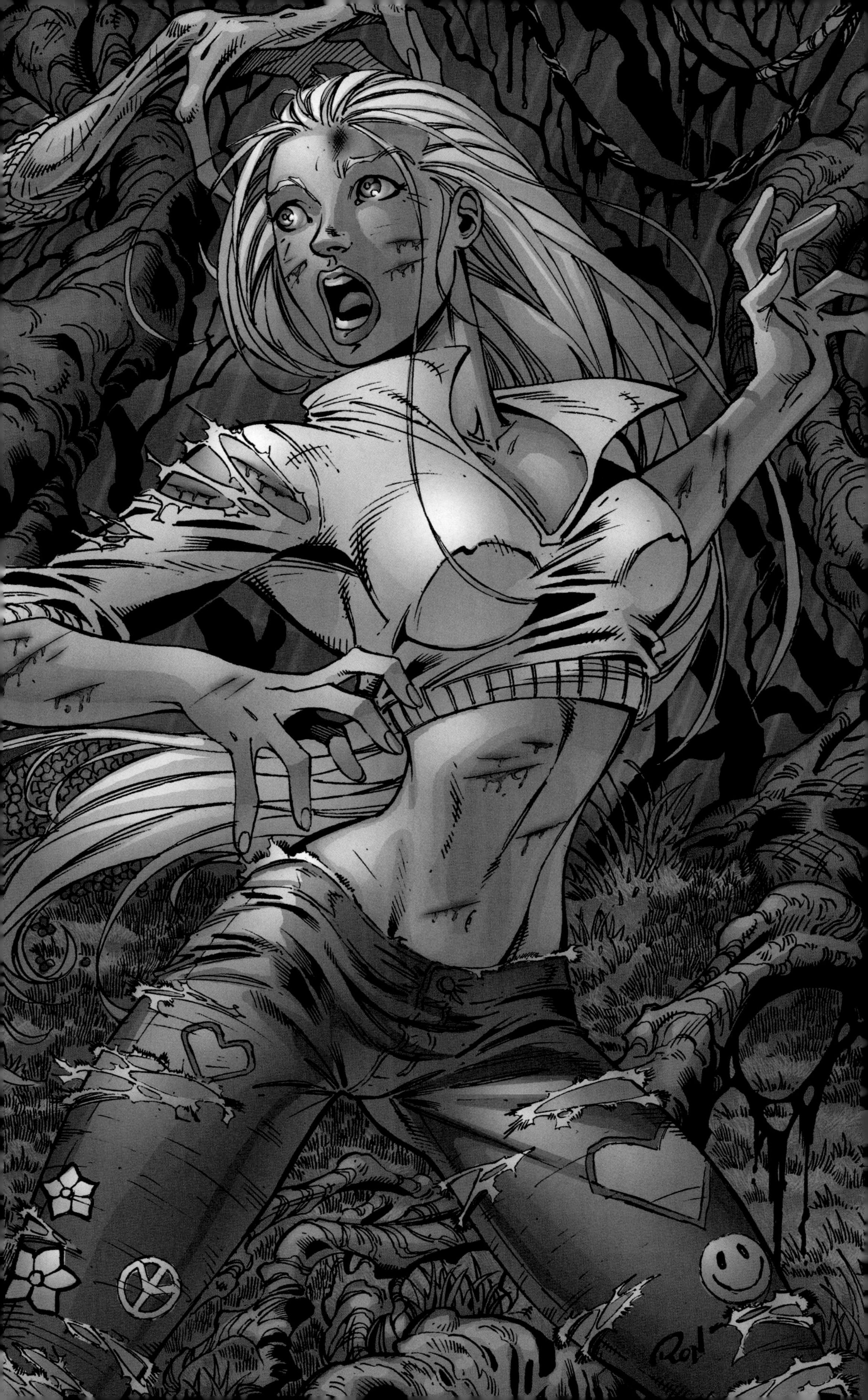

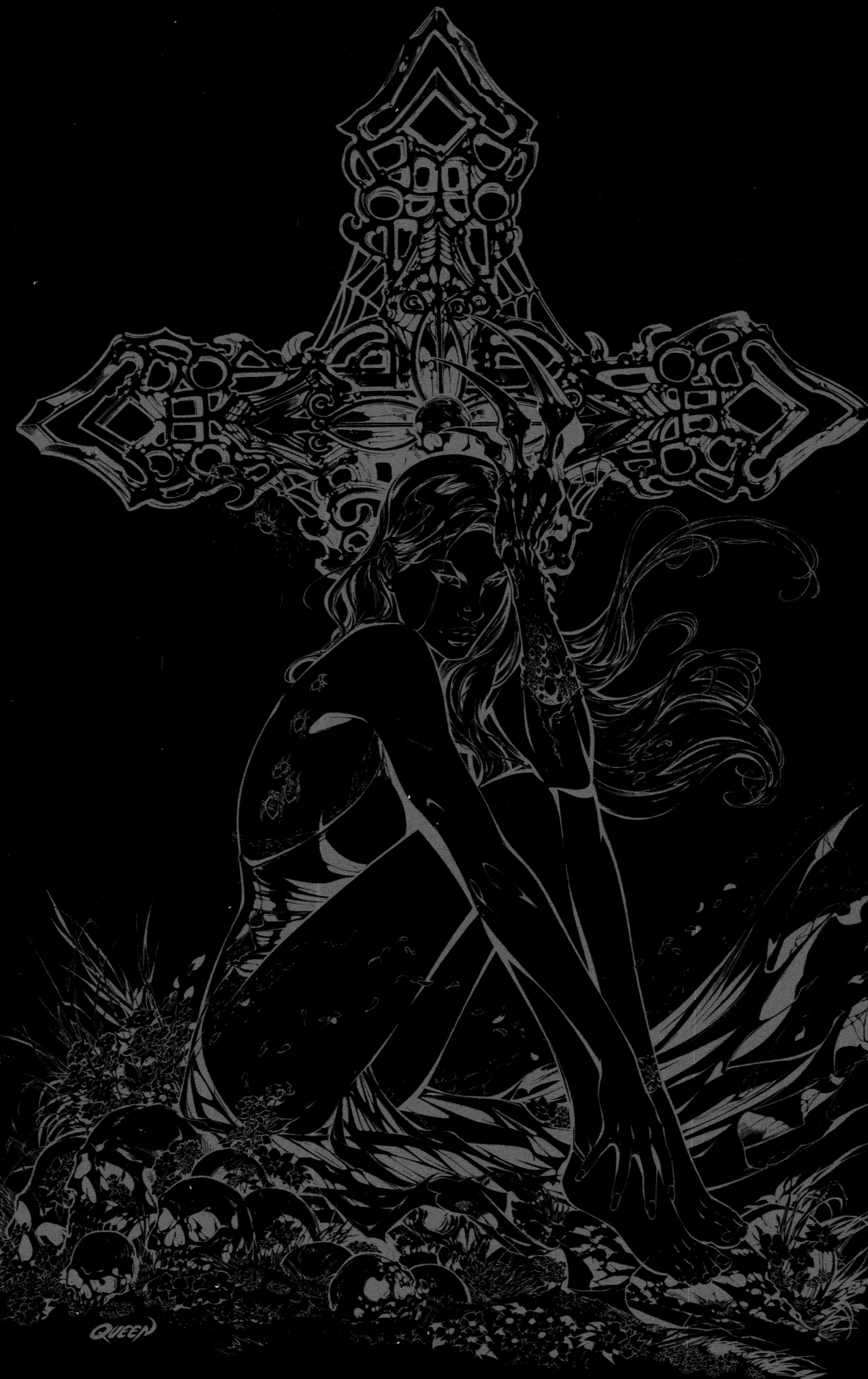
QUEEN

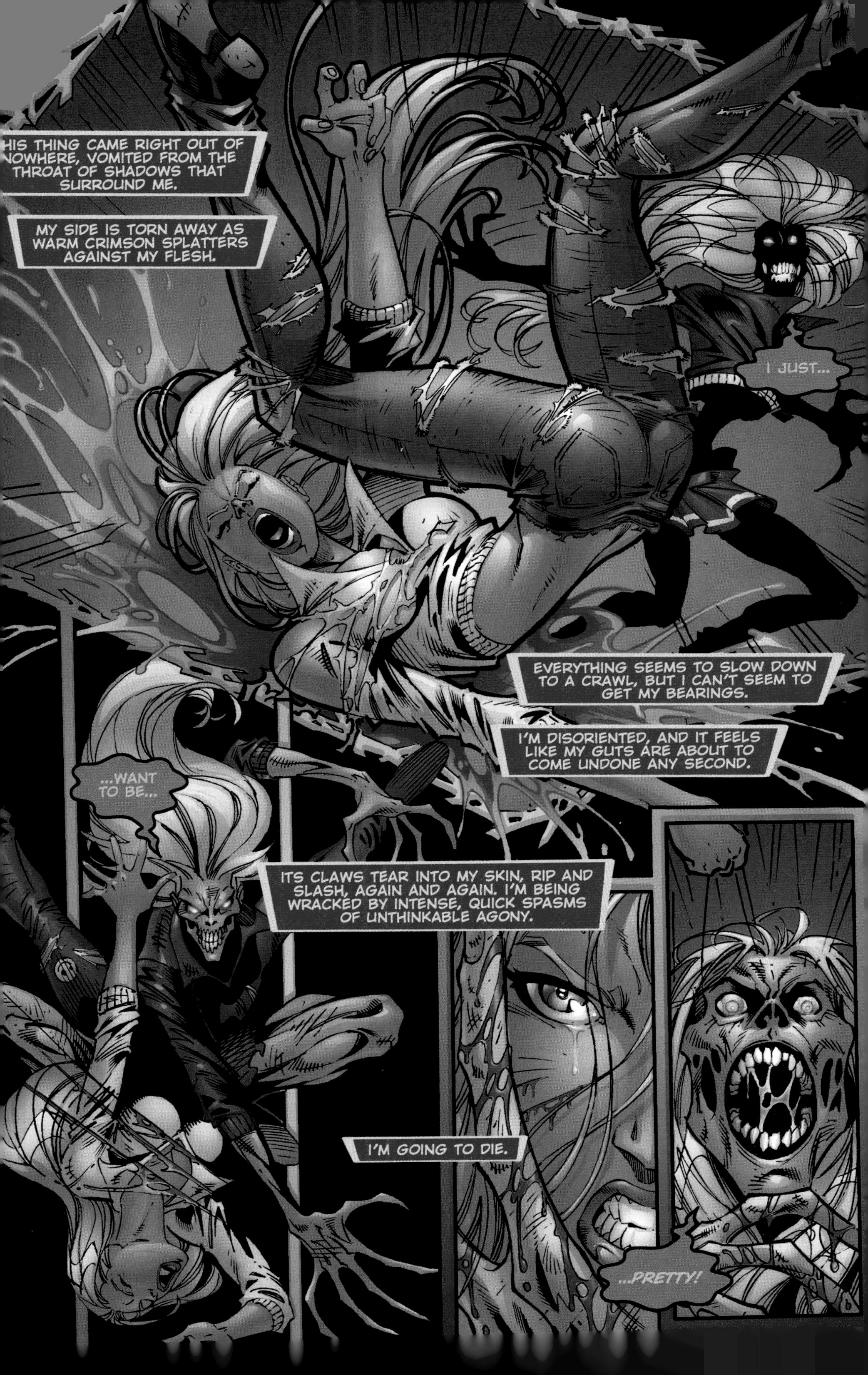
HIS THING CAME RIGHT OUT OF NOWHERE, VOMITED FROM THE THROAT OF SHADOWS THAT SURROUND ME.
MY SIDE IS TORN AWAY AS WARM CRIMSON SPLATTERS AGAINST MY FLESH.
I JUST...
EVERYTHING SEEMS TO SLOW DOWN TO A CRAWL, BUT I CAN'T SEEM TO GET MY BEARINGS.
I'M DISORIENTED, AND IT FEELS LIKE MY GUTS ARE ABOUT TO COME UNDONE ANY SECOND.
...WANT TO BE...
ITS CLAWS TEAR INTO MY SKIN, RIP AND SLASH, AGAIN AND AGAIN. I'M BEING WRACKED BY INTENSE, QUICK SPASMS OF UNTHINKABLE AGONY.
I'M GOING TO DIE.
...PRETTY!

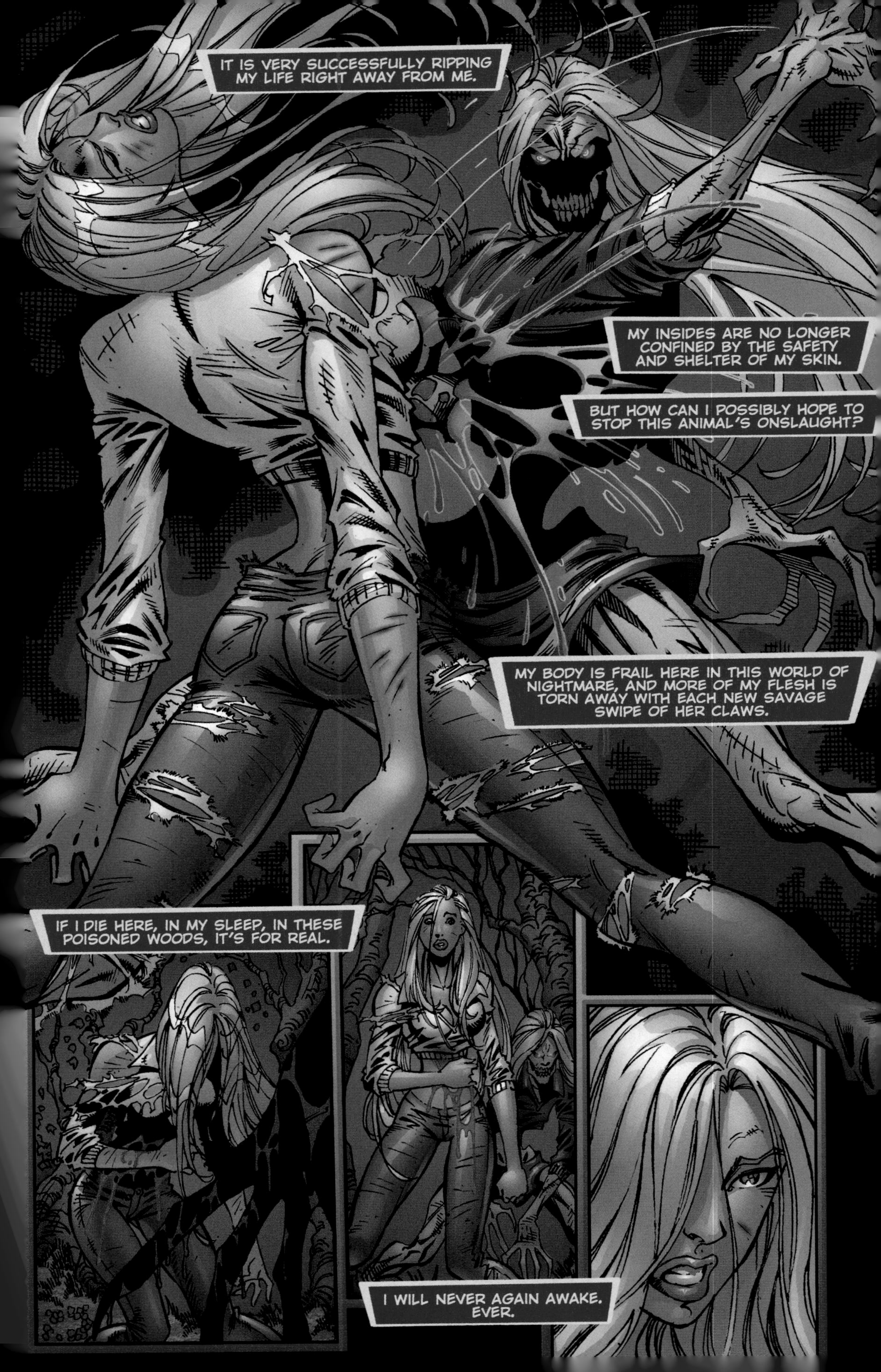

IT IS VERY SUCCESSFULLY RIPPING MY LIFE RIGHT AWAY FROM ME.
MY INSIDES ARE NO LONGER CONFINED BY THE SAFETY AND SHELTER OF MY SKIN.
BUT HOW CAN I POSSIBLY HOPE TO STOP THIS ANIMAL'S ONSLAUGHT?
MY BODY IS FRAIL HERE IN THIS WORLD OF NIGHTMARE, AND MORE OF MY FLESH IS TORN AWAY WITH EACH NEW SAVAGE SWIPE OF HER CLAWS.
IF I DIE HERE, IN MY SLEEP, IN THESE POISONED WOODS, IT'S FOR REAL.
I WILL NEVER AGAIN AWAKE. EVER.

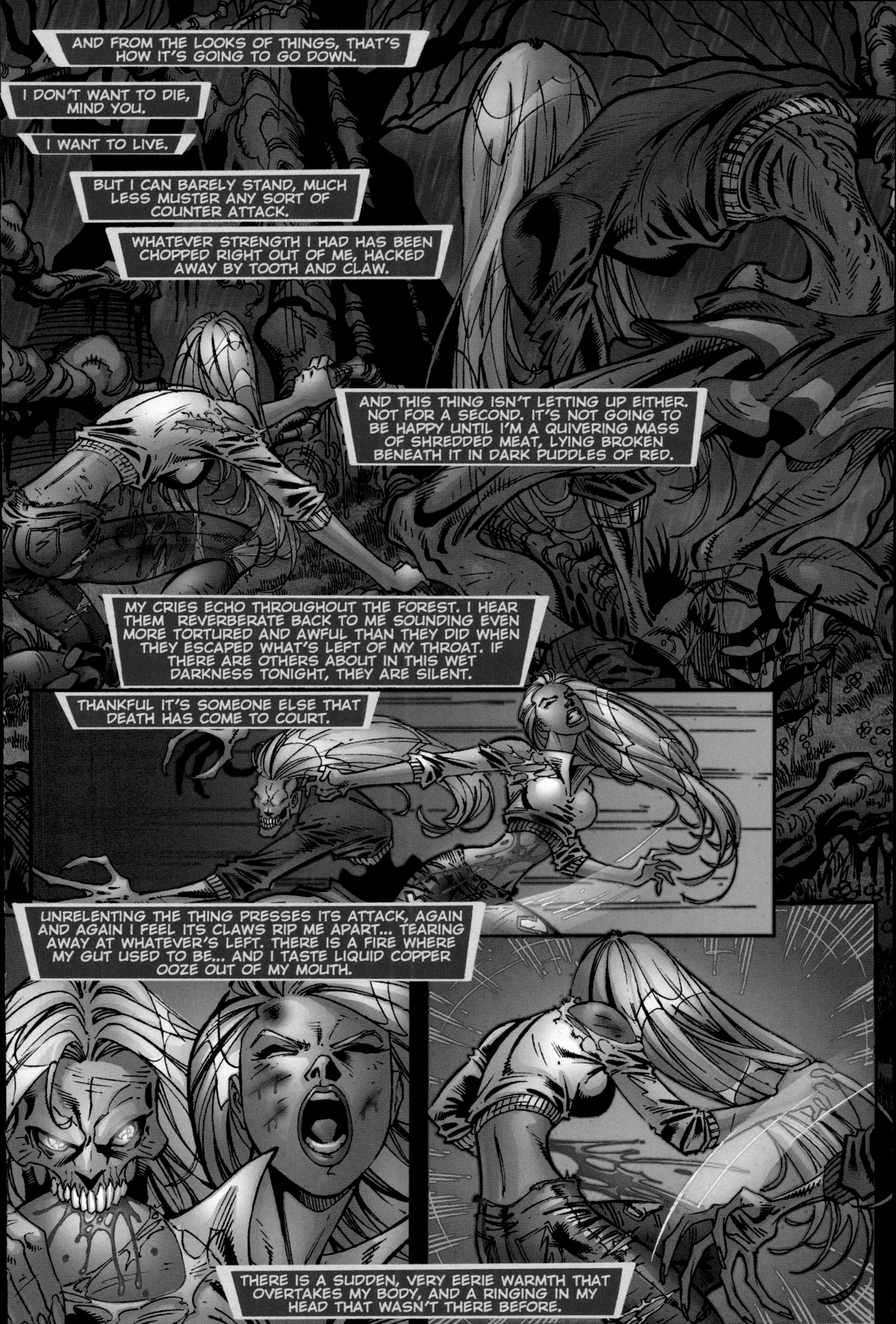
AND FROM THE LOOKS OF THINGS, THAT'S HOW IT'S GOING TO GO DOWN.
I DON'T WANT TO DIE, MIND YOU.
I WANT TO LIVE.
BUT I CAN BARELY STAND, MUCH LESS MUSTER ANY SORT OF COUNTER ATTACK.
WHATEVER STRENGTH I HAD HAS BEEN CHOPPED RIGHT OUT OF ME, HACKED AWAY BY TOOTH AND CLAW.
AND THIS THING ISN'T LETTING UP EITHER. NOT FOR A SECOND. IT'S NOT GOING TO BE HAPPY UNTIL I'M A QUIVERING MASS OF SHREDDED MEAT, LYING BROKEN BENEATH IT IN DARK PUDDLES OF RED.
MY CRIES ECHO THROUGHOUT THE FOREST. I HEAR THEM REVERBERATE BACK TO ME SOUNDING EVEN MORE TORTURED AND AWFUL THAN THEY DID WHEN THEY ESCAPED WHAT'S LEFT OF MY THROAT. IF THERE ARE OTHERS ABOUT IN THIS WET DARKNESS TONIGHT, THEY ARE SILENT.
THANKFUL IT'S SOMEONE ELSE THAT DEATH HAS COME TO COURT.
UNRELENTING THE THING PRESSES ITS ATTACK, AGAIN AND AGAIN I FEEL ITS CLAWS RIP ME APART... TEARING AWAY AT WHATEVER'S LEFT. THERE IS A FIRE WHERE MY GUT USED TO BE... AND I TASTE LIQUID COPPER OOZE OUT OF MY MOUTH.
THERE IS A SUDDEN, VERY EERIE WARMTH THAT OVERTAKES MY BODY, AND A RINGING IN MY HEAD THAT WASN'T THERE BEFORE.

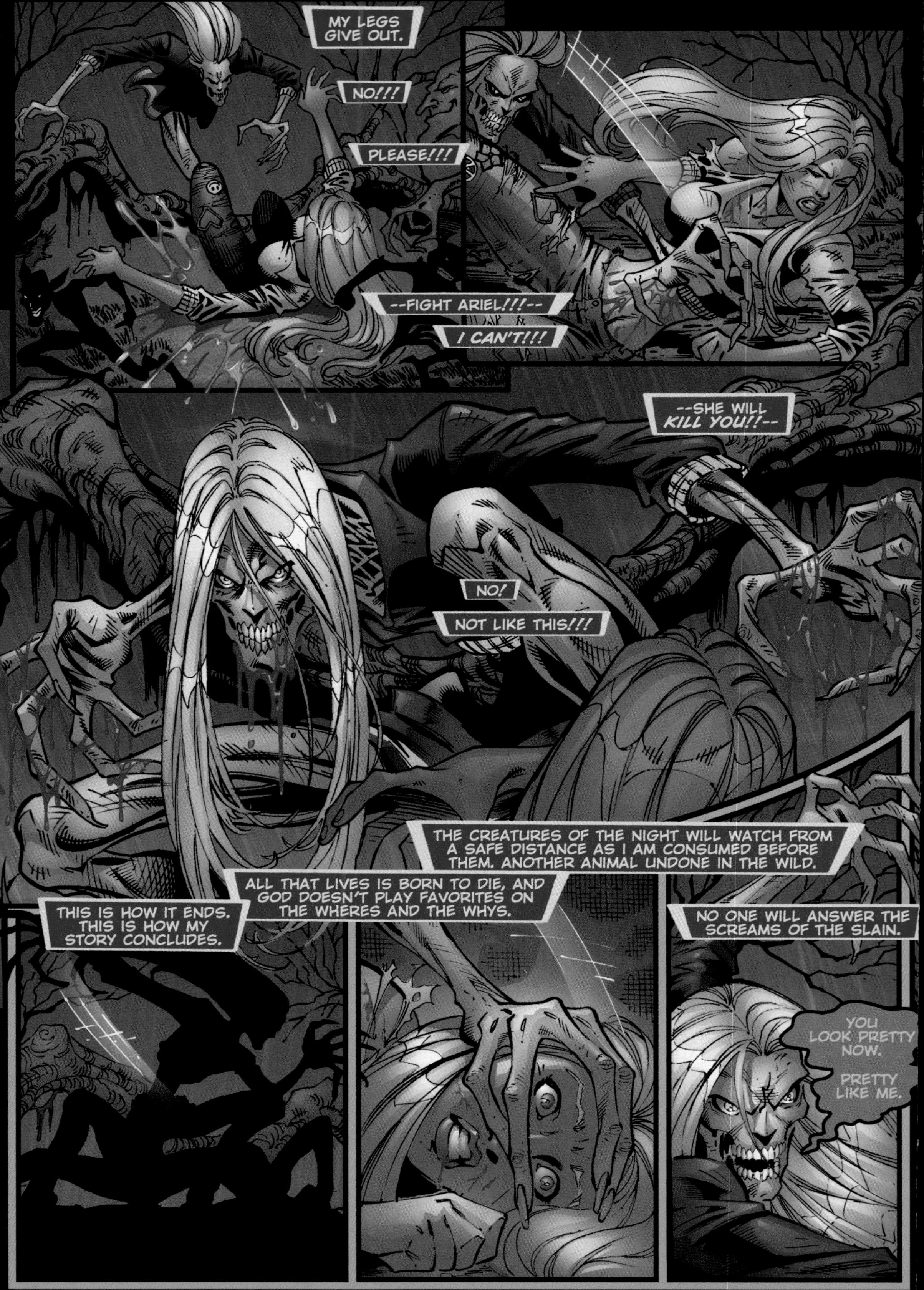
MY LEGS GIVE OUT.
NO!!!
PLEASE!!!
--FIGHT ARIEL!!!--
I CAN'T!!!
--SHE WILL KILL YOU!!--
NO!
NOT LIKE THIS!!!
THE CREATURES OF THE NIGHT WILL WATCH FROM A SAFE DISTANCE AS I AM CONSUMED BEFORE THEM. ANOTHER ANIMAL UNDONE IN THE WILD.
THIS IS HOW IT ENDS. THIS IS HOW MY STORY CONCLUDES.
ALL THAT LIVES IS BORN TO DIE, AND GOD DOESN'T PLAY FAVORITES ON THE WHERES AND THE WHYS.
NO ONE WILL ANSWER THE SCREAMS OF THE SLAIN.
YOU LOOK PRETTY NOW.
PRETTY LIKE ME.

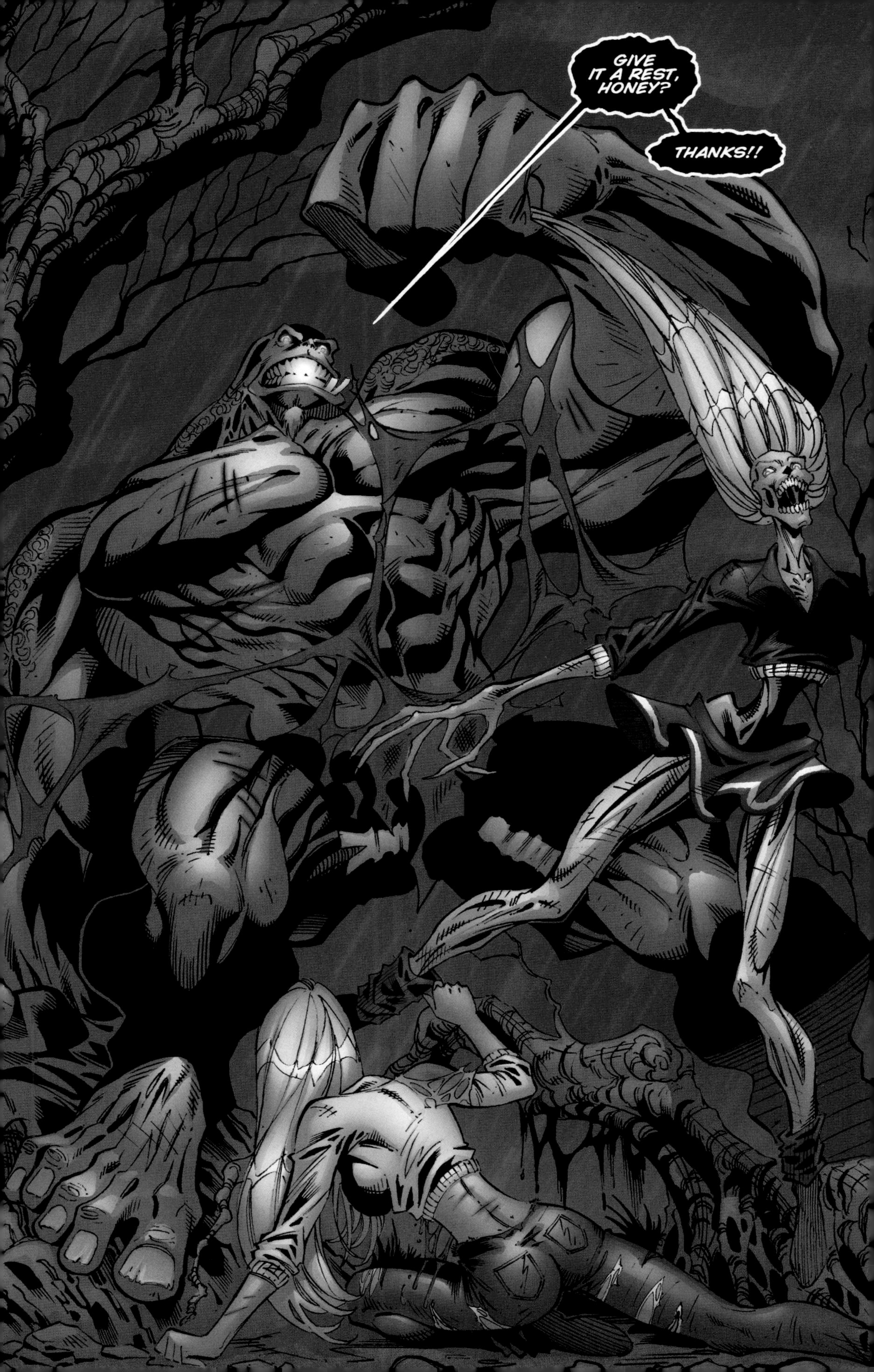
GIVE IT A REST, HONEY?
THANKS!!

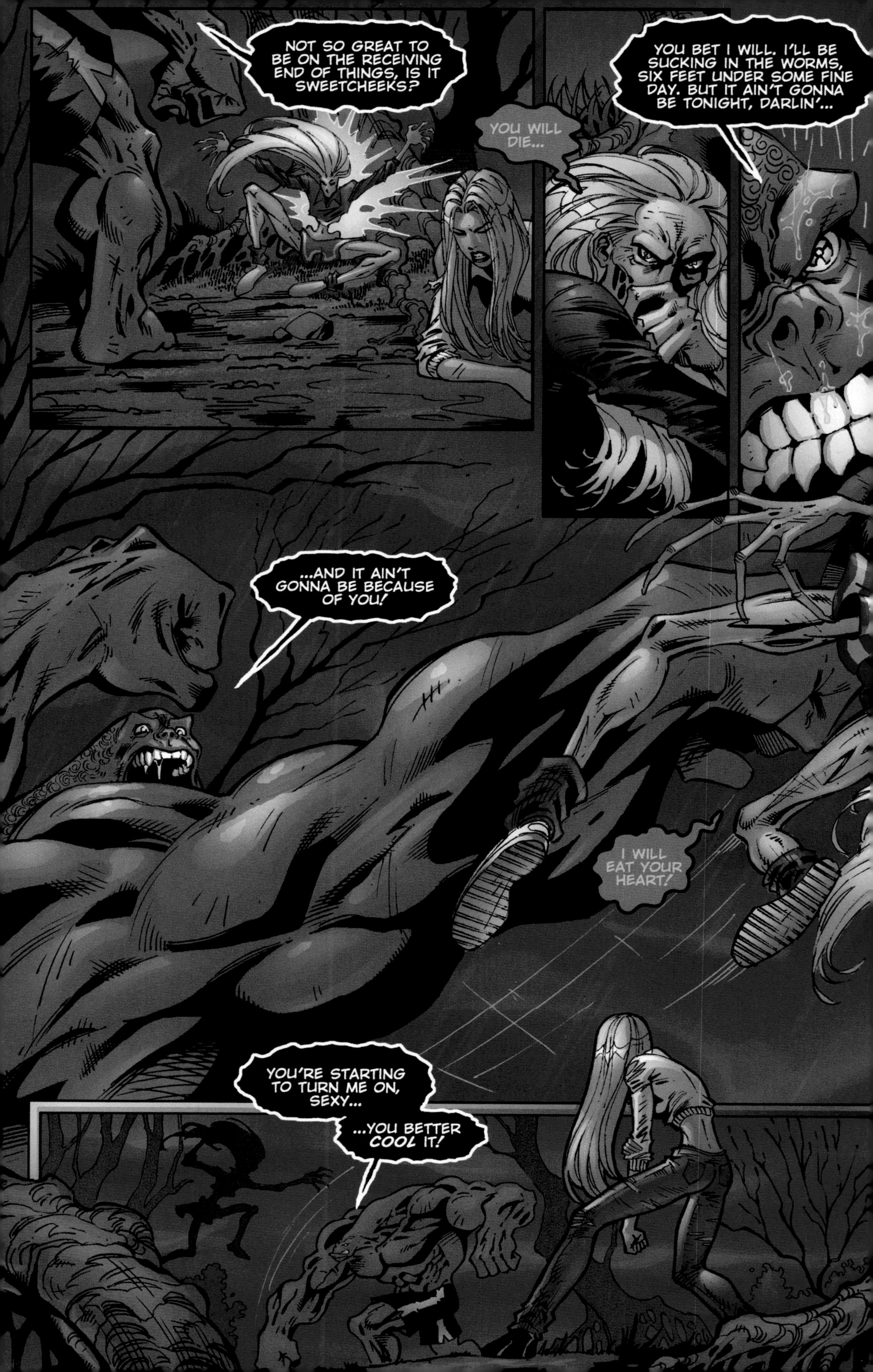
NOT SO GREAT TO BE ON THE RECEIVING END OF THINGS, IS IT SWEETCHEEKS?
YOU WILL DIE...
YOU BET I WILL. I'LL BE SUCKING IN THE WORMS, SIX FEET UNDER SOME FINE DAY. BUT IT AIN'T GONNA BE TONIGHT, DARLIN'...
...AND IT AIN'T GONNA BE BECAUSE OF YOU!
I WILL EAT YOUR HEART!
YOU'RE STARTING TO TURN ME ON, SEXY...
...YOU BETTER *COOL* IT!

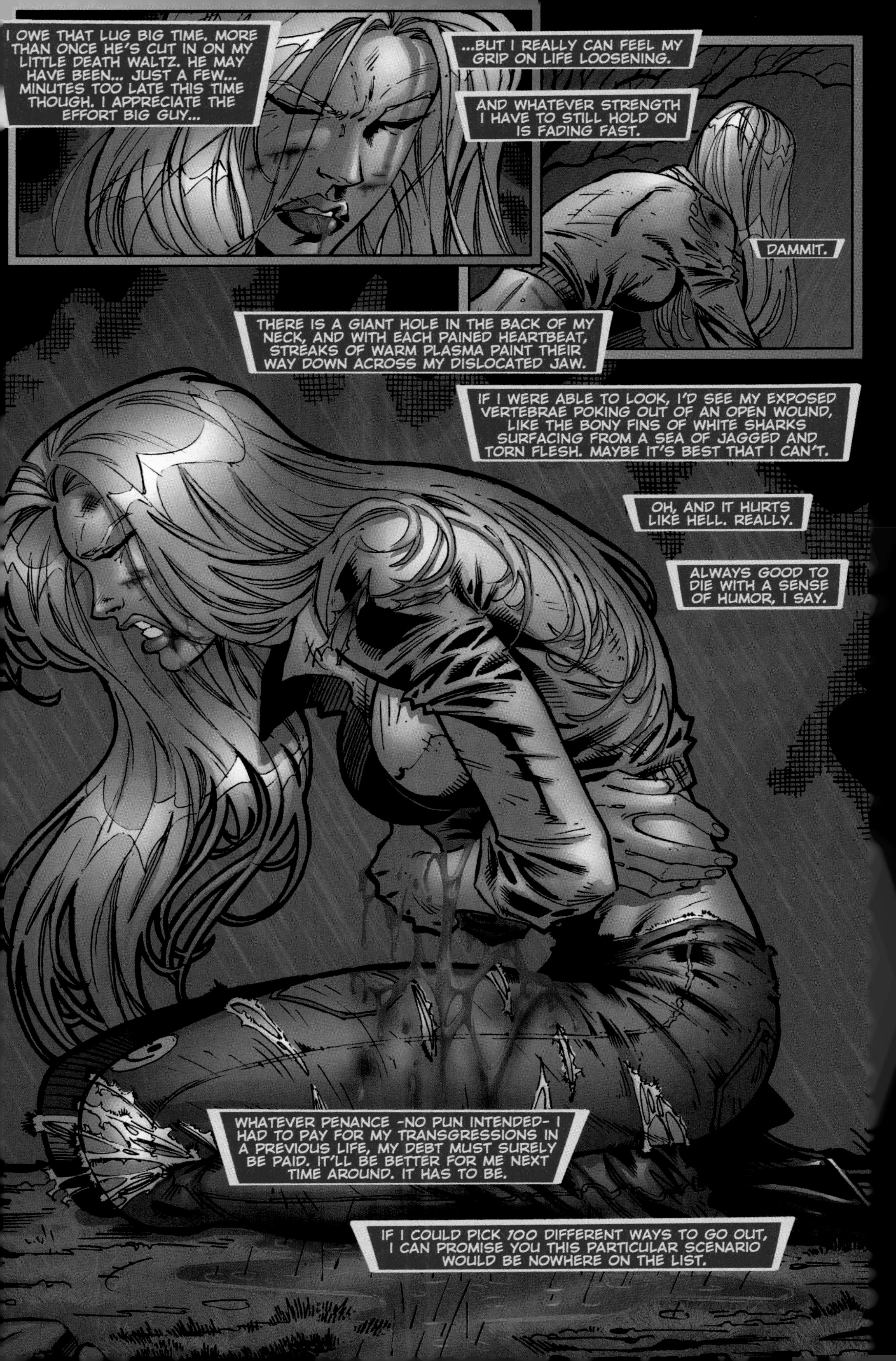
I OWE THAT LUG BIG TIME. MORE THAN ONCE HE'S CUT IN ON MY LITTLE DEATH WALTZ. HE MAY HAVE BEEN... JUST A FEW... MINUTES TOO LATE THIS TIME THOUGH. I APPRECIATE THE EFFORT BIG GUY...
...BUT I REALLY CAN FEEL MY GRIP ON LIFE LOOSENING.
AND WHATEVER STRENGTH I HAVE TO STILL HOLD ON IS FADING FAST.
DAMMIT.
THERE IS A GIANT HOLE IN THE BACK OF MY NECK, AND WITH EACH PAINED HEARTBEAT, STREAKS OF WARM PLASMA PAINT THEIR WAY DOWN ACROSS MY DISLOCATED JAW.
IF I WERE ABLE TO LOOK, I'D SEE MY EXPOSED VERTEBRAE POKING OUT OF AN OPEN WOUND, LIKE THE BONY FINS OF WHITE SHARKS SURFACING FROM A SEA OF JAGGED AND TORN FLESH. MAYBE IT'S BEST THAT I CAN'T.
OH, AND IT HURTS LIKE HELL. REALLY.
ALWAYS GOOD TO DIE WITH A SENSE OF HUMOR, I SAY.
WHATEVER PENANCE -NO PUN INTENDED- I HAD TO PAY FOR MY TRANSGRESSIONS IN A PREVIOUS LIFE, MY DEBT MUST SURELY BE PAID. IT'LL BE BETTER FOR ME NEXT TIME AROUND. IT HAS TO BE.
IF I COULD PICK 100 DIFFERENT WAYS TO GO OUT, I CAN PROMISE YOU THIS PARTICULAR SCENARIO WOULD BE NOWHERE ON THE LIST.

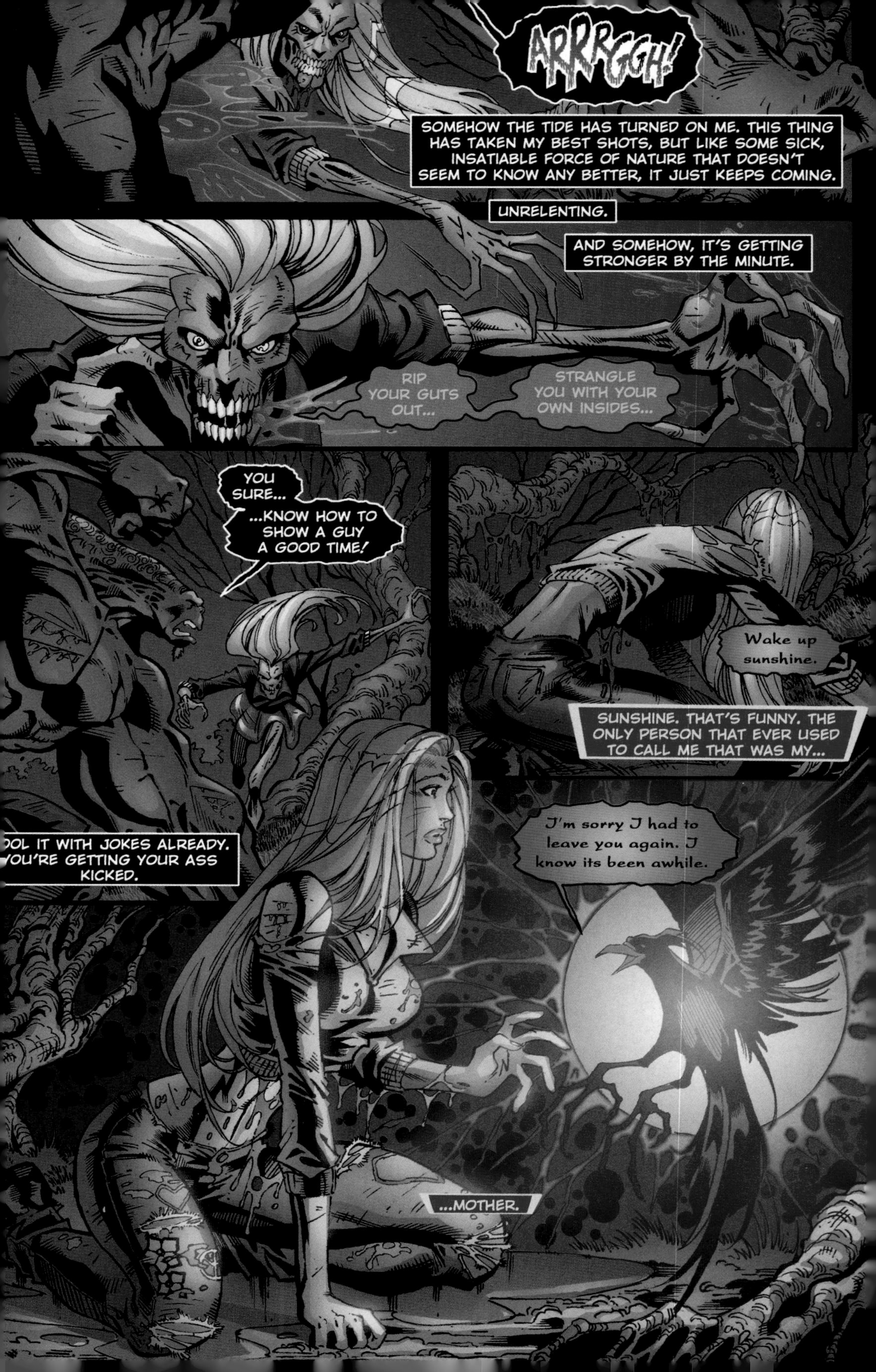

ARRRGGH!
SOMEHOW THE TIDE HAS TURNED ON ME. THIS THING HAS TAKEN MY BEST SHOTS, BUT LIKE SOME SICK, INSATIABLE FORCE OF NATURE THAT DOESN'T SEEM TO KNOW ANY BETTER, IT JUST KEEPS COMING.
UNRELENTING.
AND SOMEHOW, IT'S GETTING STRONGER BY THE MINUTE.
RIP YOUR GUTS OUT...
STRANGLE YOU WITH YOUR OWN INSIDES...
YOU SURE...
...KNOW HOW TO SHOW A GUY A GOOD TIME!
OL IT WITH JOKES ALREADY. YOU'RE GETTING YOUR ASS KICKED.
Wake up sunshine.
SUNSHINE. THAT'S FUNNY. THE ONLY PERSON THAT EVER USED TO CALL ME THAT WAS MY...
I'm sorry I had to leave you again. I know its been awhile.
...MOTHER.

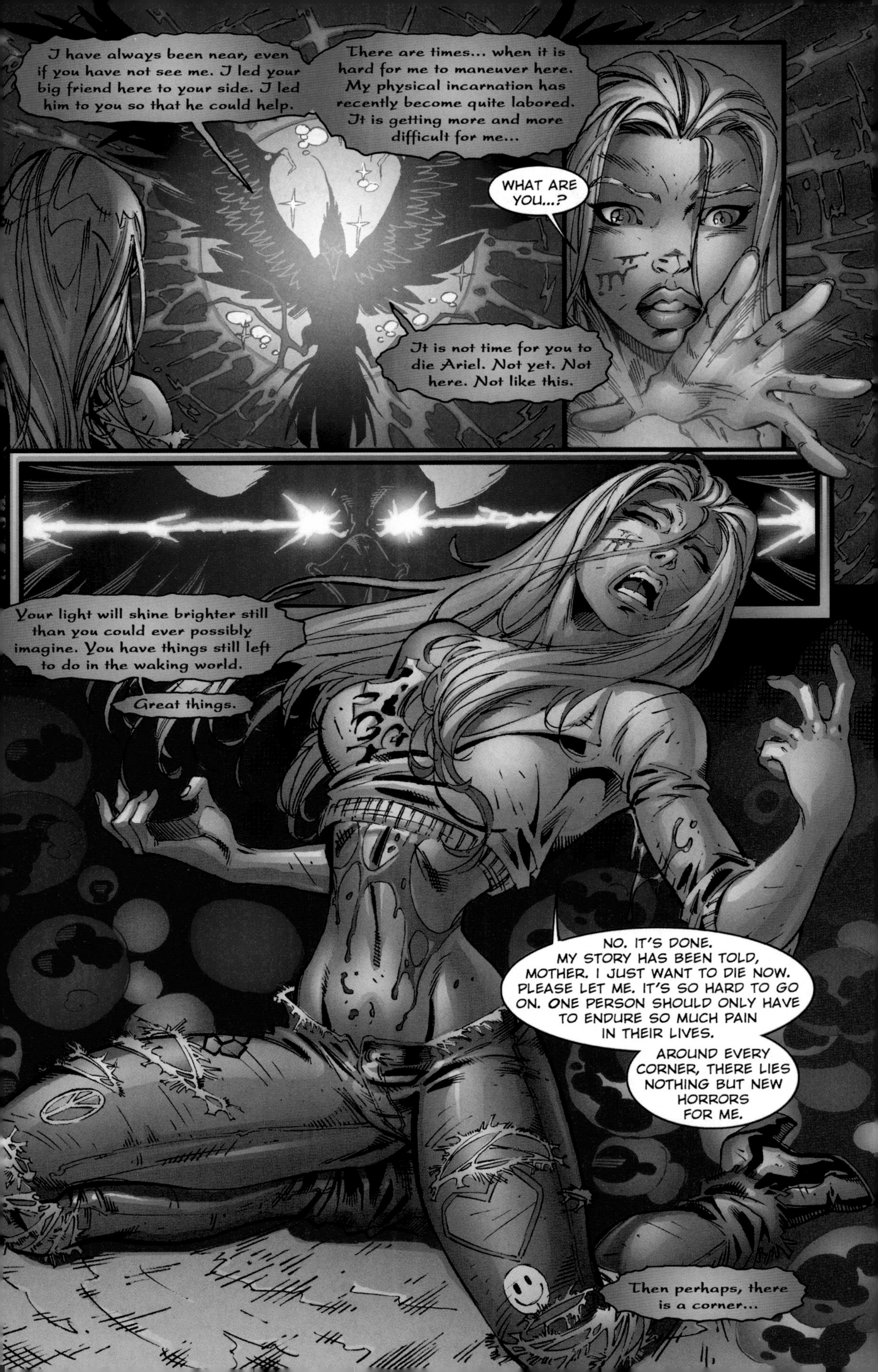
I have always been near, even if you have not see me. I led your big friend here to your side. I led him to you so that he could help.
There are times... when it is hard for me to maneuver here. My physical incarnation has recently become quite labored. It is getting more and more difficult for me...
WHAT ARE YOU...?
It is not time for you to die Ariel. Not yet. Not here. Not like this.
Your light will shine brighter still than you could ever possibly imagine. You have things still left to do in the waking world.
Great things.
NO. IT'S DONE. MY STORY HAS BEEN TOLD, MOTHER. I JUST WANT TO DIE NOW. PLEASE LET ME. IT'S SO HARD TO GO ON. ONE PERSON SHOULD ONLY HAVE TO ENDURE SO MUCH PAIN IN THEIR LIVES.
AROUND EVERY CORNER, THERE LIES NOTHING BUT NEW HORRORS FOR ME.
Then perhaps, there is a corner...

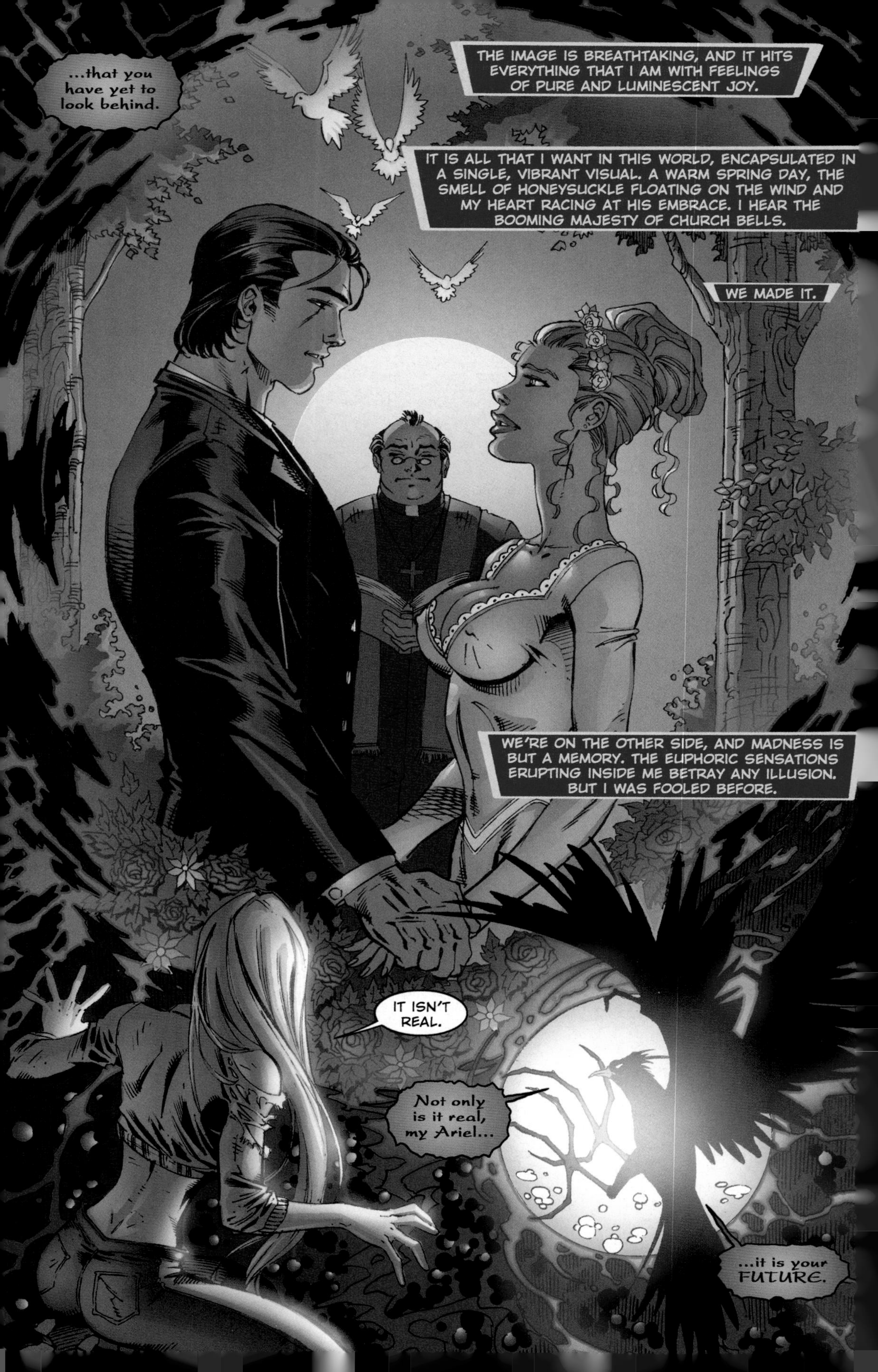
...that you have yet to look behind.
THE IMAGE IS BREATHTAKING, AND IT HITS EVERYTHING THAT I AM WITH FEELINGS OF PURE AND LUMINESCENT JOY.
IT IS ALL THAT I WANT IN THIS WORLD, ENCAPSULATED IN A SINGLE, VIBRANT VISUAL. A WARM SPRING DAY, THE SMELL OF HONEYSUCKLE FLOATING ON THE WIND AND MY HEART RACING AT HIS EMBRACE. I HEAR THE BOOMING MAJESTY OF CHURCH BELLS.
WE MADE IT.
WE'RE ON THE OTHER SIDE, AND MADNESS IS BUT A MEMORY. THE EUPHORIC SENSATIONS ERUPTING INSIDE ME BETRAY ANY ILLUSION. BUT I WAS FOOLED BEFORE.
IT ISN'T REAL.
Not only is it real, my Ariel...
...it is your FUTURE.

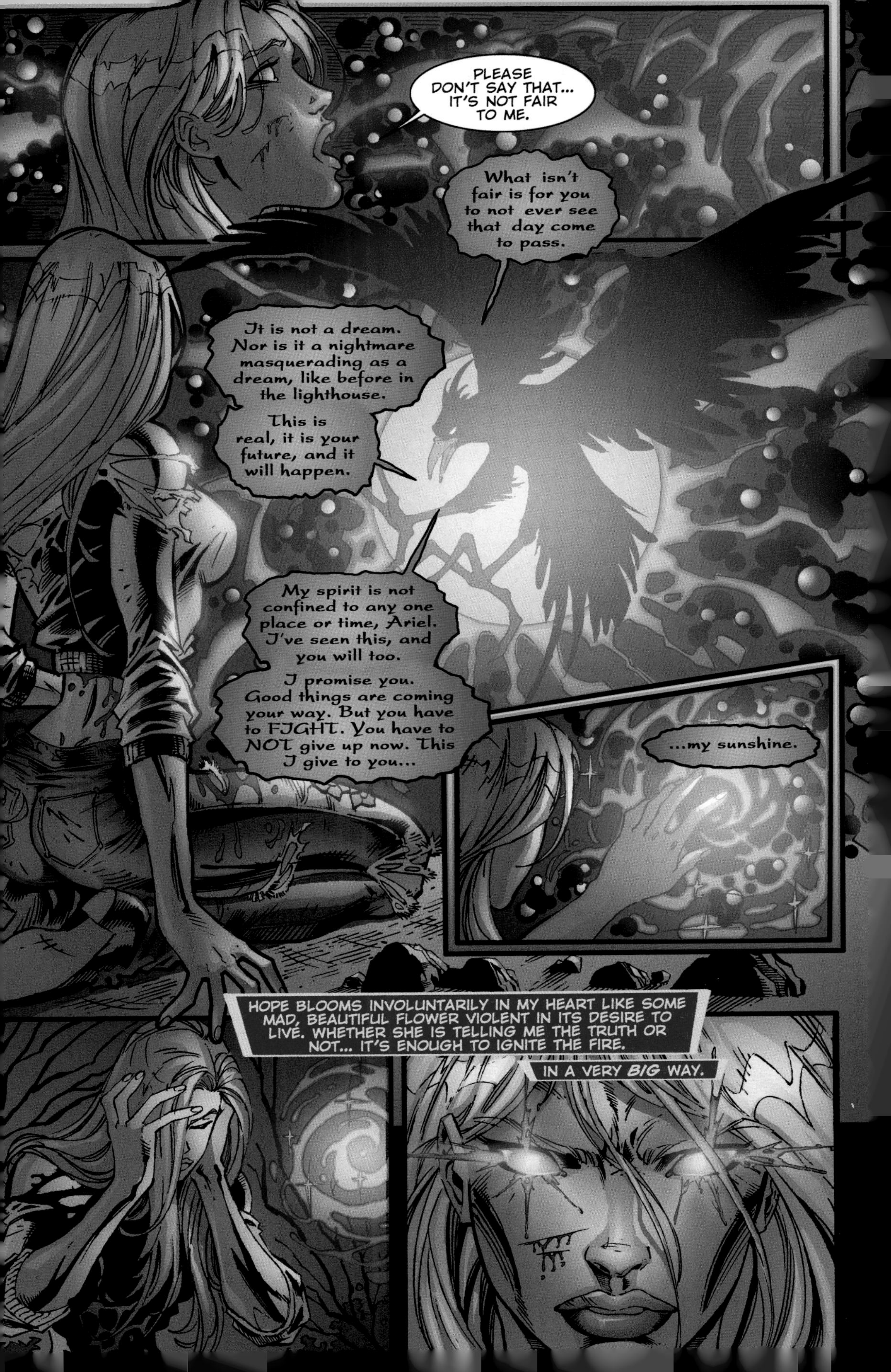
PLEASE DON'T SAY THAT... IT'S NOT FAIR TO ME.
What isn't fair is for you to not ever see that day come to pass.
It is not a dream. Nor is it a nightmare masquerading as a dream, like before in the lighthouse.
This is real, it is your future, and it will happen.
My spirit is not confined to any one place or time, Ariel. I've seen this, and you will too.
I promise you. Good things are coming your way. But you have to FIGHT. You have to NOT give up now. This I give to you...
...my sunshine.
HOPE BLOOMS INVOLUNTARILY IN MY HEART LIKE SOME MAD, BEAUTIFUL FLOWER VIOLENT IN ITS DESIRE TO LIVE. WHETHER SHE IS TELLING ME THE TRUTH OR NOT... IT'S ENOUGH TO IGNITE THE FIRE.
IN A VERY *BIG* WAY.

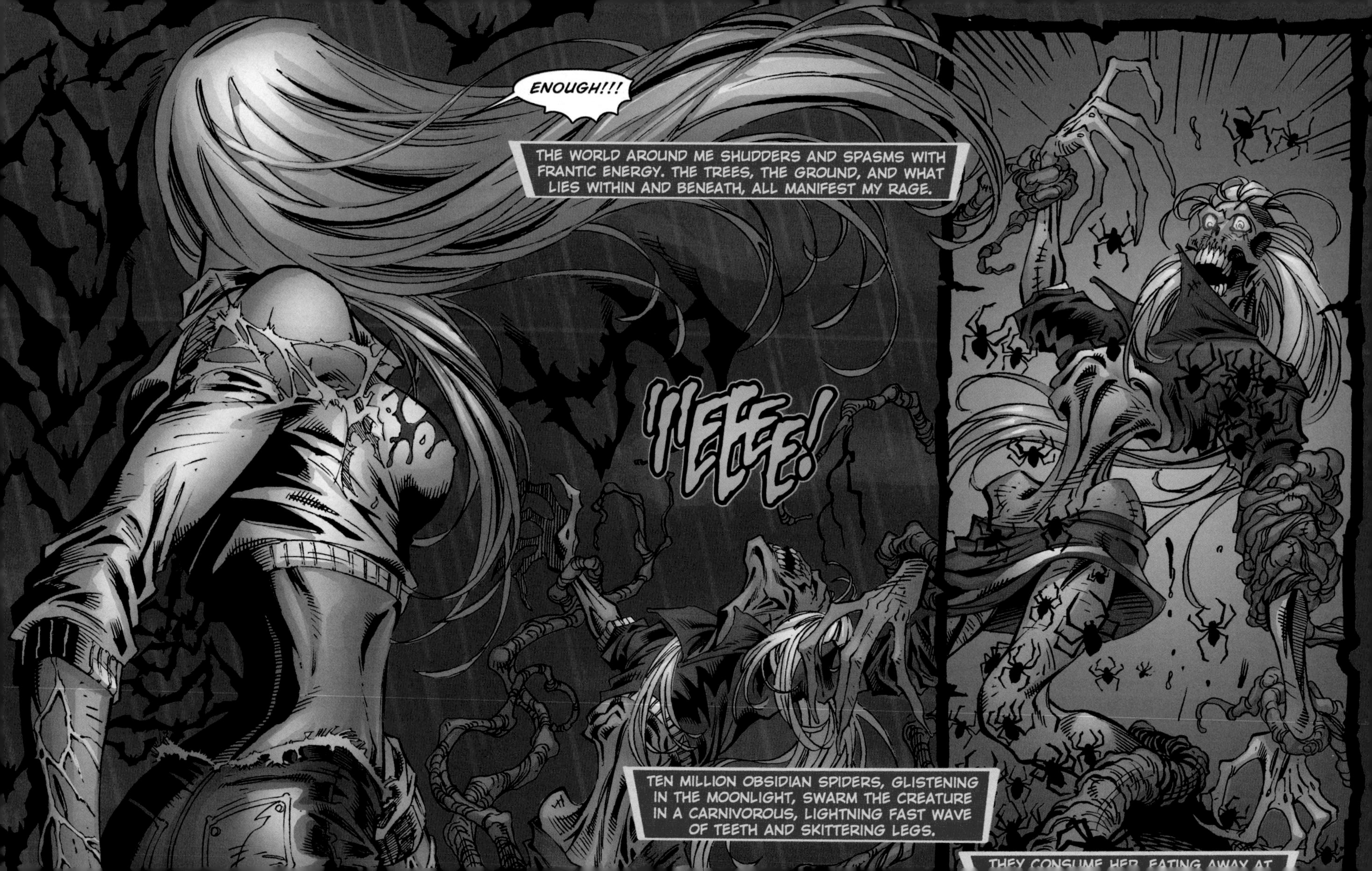
ENOUGH!!!
THE WORLD AROUND ME SHUDDERS AND SPASMS WITH FRANTIC ENERGY. THE TREES, THE GROUND, AND WHAT LIES WITHIN AND BENEATH, ALL MANIFEST MY RAGE.
!!EEEEE!
TEN MILLION OBSIDIAN SPIDERS, GLISTENING IN THE MOONLIGHT, SWARM THE CREATURE IN A CARNIVOROUS, LIGHTNING FAST WAVE OF TEETH AND SKITTERING LEGS.
THEY CONSUME HER, EATING AWAY AT

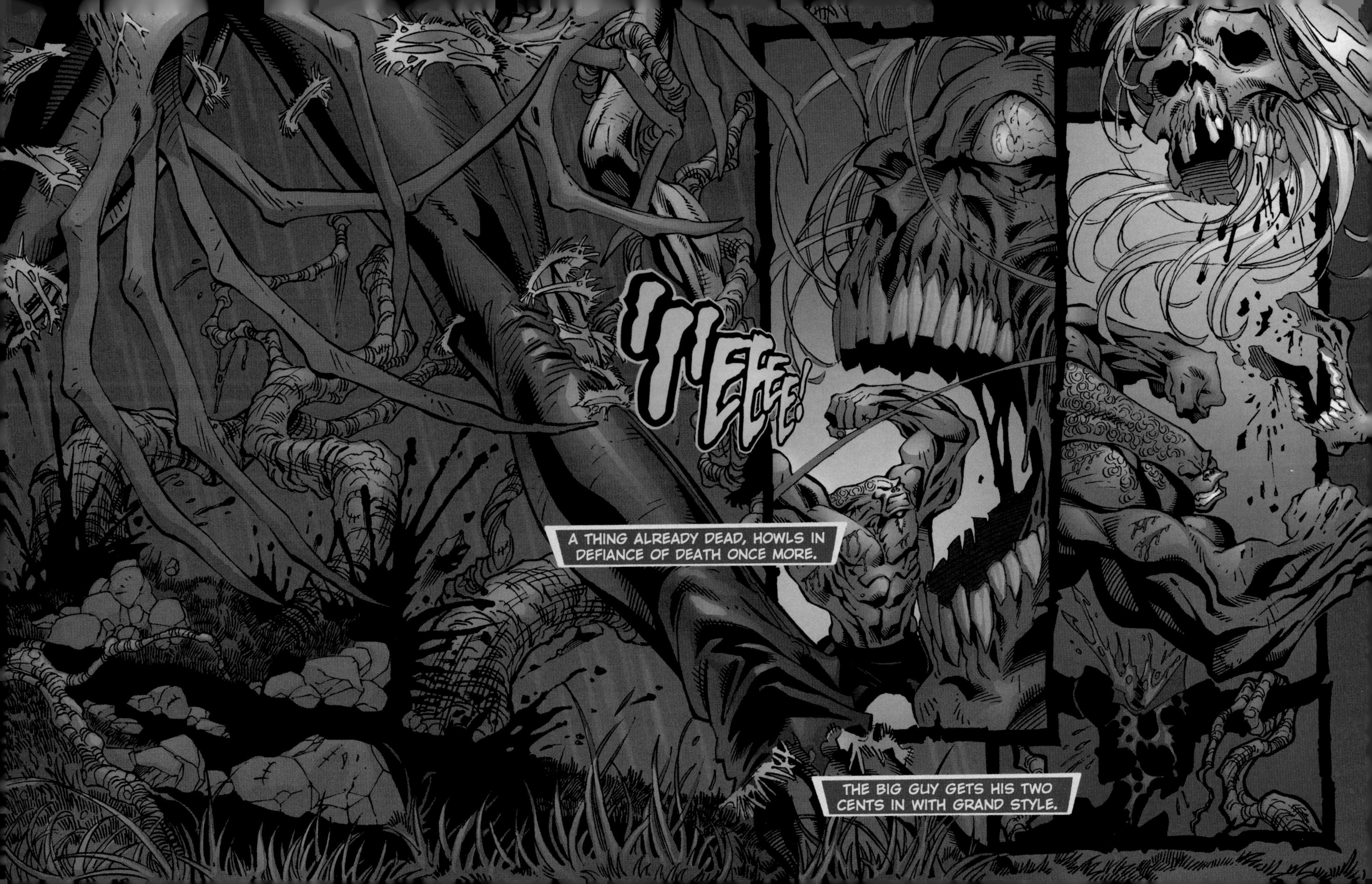
YEEEE!
A THING ALREADY DEAD, HOWLS IN DEFIANCE OF DEATH ONCE MORE.
THE BIG GUY GETS HIS TWO CENTS IN WITH GRAND STYLE.

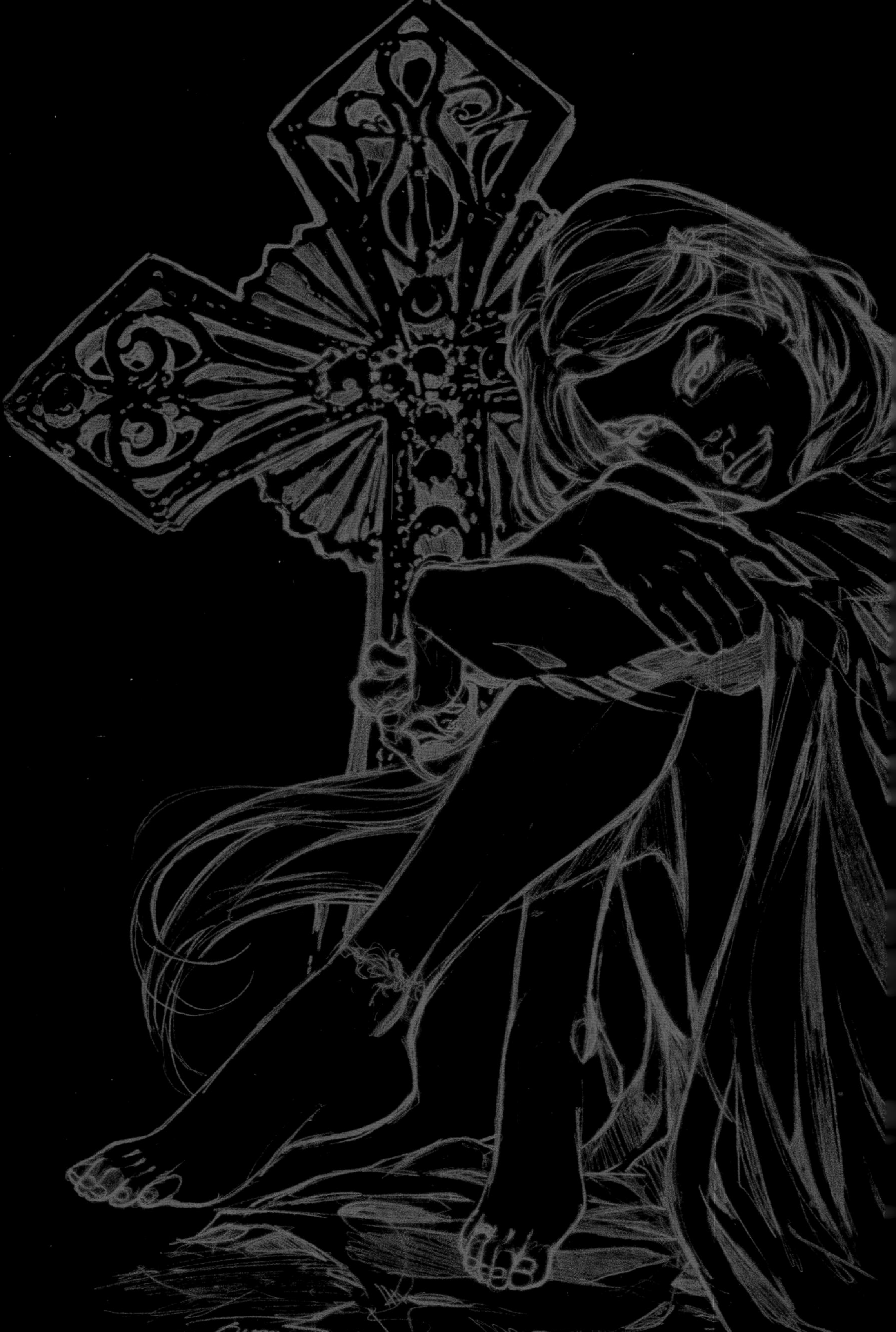

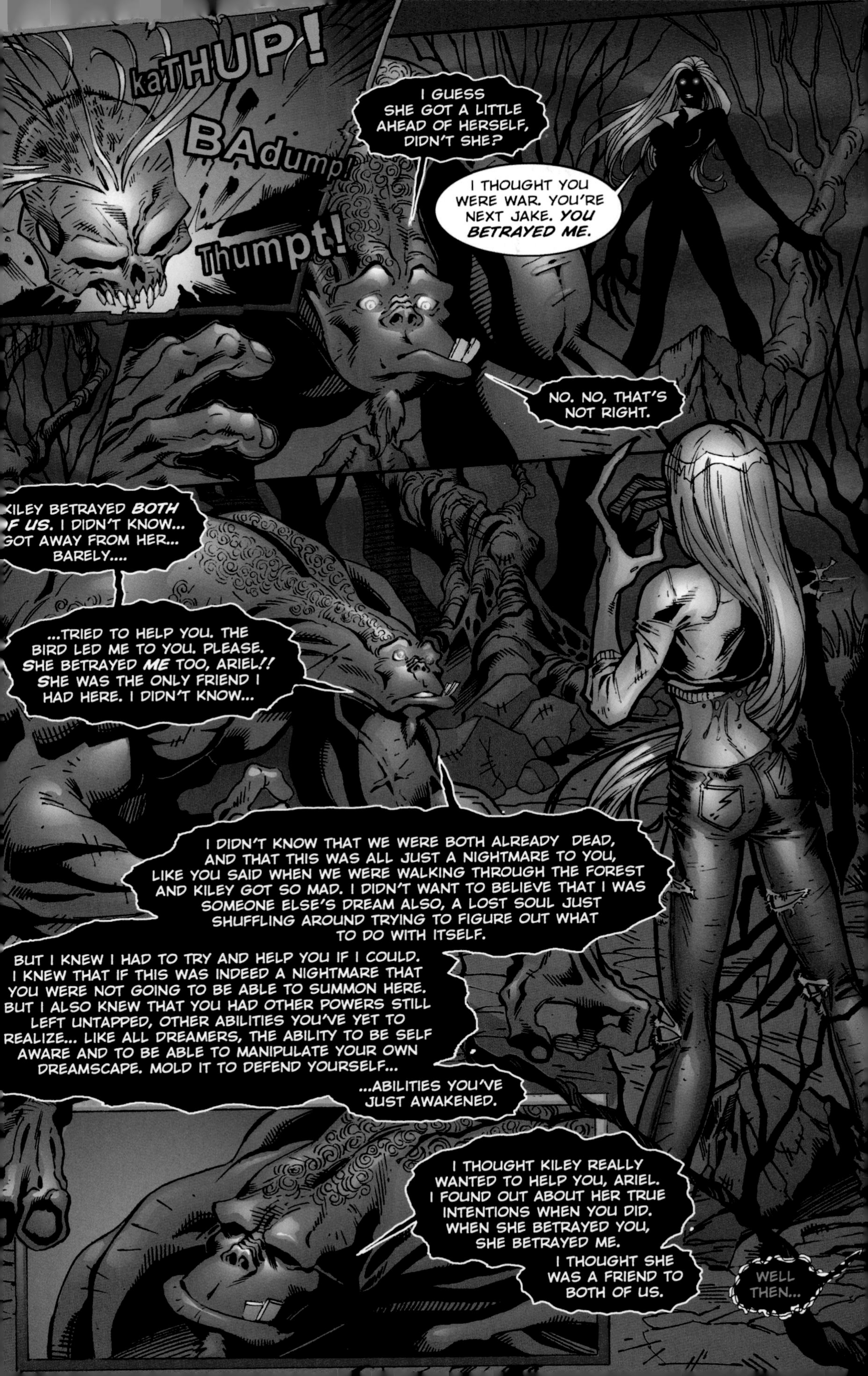
kaTHUP!
BAdump!
Thumpt!
I GUESS SHE GOT A LITTLE AHEAD OF HERSELF, DIDN'T SHE?
I THOUGHT YOU WERE WAR. YOU'RE NEXT JAKE. YOU BETRAYED ME.
NO. NO, THAT'S NOT RIGHT.
KILEY BETRAYED BOTH OF US. I DIDN'T KNOW... GOT AWAY FROM HER... BARELY....
...TRIED TO HELP YOU. THE BIRD LED ME TO YOU. PLEASE. SHE BETRAYED ME TOO, ARIEL!! SHE WAS THE ONLY FRIEND I HAD HERE. I DIDN'T KNOW...
I DIDN'T KNOW THAT WE WERE BOTH ALREADY DEAD, AND THAT THIS WAS ALL JUST A NIGHTMARE TO YOU, LIKE YOU SAID WHEN WE WERE WALKING THROUGH THE FOREST AND KILEY GOT SO MAD. I DIDN'T WANT TO BELIEVE THAT I WAS SOMEONE ELSE'S DREAM ALSO, A LOST SOUL JUST SHUFFLING AROUND TRYING TO FIGURE OUT WHAT TO DO WITH ITSELF.
BUT I KNEW I HAD TO TRY AND HELP YOU IF I COULD. I KNEW THAT IF THIS WAS INDEED A NIGHTMARE THAT YOU WERE NOT GOING TO BE ABLE TO SUMMON HERE. BUT I ALSO KNEW THAT YOU HAD OTHER POWERS STILL LEFT UNTAPPED, OTHER ABILITIES YOU'VE YET TO REALIZE... LIKE ALL DREAMERS, THE ABILITY TO BE SELF AWARE AND TO BE ABLE TO MANIPULATE YOUR OWN DREAMSCAPE. MOLD IT TO DEFEND YOURSELF...
...ABILITIES YOU'VE JUST AWAKENED.
I THOUGHT KILEY REALLY WANTED TO HELP YOU, ARIEL. I FOUND OUT ABOUT HER TRUE INTENTIONS WHEN YOU DID. WHEN SHE BETRAYED YOU, SHE BETRAYED ME.
I THOUGHT SHE WAS A FRIEND TO BOTH OF US.
WELL THEN...

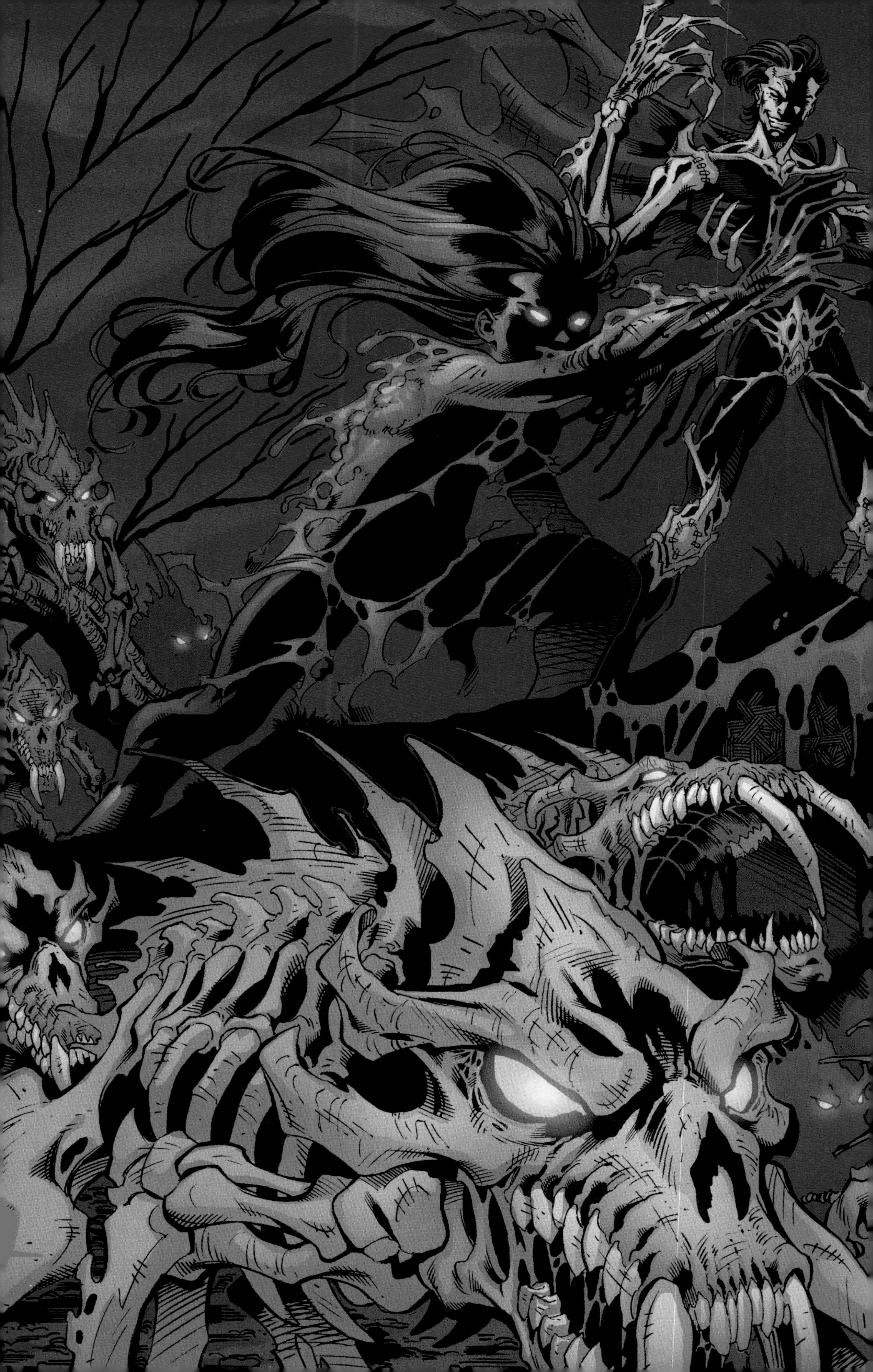

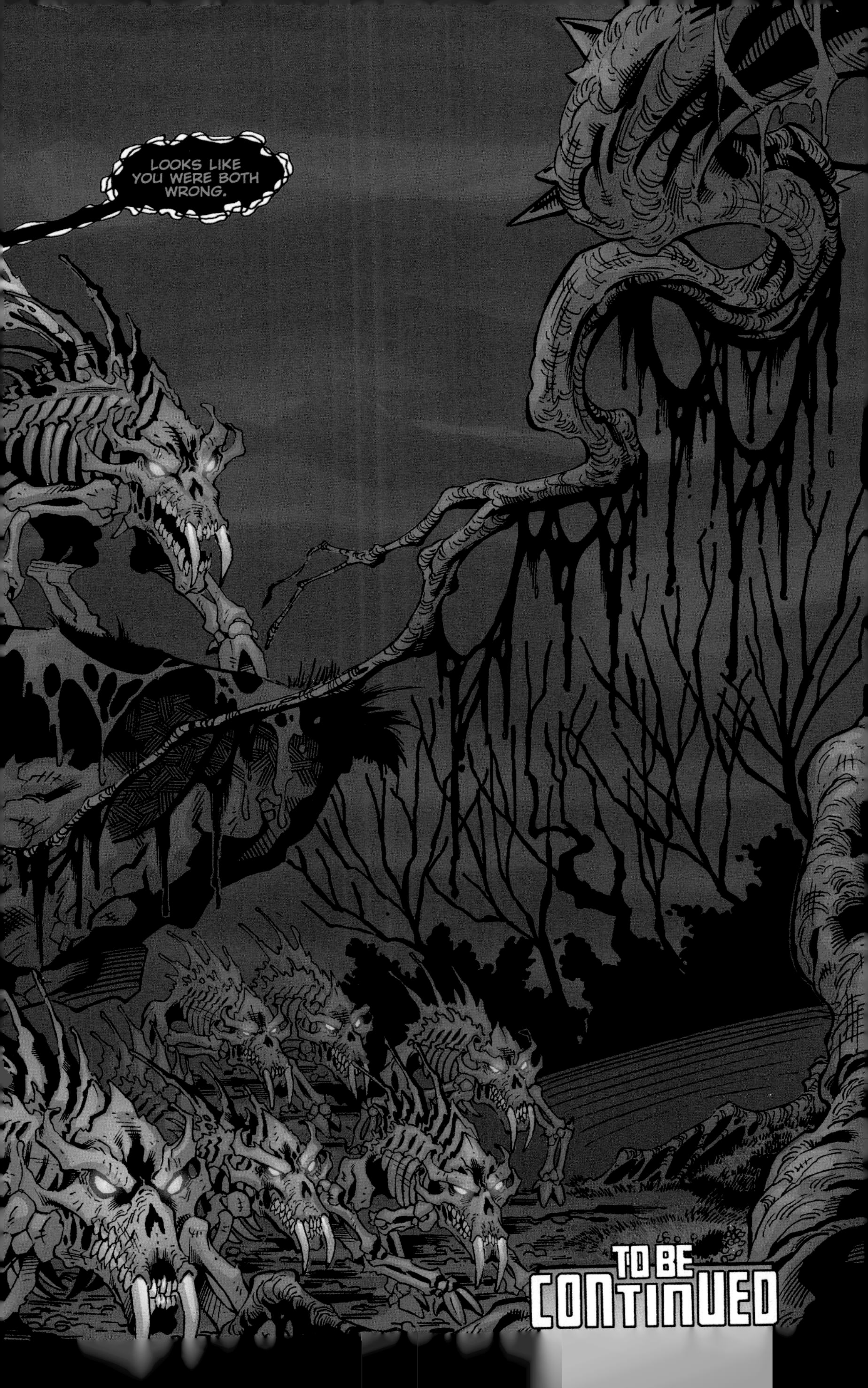
LOOKS LIKE YOU WERE BOTH WRONG.
TO BE CONTINUED

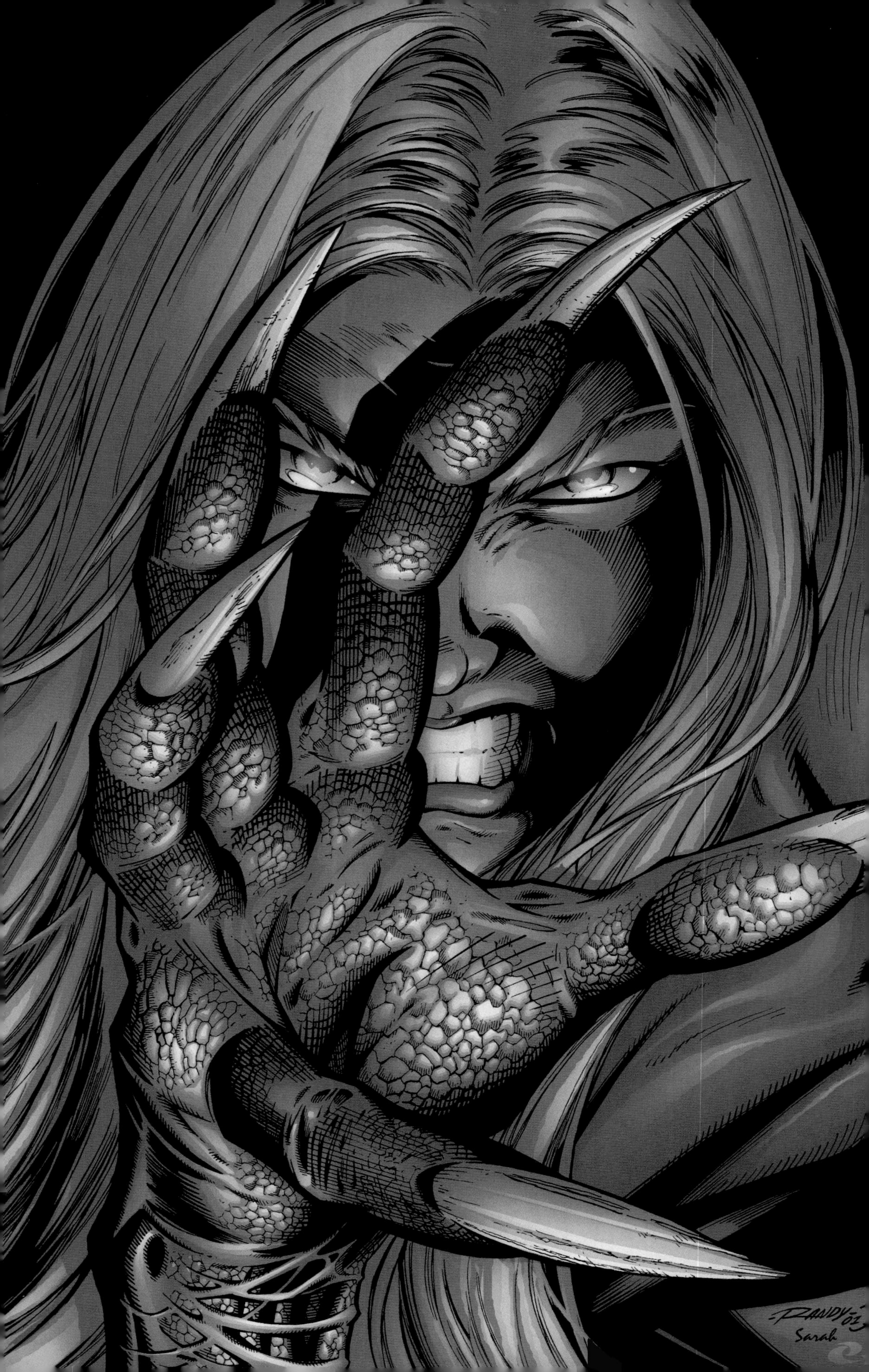
RANDY '02
Sarah

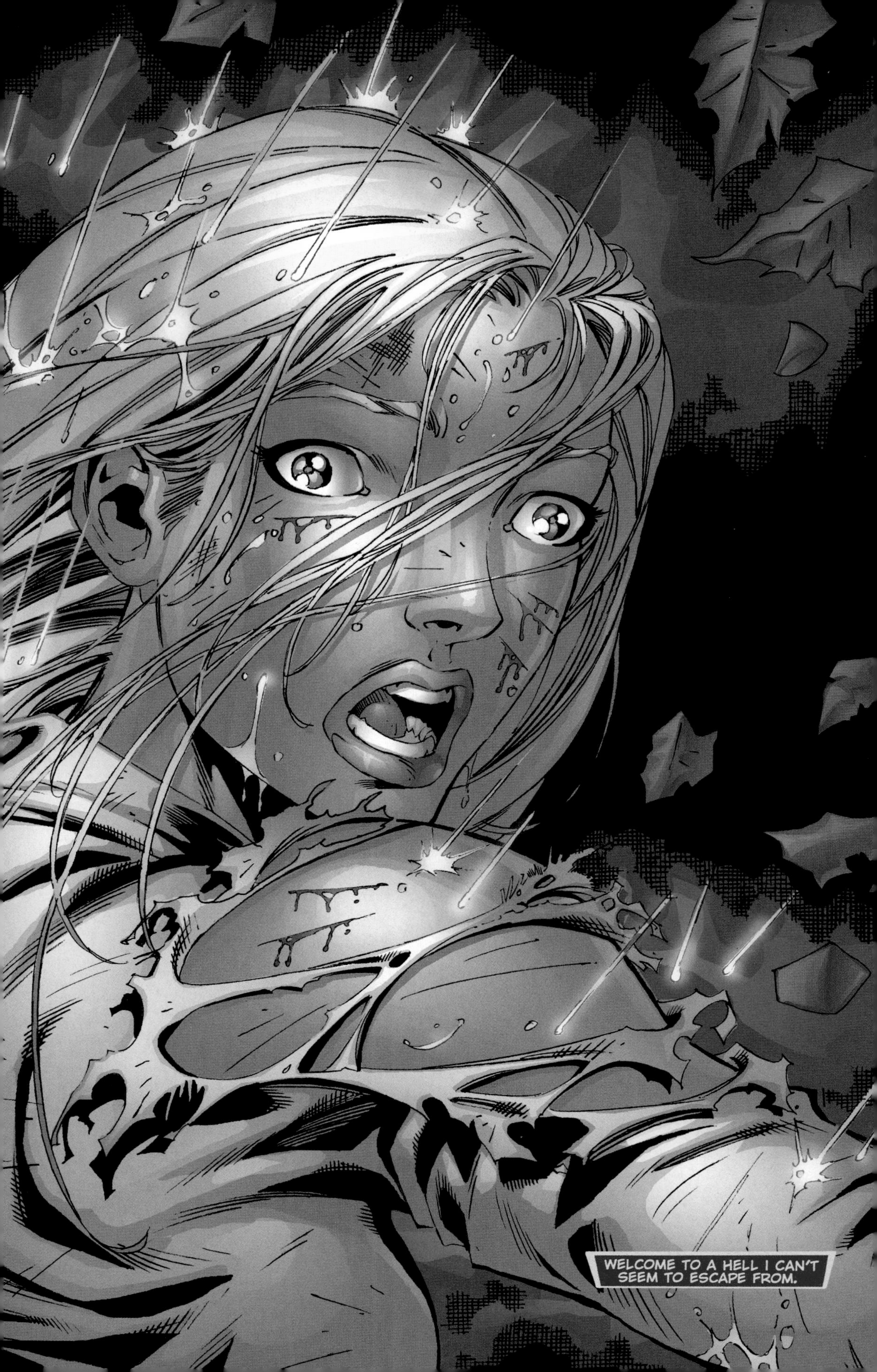
WELCOME TO A HELL I CAN'T SEEM TO ESCAPE FROM.

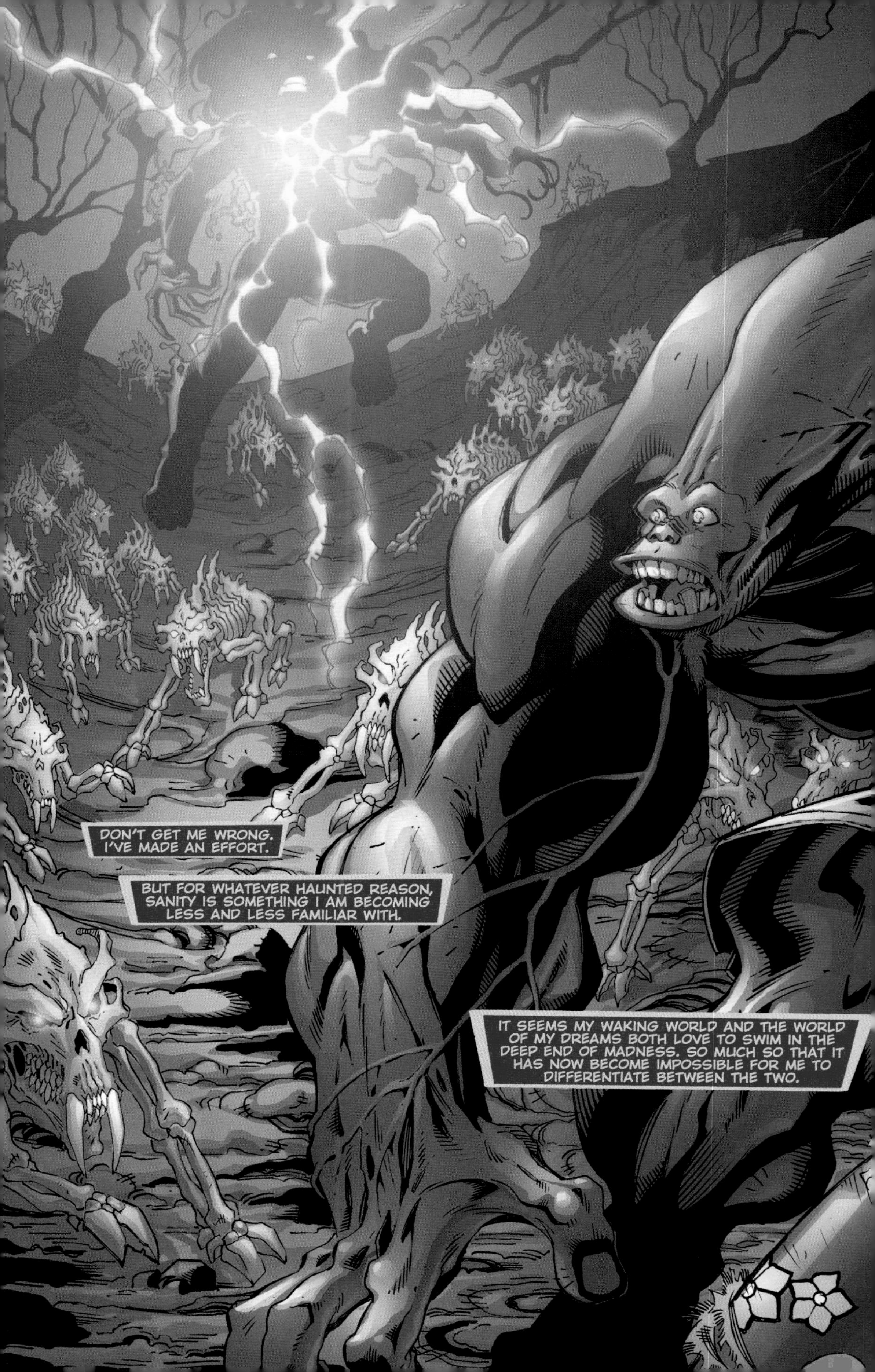
DON'T GET ME WRONG. I'VE MADE AN EFFORT.
BUT FOR WHATEVER HAUNTED REASON, SANITY IS SOMETHING I AM BECOMING LESS AND LESS FAMILIAR WITH.
IT SEEMS MY WAKING WORLD AND THE WORLD OF MY DREAMS BOTH LOVE TO SWIM IN THE DEEP END OF MADNESS. SO MUCH SO THAT IT HAS NOW BECOME IMPOSSIBLE FOR ME TO DIFFERENTIATE BETWEEN THE TWO.

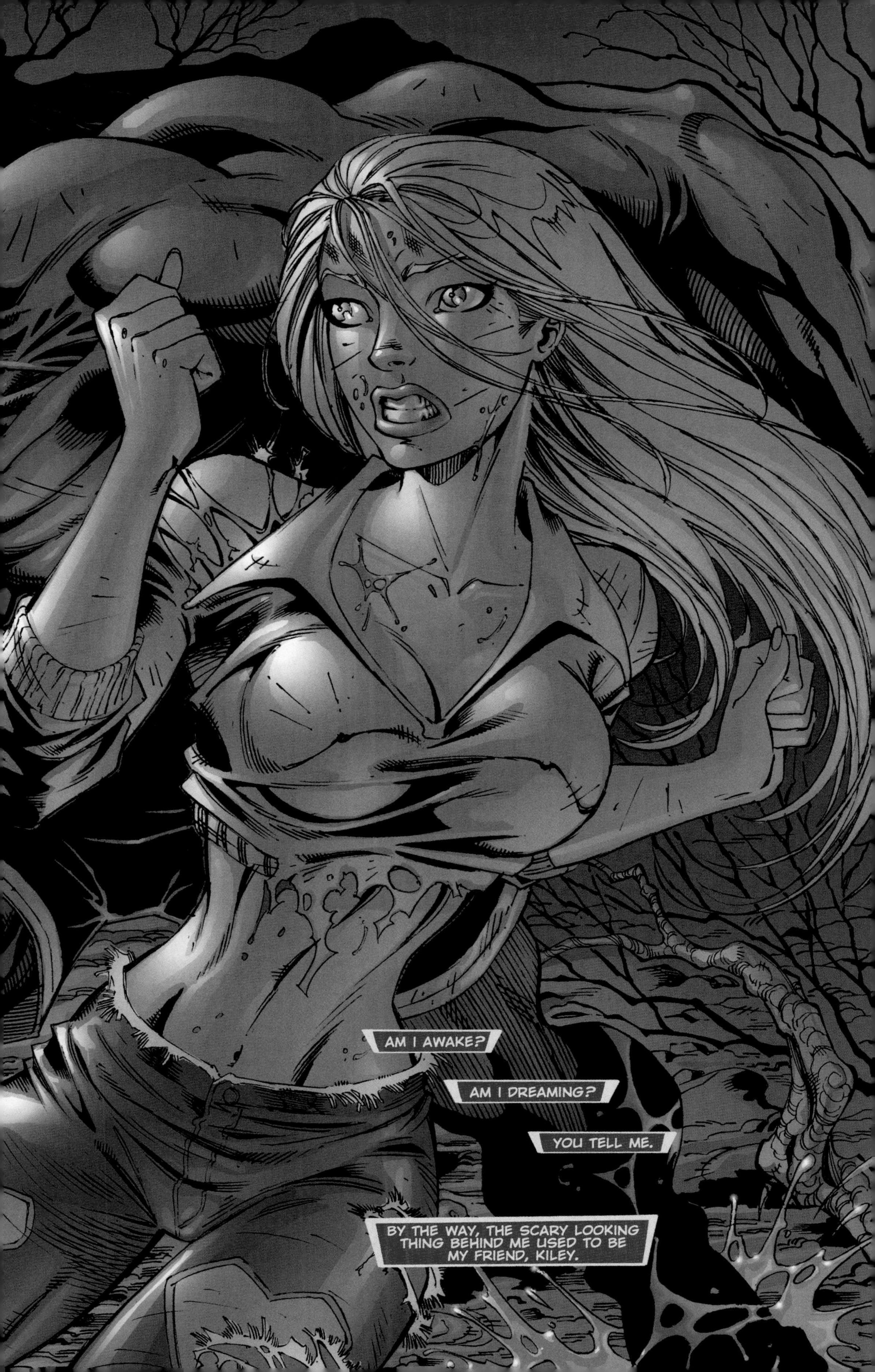
AM I AWAKE?
AM I DREAMING?
YOU TELL ME.
BY THE WAY, THE SCARY LOOKING THING BEHIND ME USED TO BE MY FRIEND, KILEY.

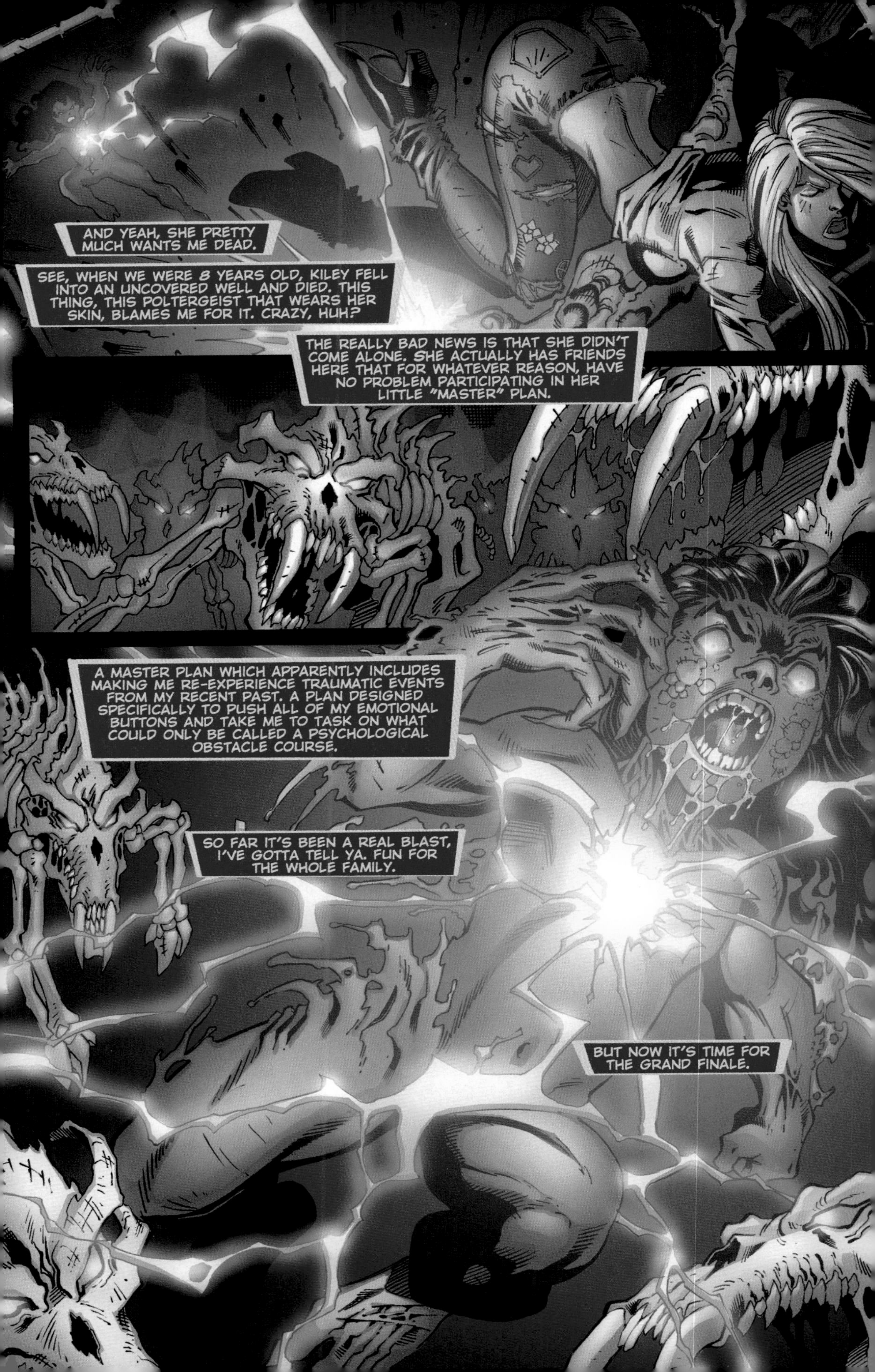
AND YEAH, SHE PRETTY MUCH WANTS ME DEAD.
SEE, WHEN WE WERE 8 YEARS OLD, KILEY FELL INTO AN UNCOVERED WELL AND DIED. THIS THING, THIS POLTERGEIST THAT WEARS HER SKIN, BLAMES ME FOR IT. CRAZY, HUH?
THE REALLY BAD NEWS IS THAT SHE DIDN'T COME ALONE. SHE ACTUALLY HAS FRIENDS HERE THAT FOR WHATEVER REASON, HAVE NO PROBLEM PARTICIPATING IN HER LITTLE "MASTER" PLAN.
A MASTER PLAN WHICH APPARENTLY INCLUDES MAKING ME RE-EXPERIENCE TRAUMATIC EVENTS FROM MY RECENT PAST. A PLAN DESIGNED SPECIFICALLY TO PUSH ALL OF MY EMOTIONAL BUTTONS AND TAKE ME TO TASK ON WHAT COULD ONLY BE CALLED A PSYCHOLOGICAL OBSTACLE COURSE.
SO FAR IT'S BEEN A REAL BLAST, I'VE GOTTA TELL YA. FUN FOR THE WHOLE FAMILY.
BUT NOW IT'S TIME FOR THE GRAND FINALE.

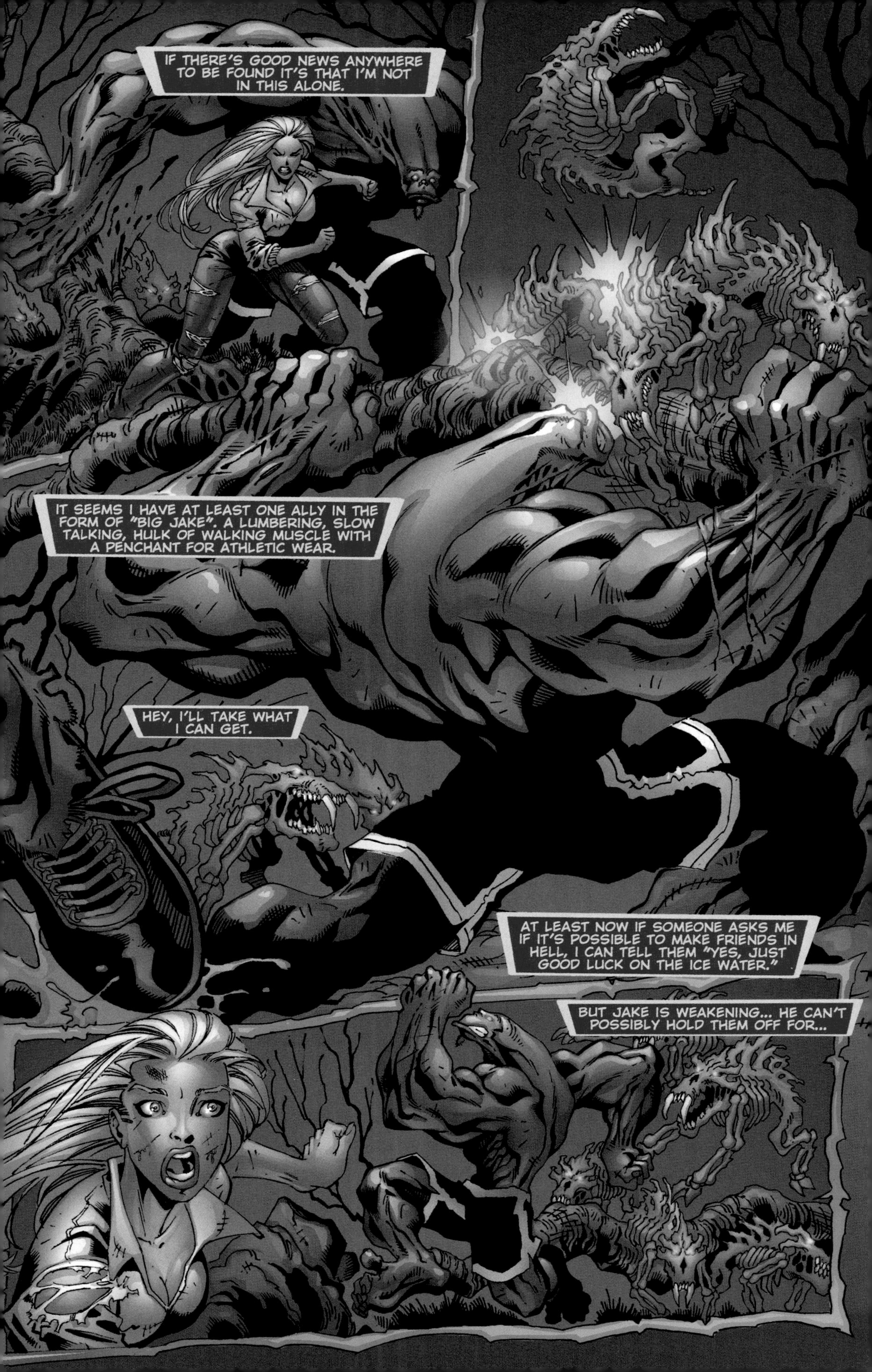
IF THERE'S GOOD NEWS ANYWHERE TO BE FOUND IT'S THAT I'M NOT IN THIS ALONE.
IT SEEMS I HAVE AT LEAST ONE ALLY IN THE FORM OF "BIG JAKE". A LUMBERING, SLOW TALKING, HULK OF WALKING MUSCLE WITH A PENCHANT FOR ATHLETIC WEAR.
HEY, I'LL TAKE WHAT I CAN GET.
AT LEAST NOW IF SOMEONE ASKS ME IF IT'S POSSIBLE TO MAKE FRIENDS IN HELL, I CAN TELL THEM "YES, JUST GOOD LUCK ON THE ICE WATER."
BUT JAKE IS WEAKENING... HE CAN'T POSSIBLY HOLD THEM OFF FOR...

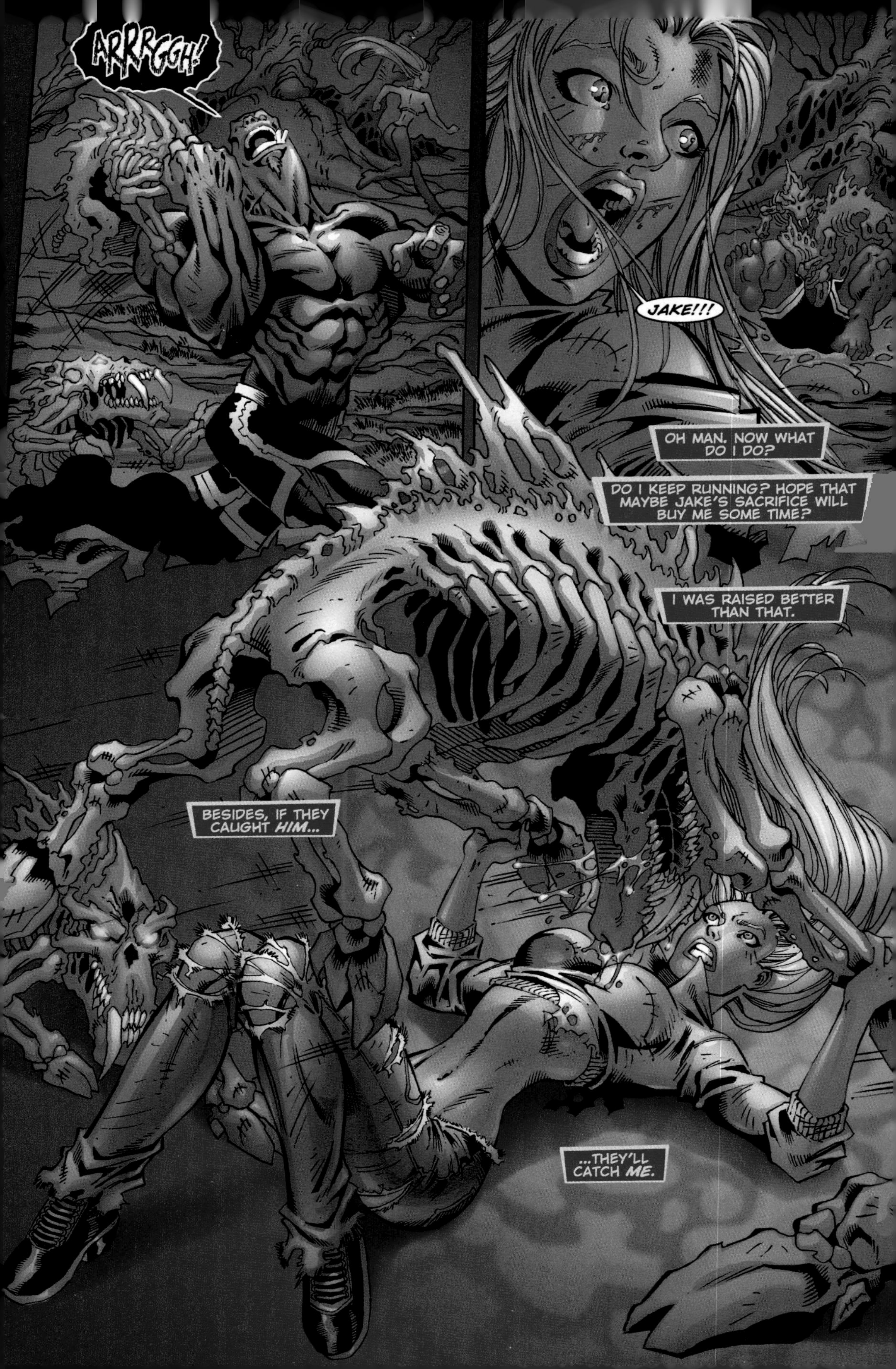
ARRRGGH!
JAKE!!!
OH MAN. NOW WHAT DO I DO?
DO I KEEP RUNNING? HOPE THAT MAYBE JAKE'S SACRIFICE WILL BUY ME SOME TIME?
I WAS RAISED BETTER THAN THAT.
BESIDES, IF THEY CAUGHT HIM...
...THEY'LL CATCH ME.

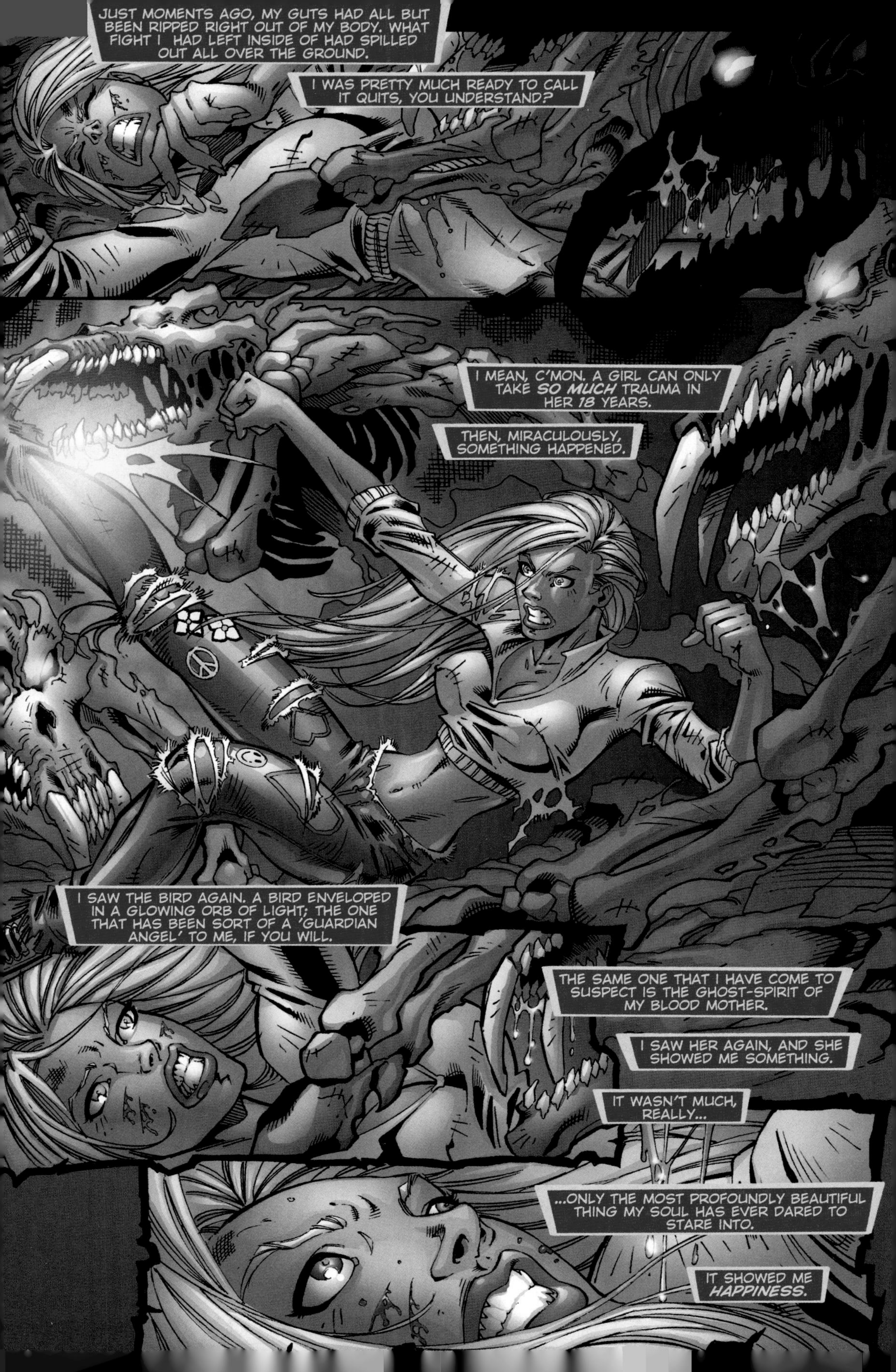
JUST MOMENTS AGO, MY GUTS HAD ALL BUT BEEN RIPPED RIGHT OUT OF MY BODY. WHAT FIGHT I HAD LEFT INSIDE OF HAD SPILLED OUT ALL OVER THE GROUND.
I WAS PRETTY MUCH READY TO CALL IT QUITS, YOU UNDERSTAND?
I MEAN, C'MON. A GIRL CAN ONLY TAKE SO MUCH TRAUMA IN HER 18 YEARS.
THEN, MIRACULOUSLY, SOMETHING HAPPENED.
I SAW THE BIRD AGAIN. A BIRD ENVELOPED IN A GLOWING ORB OF LIGHT; THE ONE THAT HAS BEEN SORT OF A 'GUARDIAN ANGEL' TO ME, IF YOU WILL.
THE SAME ONE THAT I HAVE COME TO SUSPECT IS THE GHOST-SPIRIT OF MY BLOOD MOTHER.
I SAW HER AGAIN, AND SHE SHOWED ME SOMETHING.
IT WASN'T MUCH, REALLY...
...ONLY THE MOST PROFOUNDLY BEAUTIFUL THING MY SOUL HAS EVER DARED TO STARE INTO.
IT SHOWED ME HAPPINESS.

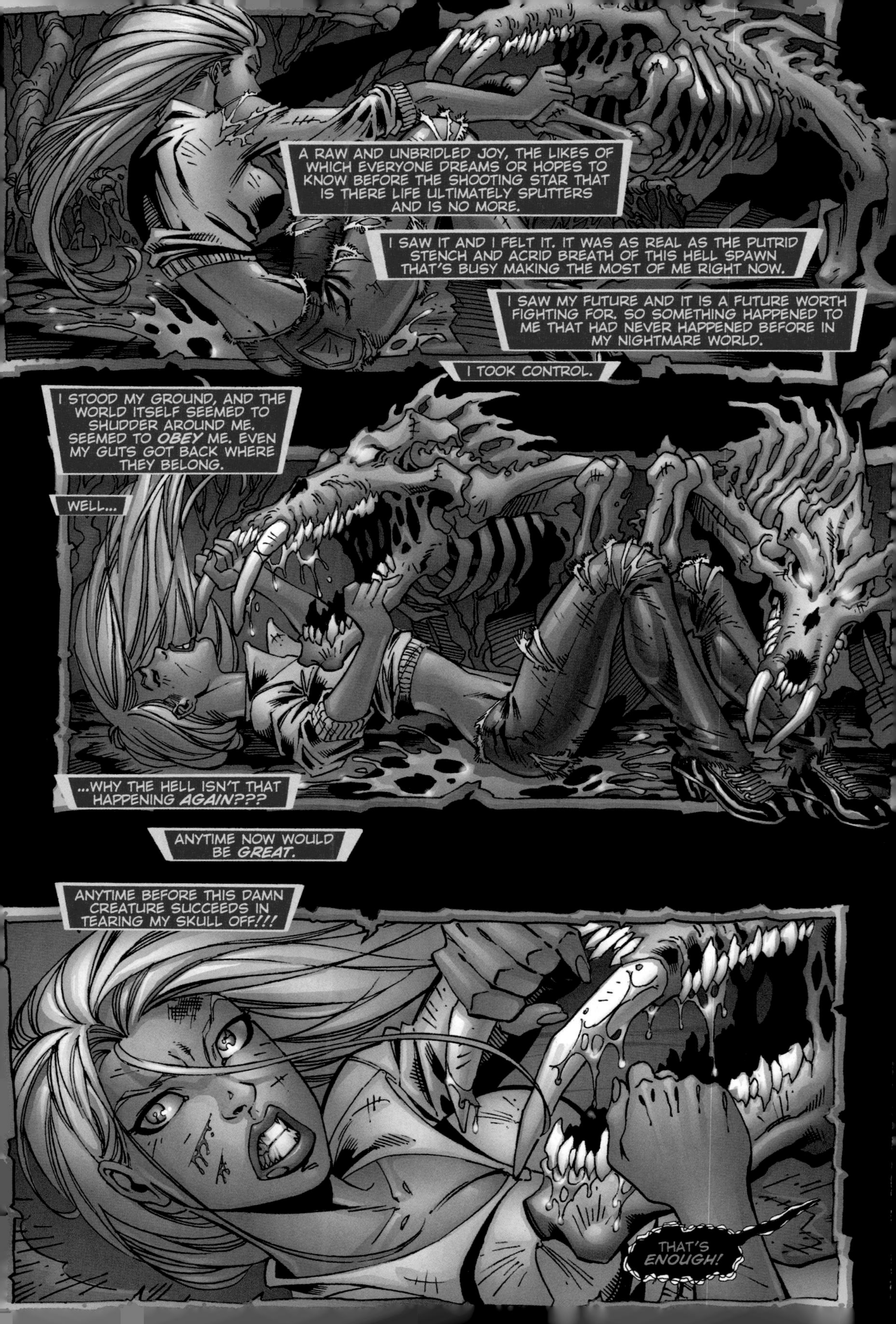
A RAW AND UNBRIDLED JOY, THE LIKES OF WHICH EVERYONE DREAMS OR HOPES TO KNOW BEFORE THE SHOOTING STAR THAT IS THERE LIFE ULTIMATELY SPUTTERS AND IS NO MORE.
I SAW IT AND I FELT IT. IT WAS AS REAL AS THE PUTRID STENCH AND ACRID BREATH OF THIS HELL SPAWN THAT'S BUSY MAKING THE MOST OF ME RIGHT NOW.
I SAW MY FUTURE AND IT IS A FUTURE WORTH FIGHTING FOR. SO SOMETHING HAPPENED TO ME THAT HAD NEVER HAPPENED BEFORE IN MY NIGHTMARE WORLD.
I TOOK CONTROL.
I STOOD MY GROUND, AND THE WORLD ITSELF SEEMED TO SHUDDER AROUND ME. SEEMED TO *OBEY* ME. EVEN MY GUTS GOT BACK WHERE THEY BELONG.
WELL...
...WHY THE HELL ISN'T THAT HAPPENING *AGAIN???*
ANYTIME NOW WOULD BE *GREAT*.
ANYTIME BEFORE THIS DAMN CREATURE SUCCEEDS IN TEARING MY SKULL OFF*!!!*
THAT'S *ENOUGH!*

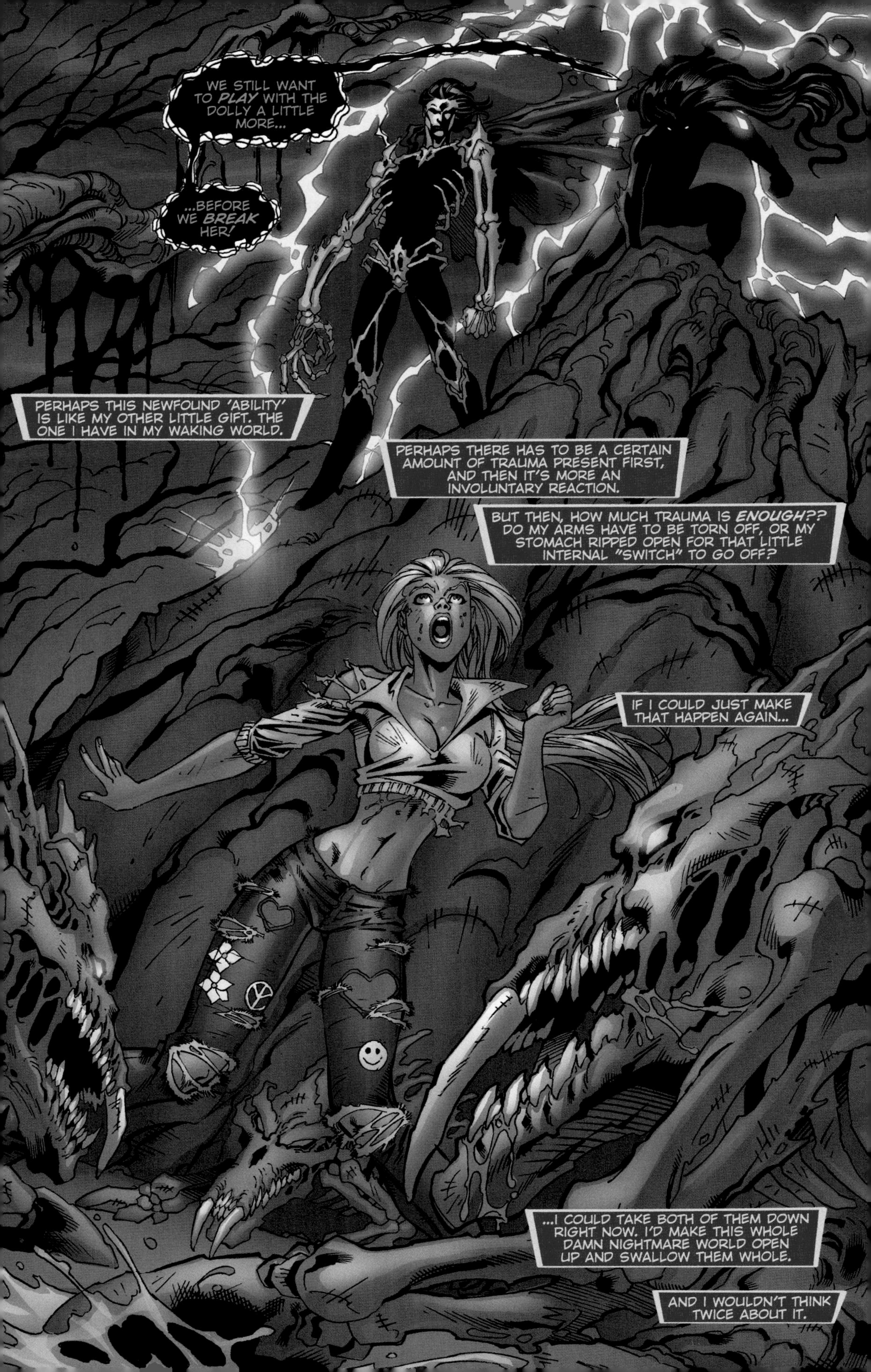
WE STILL WANT TO *PLAY* WITH THE DOLLY A LITTLE MORE...
...BEFORE WE *BREAK* HER!
PERHAPS THIS NEWFOUND 'ABILITY' IS LIKE MY OTHER LITTLE GIFT. THE ONE I HAVE IN MY WAKING WORLD.
PERHAPS THERE HAS TO BE A CERTAIN AMOUNT OF TRAUMA PRESENT FIRST, AND THEN IT'S MORE AN INVOLUNTARY REACTION.
BUT THEN, HOW MUCH TRAUMA IS *ENOUGH??* DO MY ARMS HAVE TO BE TORN OFF, OR MY STOMACH RIPPED OPEN FOR THAT LITTLE INTERNAL "SWITCH" TO GO OFF?
IF I COULD JUST MAKE THAT HAPPEN AGAIN...
...I COULD TAKE BOTH OF THEM DOWN RIGHT NOW. I'D MAKE THIS WHOLE DAMN NIGHTMARE WORLD OPEN UP AND SWALLOW THEM WHOLE.
AND I WOULDN'T THINK TWICE ABOUT IT.

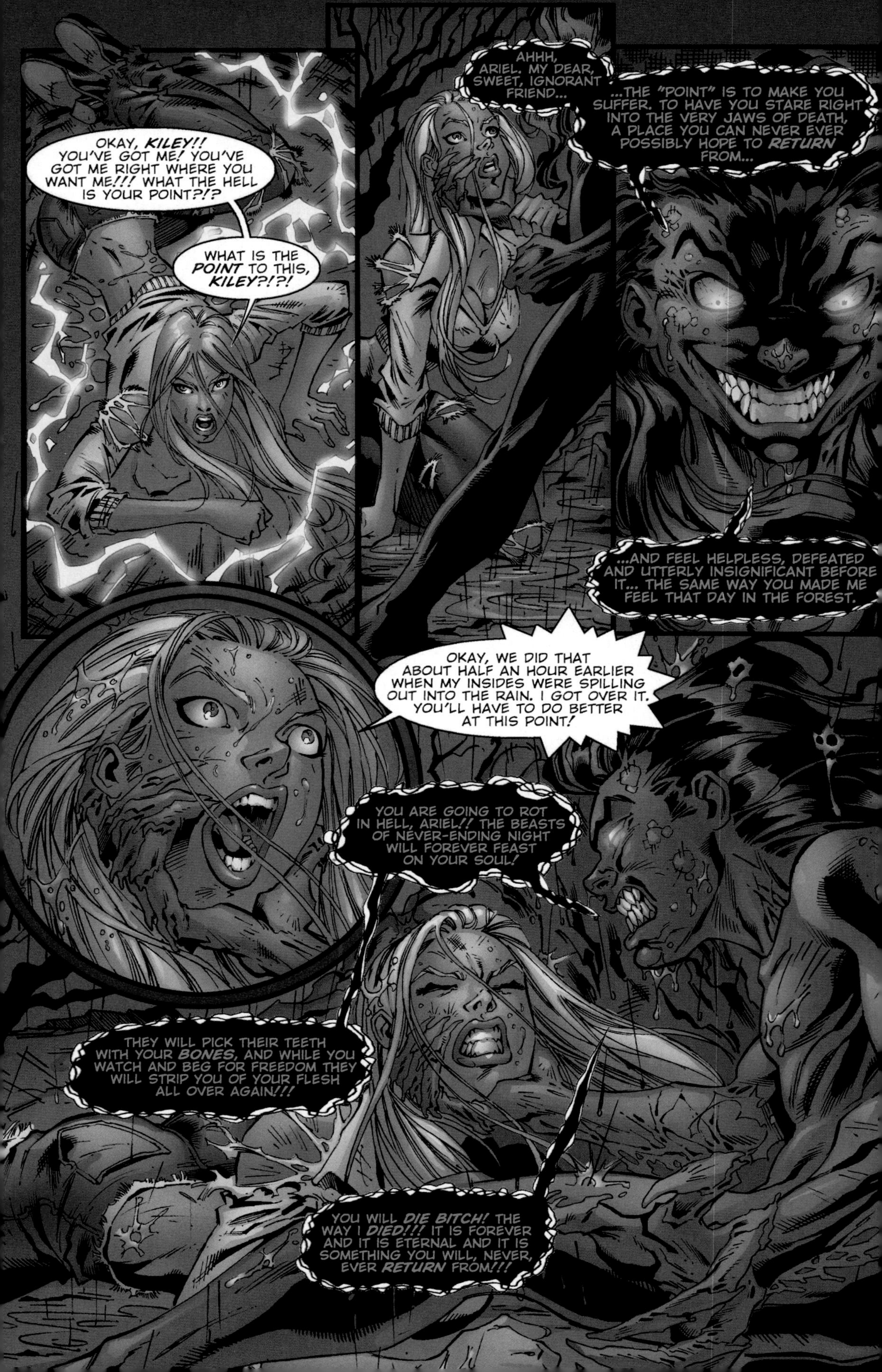

OKAY, KILEY!! YOU'VE GOT ME! YOU'VE GOT ME RIGHT WHERE YOU WANT ME!!! WHAT THE HELL IS YOUR POINT?!?
WHAT IS THE POINT TO THIS, KILEY?!?!
AHHH, ARIEL. MY DEAR, SWEET, IGNORANT FRIEND...
...THE "POINT" IS TO MAKE YOU SUFFER. TO HAVE YOU STARE RIGHT INTO THE VERY JAWS OF DEATH, A PLACE YOU CAN NEVER EVER POSSIBLY HOPE TO RETURN FROM...
...AND FEEL HELPLESS, DEFEATED AND UTTERLY INSIGNIFICANT BEFORE IT... THE SAME WAY YOU MADE ME FEEL THAT DAY IN THE FOREST.
OKAY, WE DID THAT ABOUT HALF AN HOUR EARLIER WHEN MY INSIDES WERE SPILLING OUT INTO THE RAIN. I GOT OVER IT. YOU'LL HAVE TO DO BETTER AT THIS POINT!
YOU ARE GOING TO ROT IN HELL, ARIEL!! THE BEASTS OF NEVER-ENDING NIGHT WILL FOREVER FEAST ON YOUR SOUL!
THEY WILL PICK THEIR TEETH WITH YOUR BONES, AND WHILE YOU WATCH AND BEG FOR FREEDOM THEY WILL STRIP YOU OF YOUR FLESH ALL OVER AGAIN!!!
YOU WILL DIE BITCH! THE WAY I DIED!!! IT IS FOREVER AND IT IS ETERNAL AND IT IS SOMETHING YOU WILL, NEVER, EVER RETURN FROM!!!

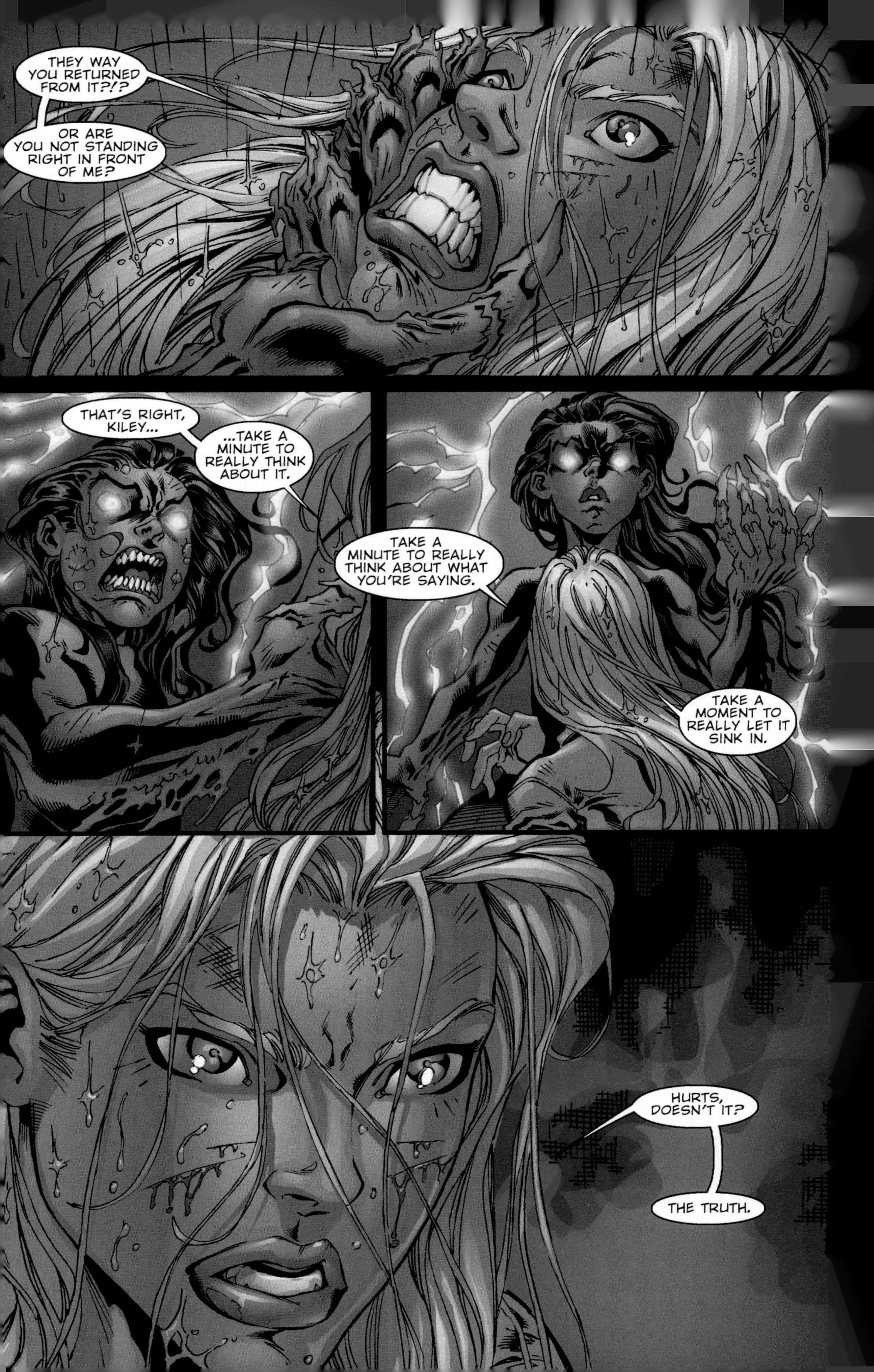
THEY WAY YOU RETURNED FROM IT?!?
OR ARE YOU NOT STANDING RIGHT IN FRONT OF ME?
THAT'S RIGHT, KILEY...
...TAKE A MINUTE TO REALLY THINK ABOUT IT.
TAKE A MINUTE TO REALLY THINK ABOUT WHAT YOU'RE SAYING.
TAKE A MOMENT TO REALLY LET IT SINK IN.
HURTS, DOESN'T IT?
THE TRUTH.

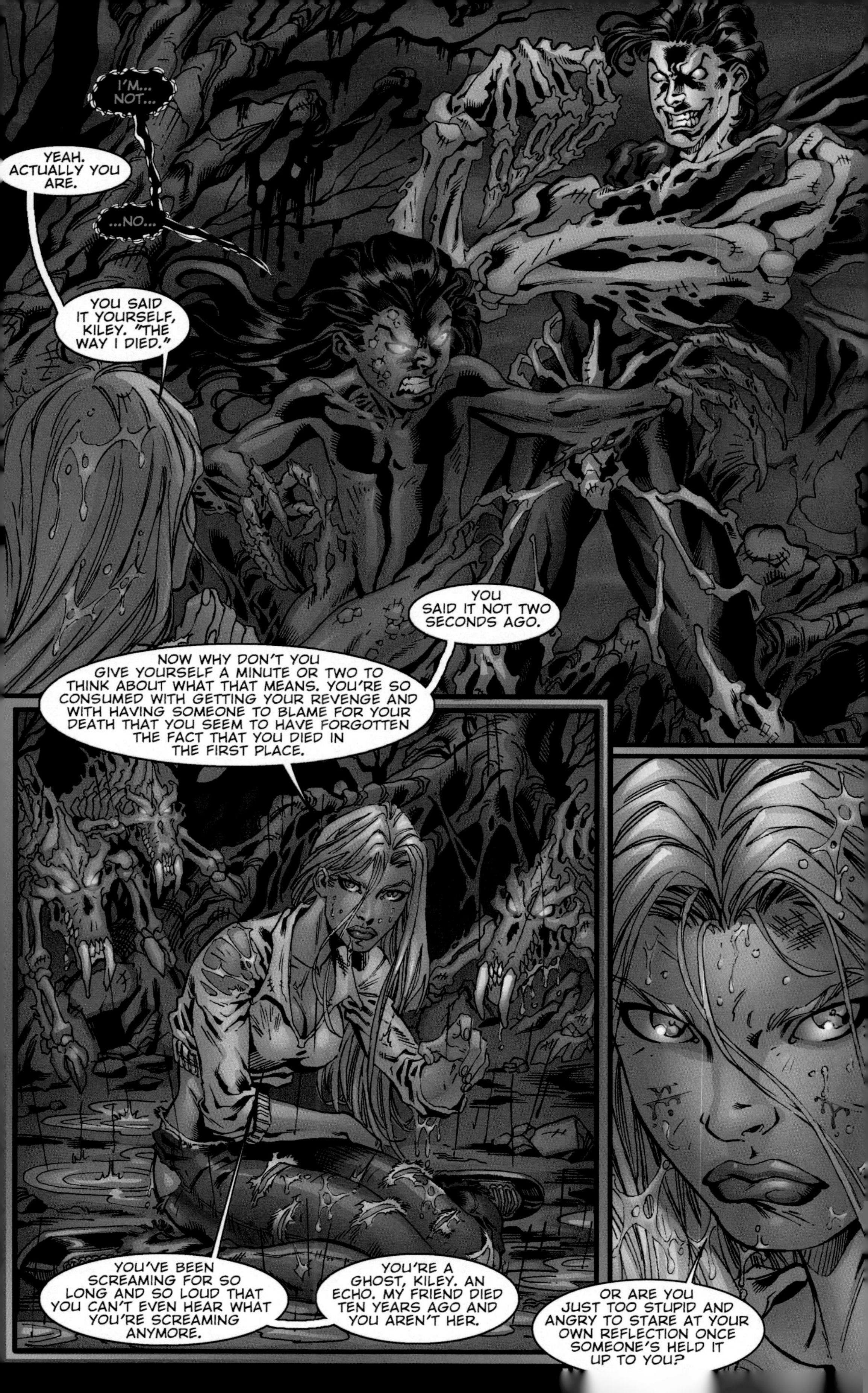
I'M... NOT...
YEAH. ACTUALLY YOU ARE.
...NO...
YOU SAID IT YOURSELF, KILEY. "THE WAY I DIED."
YOU SAID IT NOT TWO SECONDS AGO.
NOW WHY DON'T YOU GIVE YOURSELF A MINUTE OR TWO TO THINK ABOUT WHAT THAT MEANS. YOU'RE SO CONSUMED WITH GETTING YOUR REVENGE AND WITH HAVING SOMEONE TO BLAME FOR YOUR DEATH THAT YOU SEEM TO HAVE FORGOTTEN THE FACT THAT YOU DIED IN THE FIRST PLACE.
YOU'VE BEEN SCREAMING FOR SO LONG AND SO LOUD THAT YOU CAN'T EVEN HEAR WHAT YOU'RE SCREAMING ANYMORE.
YOU'RE A GHOST, KILEY. AN ECHO. MY FRIEND DIED TEN YEARS AGO AND YOU AREN'T HER.
OR ARE YOU JUST TOO STUPID AND ANGRY TO STARE AT YOUR OWN REFLECTION ONCE SOMEONE'S HELD IT UP TO YOU?

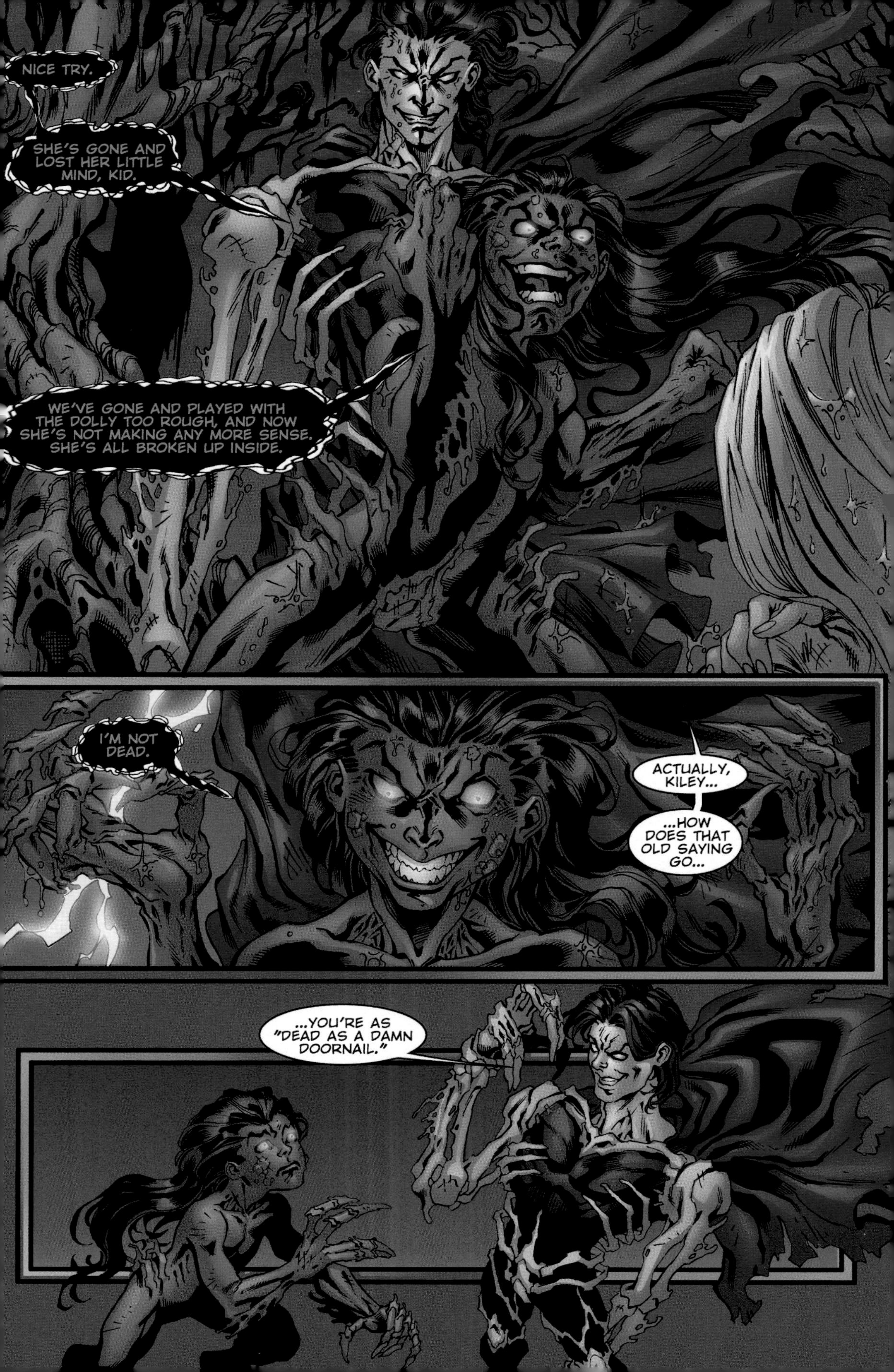
NICE TRY.
SHE'S GONE AND LOST HER LITTLE MIND, KID.
WE'VE GONE AND PLAYED WITH THE DOLLY TOO ROUGH, AND NOW SHE'S NOT MAKING ANY MORE SENSE. SHE'S ALL BROKEN UP INSIDE.
I'M NOT DEAD.
ACTUALLY, KILEY...
...HOW DOES THAT OLD SAYING GO...
...YOU'RE AS "DEAD AS A DAMN DOORNAIL."

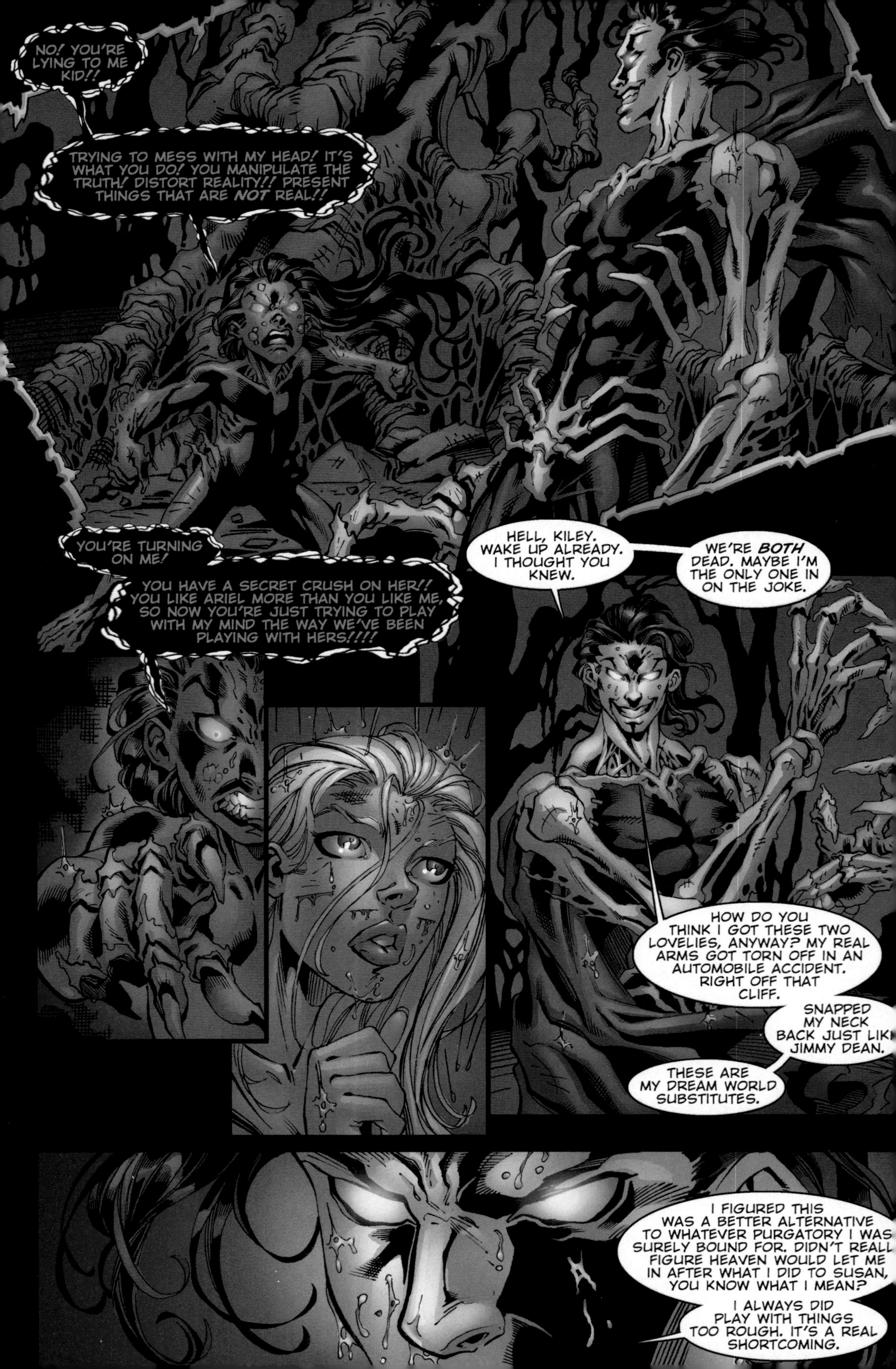
NO! YOU'RE LYING TO ME KID!!
TRYING TO MESS WITH MY HEAD! IT'S WHAT YOU DO! YOU MANIPULATE THE TRUTH! DISTORT REALITY!! PRESENT THINGS THAT ARE NOT REAL!!
YOU'RE TURNING ON ME!
YOU HAVE A SECRET CRUSH ON HER!! YOU LIKE ARIEL MORE THAN YOU LIKE ME, SO NOW YOU'RE JUST TRYING TO PLAY WITH MY MIND THE WAY WE'VE BEEN PLAYING WITH HERS!!!!
HELL, KILEY. WAKE UP ALREADY. I THOUGHT YOU KNEW.
WE'RE BOTH DEAD. MAYBE I'M THE ONLY ONE IN ON THE JOKE.
HOW DO YOU THINK I GOT THESE TWO LOVELIES, ANYWAY? MY REAL ARMS GOT TORN OFF IN AN AUTOMOBILE ACCIDENT. RIGHT OFF THAT CLIFF.
SNAPPED MY NECK BACK JUST LIK JIMMY DEAN.
THESE ARE MY DREAM WORLD SUBSTITUTES.
I FIGURED THIS WAS A BETTER ALTERNATIVE TO WHATEVER PURGATORY I WAS SURELY BOUND FOR. DIDN'T REALL FIGURE HEAVEN WOULD LET ME IN AFTER WHAT I DID TO SUSAN, YOU KNOW WHAT I MEAN?
I ALWAYS DID PLAY WITH THINGS TOO ROUGH. IT'S A REAL SHORTCOMING.

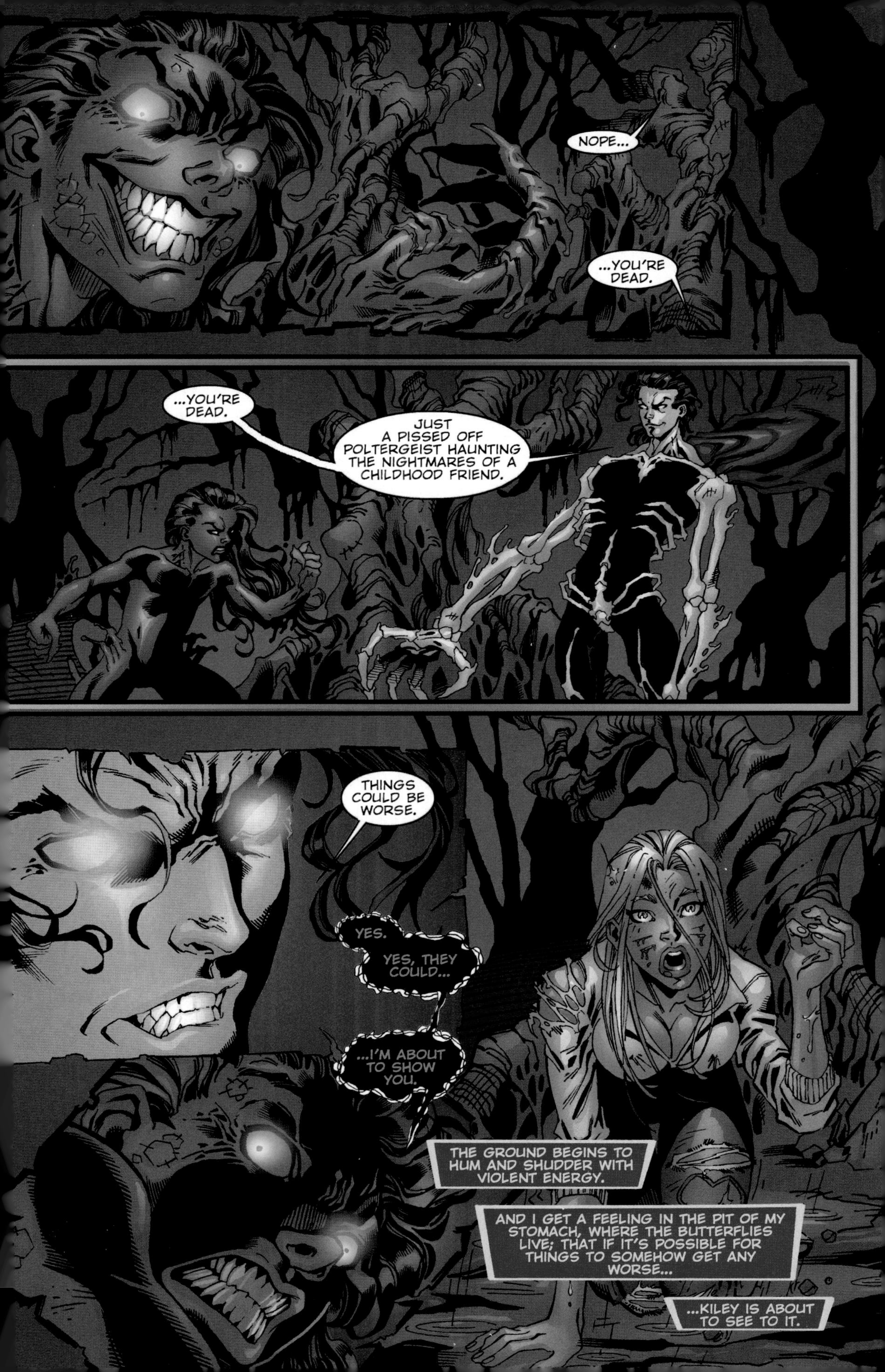
NOPE...
...YOU'RE DEAD.
...YOU'RE DEAD.
JUST A PISSED OFF POLTERGEIST HAUNTING THE NIGHTMARES OF A CHILDHOOD FRIEND.
THINGS COULD BE WORSE.
YES.
YES, THEY COULD...
...I'M ABOUT TO SHOW YOU.
THE GROUND BEGINS TO HUM AND SHUDDER WITH VIOLENT ENERGY.
AND I GET A FEELING IN THE PIT OF MY STOMACH, WHERE THE BUTTERFLIES LIVE; THAT IF IT'S POSSIBLE FOR THINGS TO SOMEHOW GET ANY WORSE...
...KILEY IS ABOUT TO SEE TO IT.

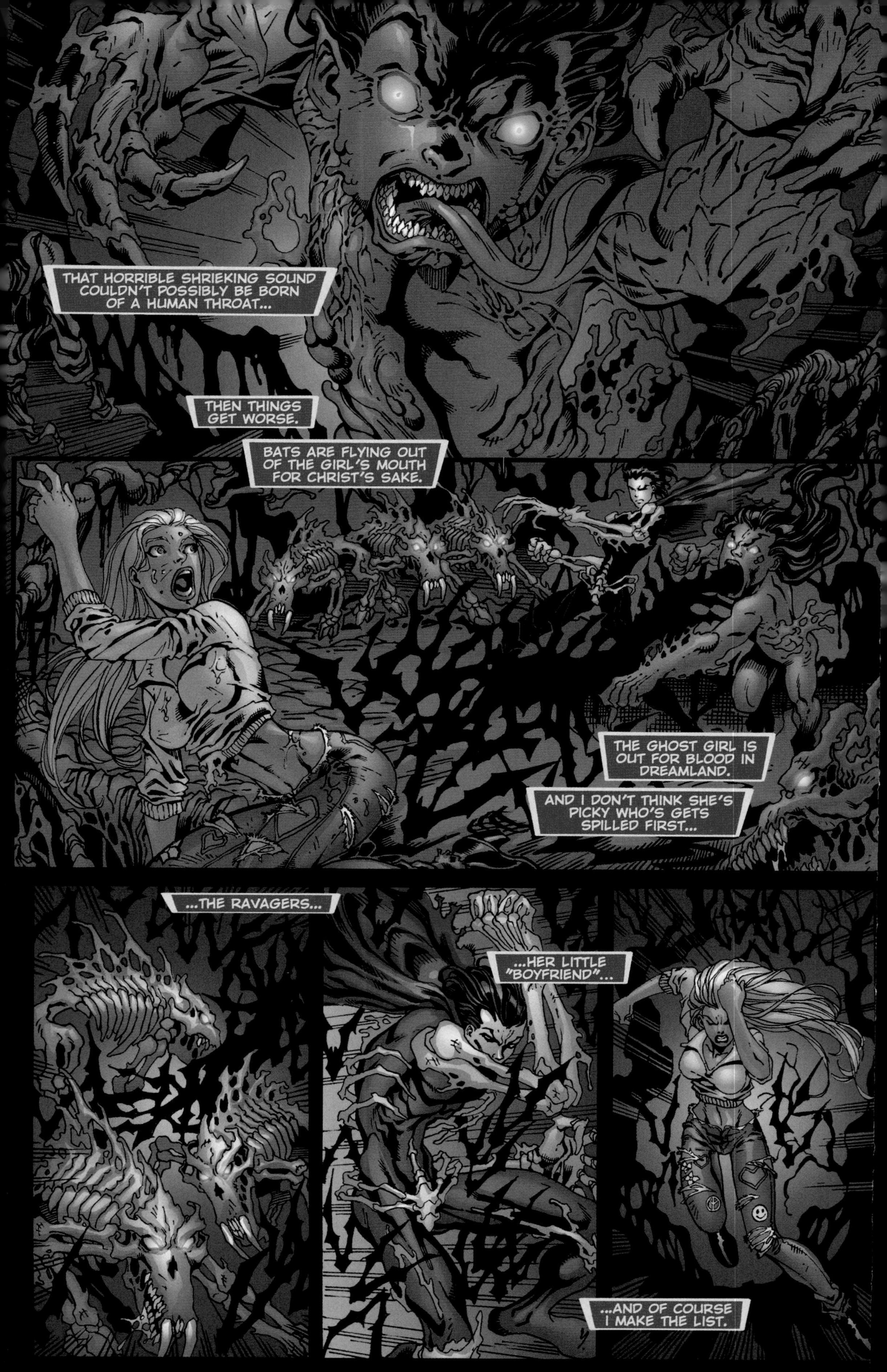
THAT HORRIBLE SHRIEKING SOUND COULDN'T POSSIBLY BE BORN OF A HUMAN THROAT...
THEN THINGS GET WORSE.
BATS ARE FLYING OUT OF THE GIRL'S MOUTH FOR CHRIST'S SAKE.
THE GHOST GIRL IS OUT FOR BLOOD IN DREAMLAND.
AND I DON'T THINK SHE'S PICKY WHO'S GETS SPILLED FIRST...
...THE RAVAGERS...
...HER LITTLE "BOYFRIEND"...
...AND OF COURSE I MAKE THE LIST.

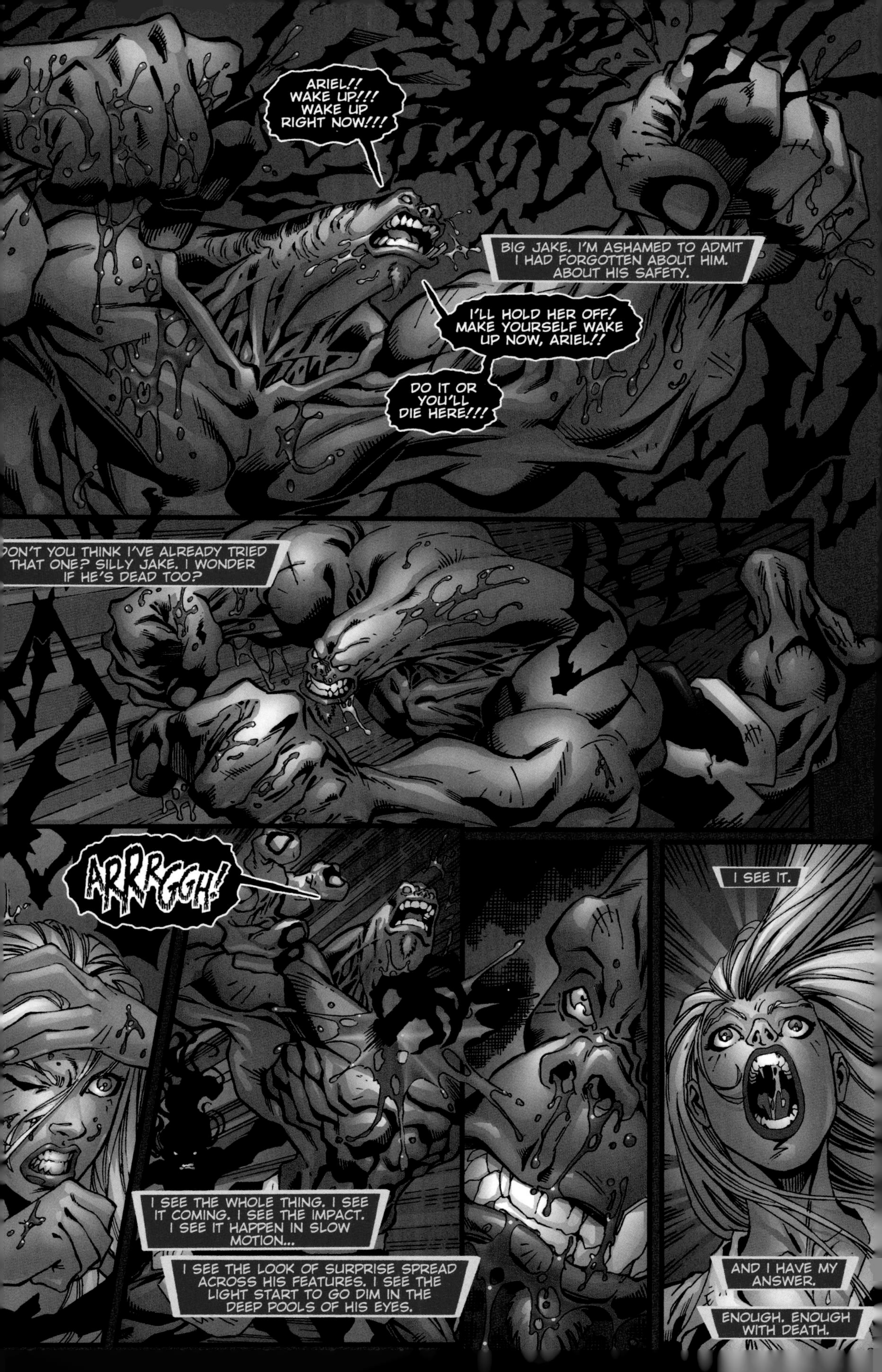
ARIEL!! WAKE UP!!! WAKE UP RIGHT NOW!!!
BIG JAKE. I'M ASHAMED TO ADMIT I HAD FORGOTTEN ABOUT HIM. ABOUT HIS SAFETY.
I'LL HOLD HER OFF! MAKE YOURSELF WAKE UP NOW, ARIEL!!
DO IT OR YOU'LL DIE HERE!!!
DON'T YOU THINK I'VE ALREADY TRIED THAT ONE? SILLY JAKE. I WONDER IF HE'S DEAD TOO?
ARRRGGH!
I SEE THE WHOLE THING. I SEE IT COMING. I SEE THE IMPACT. I SEE IT HAPPEN IN SLOW MOTION...
I SEE THE LOOK OF SURPRISE SPREAD ACROSS HIS FEATURES. I SEE THE LIGHT START TO GO DIM IN THE DEEP POOLS OF HIS EYES.
I SEE IT.
AND I HAVE MY ANSWER.
ENOUGH. ENOUGH WITH DEATH.

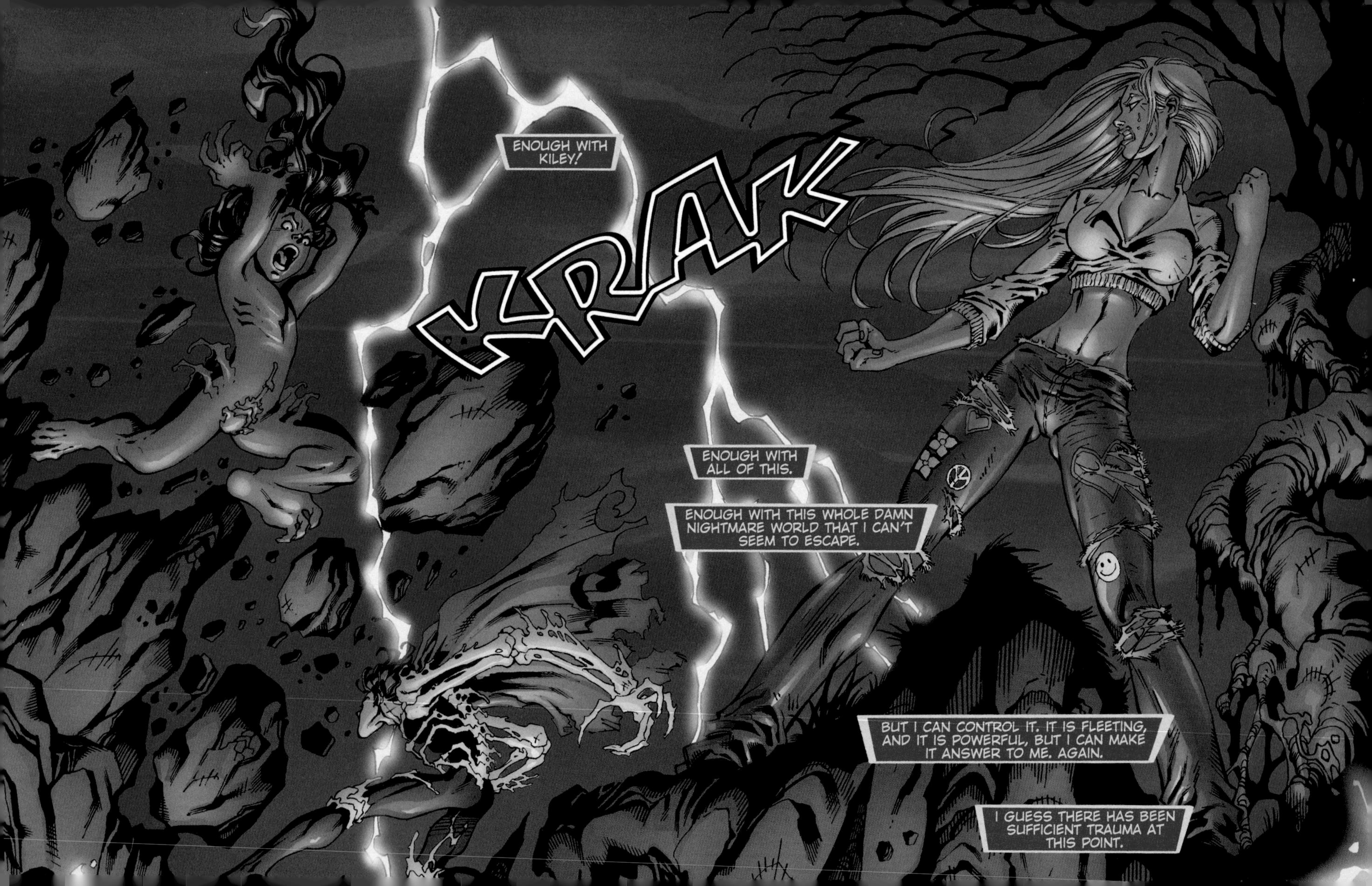
ENOUGH WITH KILEY!
KRAK
ENOUGH WITH ALL OF THIS.
ENOUGH WITH THIS WHOLE DAMN NIGHTMARE WORLD THAT I CAN'T SEEM TO ESCAPE.
BUT I CAN CONTROL IT. IT IS FLEETING, AND IT IS POWERFUL, BUT I CAN MAKE IT ANSWER TO ME. AGAIN.
I GUESS THERE HAS BEEN SUFFICIENT TRAUMA AT THIS POINT.

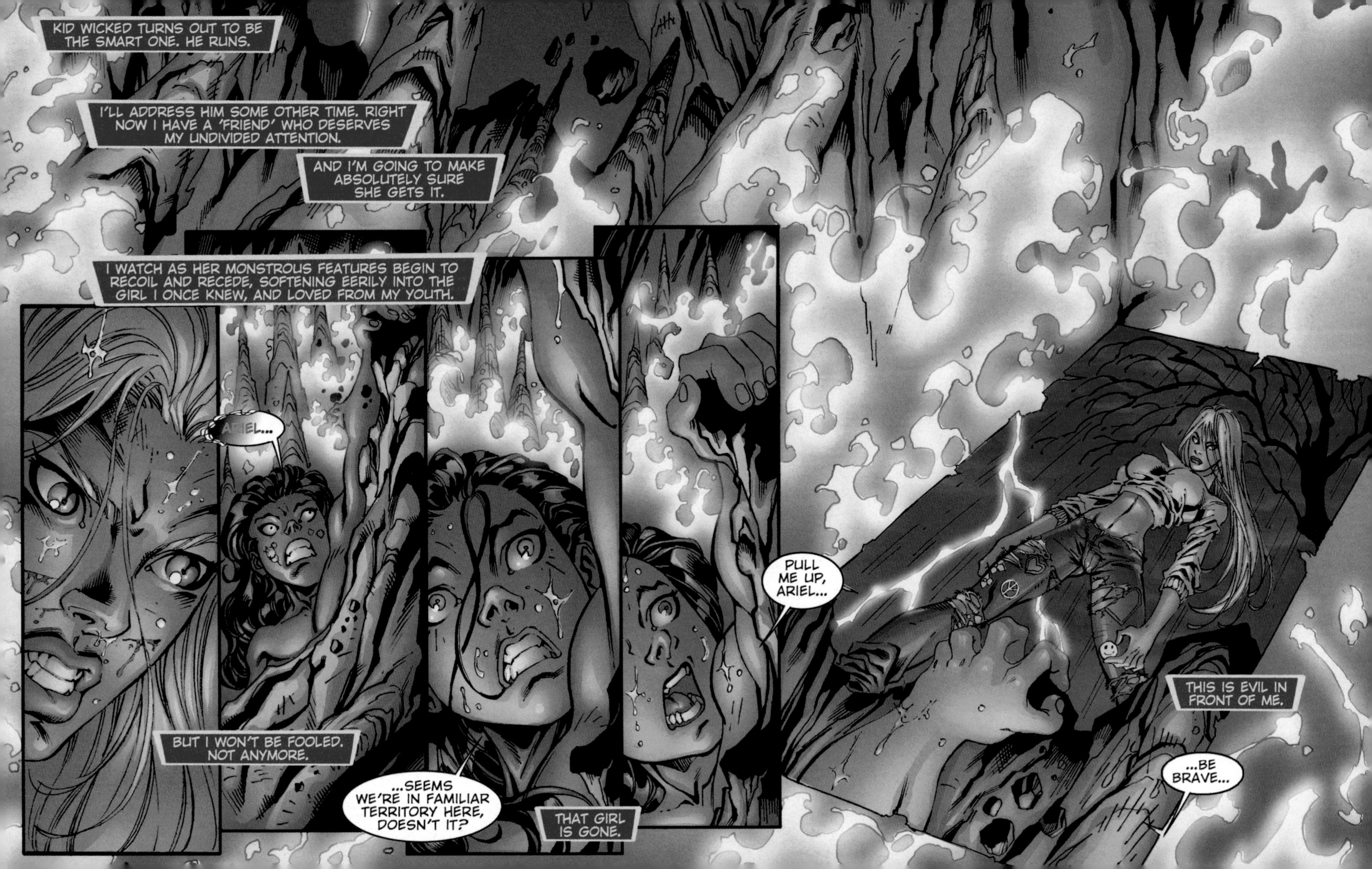
KID WICKED TURNS OUT TO BE THE SMART ONE. HE RUNS.
I'LL ADDRESS HIM SOME OTHER TIME. RIGHT NOW I HAVE A 'FRIEND' WHO DESERVES MY UNDIVIDED ATTENTION.
AND I'M GOING TO MAKE ABSOLUTELY SURE SHE GETS IT.
I WATCH AS HER MONSTROUS FEATURES BEGIN TO RECOIL AND RECEDE, SOFTENING EERILY INTO THE GIRL I ONCE KNEW, AND LOVED FROM MY YOUTH.
ARIEL...
BUT I WON'T BE FOOLED. NOT ANYMORE.
...SEEMS WE'RE IN FAMILIAR TERRITORY HERE, DOESN'T IT?
THAT GIRL IS GONE.
PULL ME UP, ARIEL...
THIS IS EVIL IN FRONT OF ME.
...BE BRAVE...

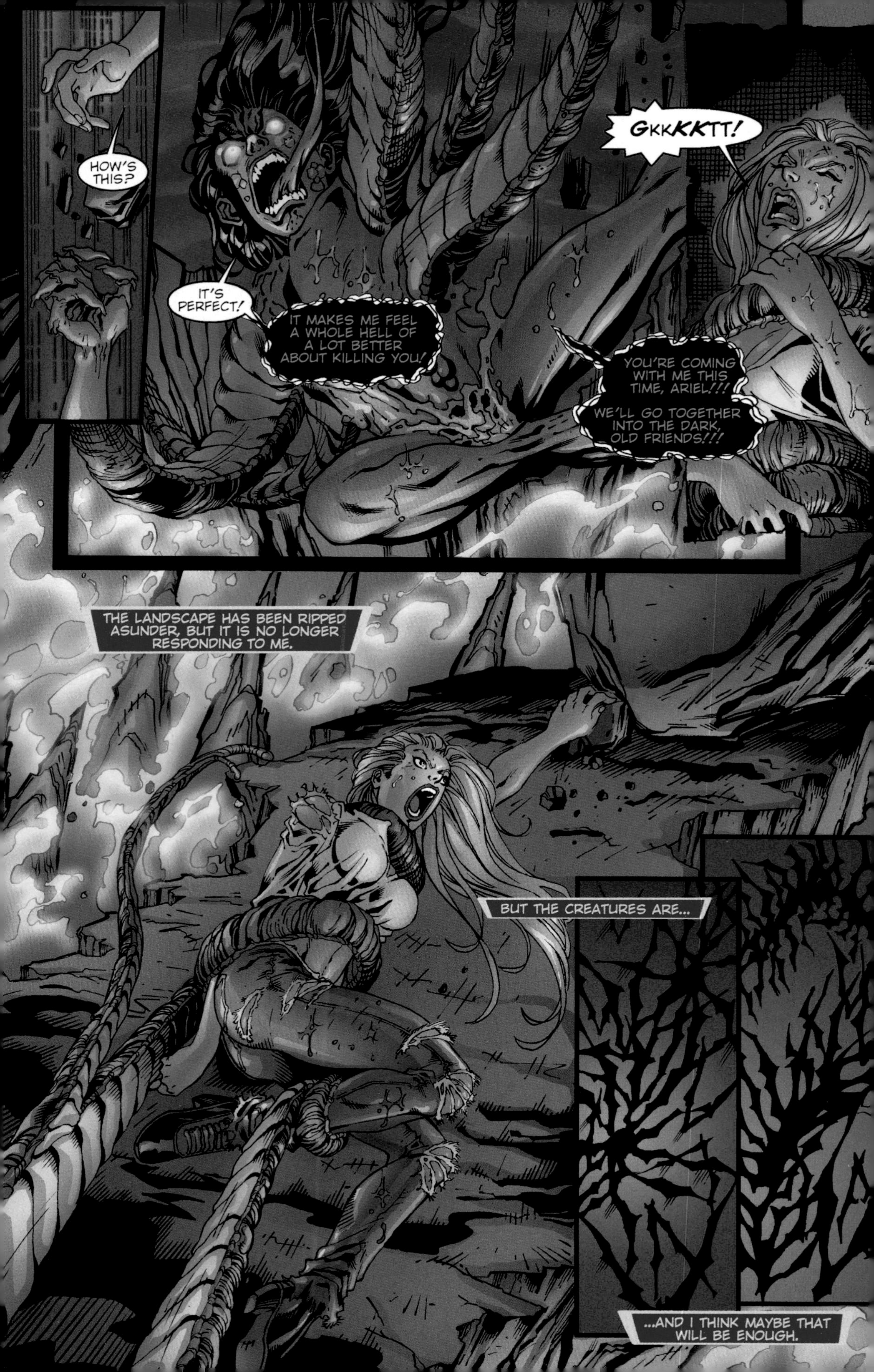
HOW'S THIS?
IT'S PERFECT!
IT MAKES ME FEEL A WHOLE HELL OF A LOT BETTER ABOUT KILLING YOU!
GKKKKTT!
YOU'RE COMING WITH ME THIS TIME, ARIEL!!!
WE'LL GO TOGETHER INTO THE DARK, OLD FRIENDS!!!
THE LANDSCAPE HAS BEEN RIPPED ASUNDER, BUT IT IS NO LONGER RESPONDING TO ME.
BUT THE CREATURES ARE...
...AND I THINK MAYBE THAT WILL BE ENOUGH.

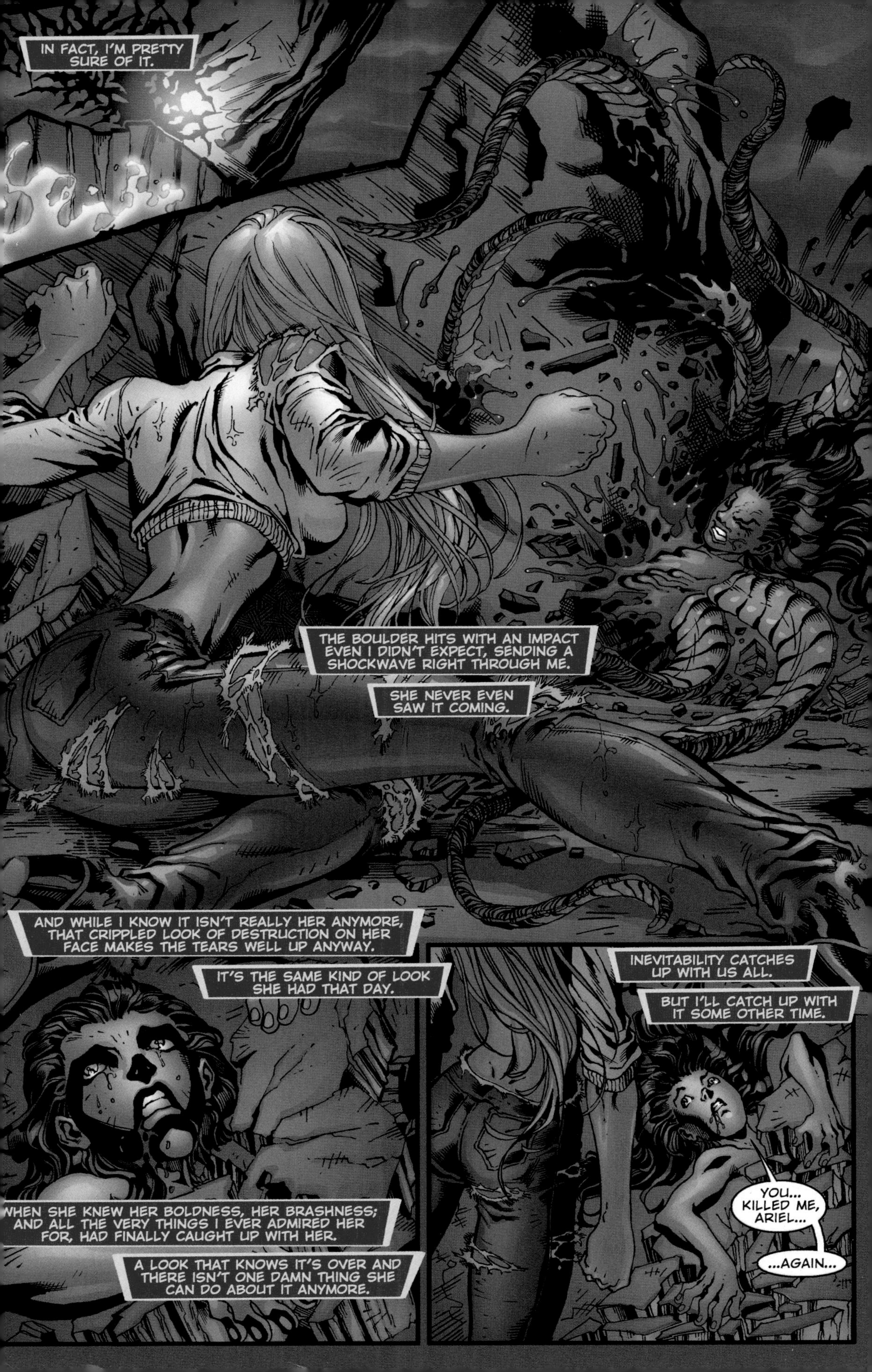
IN FACT, I'M PRETTY SURE OF IT.
THE BOULDER HITS WITH AN IMPACT EVEN I DIDN'T EXPECT, SENDING A SHOCKWAVE RIGHT THROUGH ME.
SHE NEVER EVEN SAW IT COMING.
AND WHILE I KNOW IT ISN'T REALLY HER ANYMORE, THAT CRIPPLED LOOK OF DESTRUCTION ON HER FACE MAKES THE TEARS WELL UP ANYWAY.
IT'S THE SAME KIND OF LOOK SHE HAD THAT DAY.
WHEN SHE KNEW HER BOLDNESS, HER BRASHNESS; AND ALL THE VERY THINGS I EVER ADMIRED HER FOR, HAD FINALLY CAUGHT UP WITH HER.
A LOOK THAT KNOWS IT'S OVER AND THERE ISN'T ONE DAMN THING SHE CAN DO ABOUT IT ANYMORE.
INEVITABILITY CATCHES UP WITH US ALL.
BUT I'LL CATCH UP WITH IT SOME OTHER TIME.
YOU... KILLED ME, ARIEL...
...AGAIN...

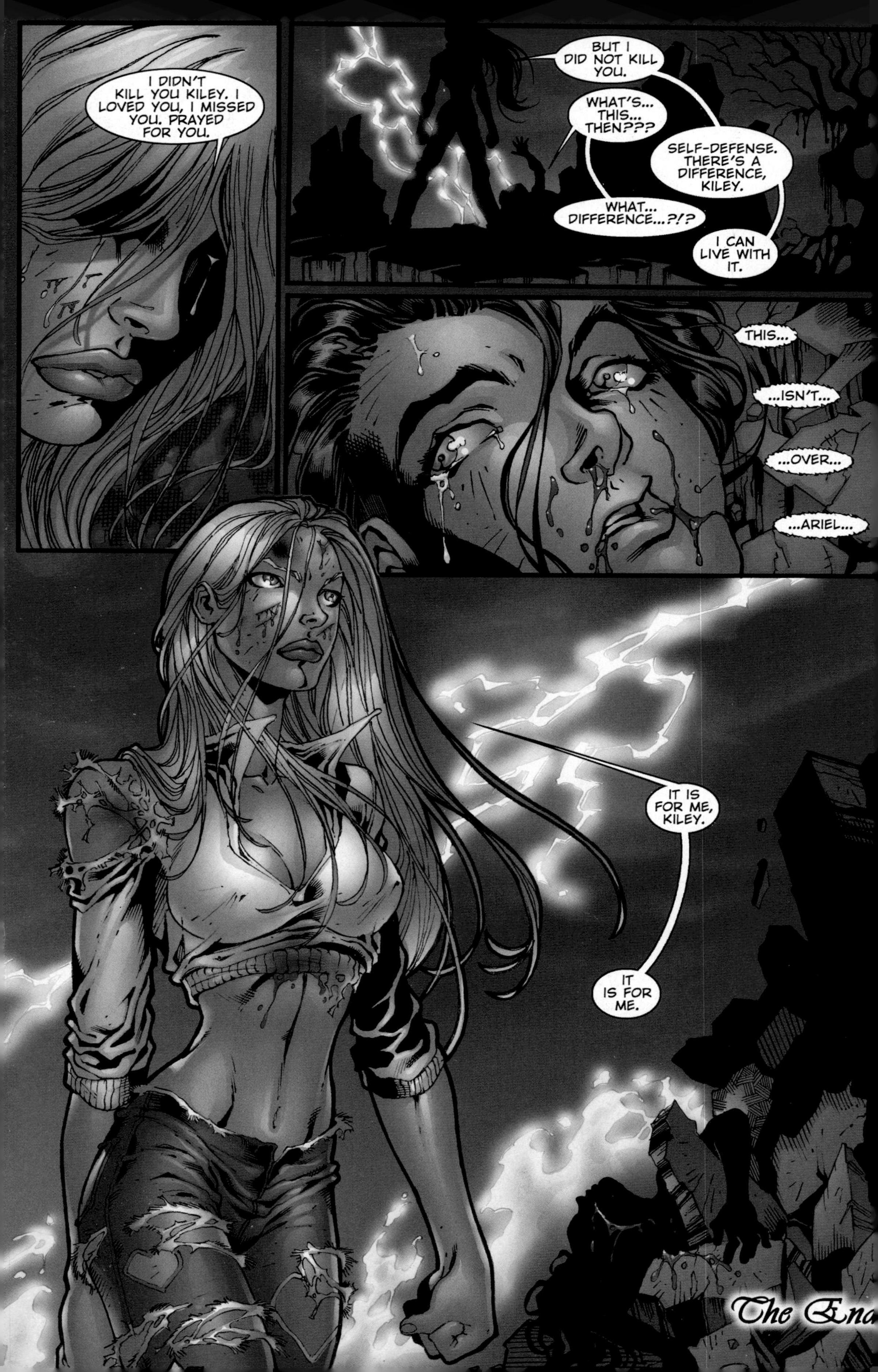
I DIDN'T KILL YOU KILEY. I LOVED YOU, I MISSED YOU. PRAYED FOR YOU.
BUT I DID NOT KILL YOU.
WHAT'S... THIS... THEN???
SELF-DEFENSE. THERE'S A DIFFERENCE, KILEY.
WHAT... DIFFERENCE...?!?
I CAN LIVE WITH IT.
THIS...
...ISN'T...
...OVER...
...ARIEL...
IT IS FOR ME, KILEY.
IT IS FOR ME.
The End